THE BASICS
OF
LIBRARIANSHIP

THE BASICS
OF
LIBRARIANSHIP

Third edition

ROSEMARY BEENHAM

Formerly Senior Lecturer, Anglia Higher Education College

and

COLIN HARRISON

Head of Department of Educational Services,
Anglia Higher Education College

CLIVE BINGLEY  LONDON

Published by
Library Association Publishing Ltd
7 Ridgmount Street
London WC1E 7AE

First published 1990

British Library Cataloguing in Publication Data

Harrison, Colin T. (Colin Thomas)
  The basics of librarianship. — 3rd ed.
  1. Librarianship
  I. Title II. Beenham, Rosemary
  020

  ISBN 0-85157-465-3

Typeset in 10/12pt Times by Library Association Publishing Ltd
Printed and made in Great Britain by Billing and Sons Ltd, Worcester

Contents

The functions and purposes of libraries, information services and other related organizations

Libraries and information services do not exist simply because they are 'good things'. They are costly enterprises and therefore need a sound rationale both to continue and to be started. Therefore the purpose of the service will be defined closely; often this will be enshrined in a set of aims and objectives against which the service can later be measured. The purpose may be to provide information to a research company or industrial organization; it may be to help learning in a college or provide information and recreation to the general public. Whatever the purpose of the service, it should be clearly stated and be a guide to staff in their operation of that service.

The function of libraries and information services will vary according to the purpose: some will be reference collections, some will actively circulate collated data for research, some will hold leaflets for tourists, some will be lending libraries and some will have all of these functions and more. Put simply, the function relates to what the library actually does for its users.

To consider the role and purpose of libraries and information services, it is helpful to group them into different types of services, while recognizing that this is often too simplistic a grouping of a complex set of services. In this book we have kept this broad classification down to a minimum number of types, namely, public libraries, academic libraries, industrial/commercial libraries, national libraries and some examples of related organizations.

Some libraries may at first seem difficult to fit into this list of types: an example is a community library that is a branch of a public library but also serves as a school library. Obviously it could fit into the public or the academic classification. In fact, it goes into both and fulfils the functions of both, directing special services to the appropriate group of users. It is possible to list the functions it provides for the general public and those it provides for the teachers and pupils — they will probably show some differences.

The broad function that lies at the heart of almost all library services is the provision of information and/or cultural materials. The proportion varies according to the aims and objectives of the particular service. For example, the public library service might be said to have a 40:60 split, while an industrial library will be wholly information-based.

The factors that decide this changing balance relate directly to the reasons for the existence of the service in the first place. Normally these reasons are embodied in a statement of policy or a series of aims and objectives that guide the day-to-day development and running of the service. We often find that 'industrial' libraries have more clearly defined terms of reference than public libraries. To some extent this reflects the environment in which the library operates, that is, the economic world of industry where information is costed as part of the overall product price.

From this it follows that, whatever the type of library, it has a controlling body that monitors performance and development against the yardstick of the original objectives of the service. In almost no circumstances can the librarian be said to be the sole arbiter of what is or is not acceptable to the user. We are all answerable to a higher authority for the performance of ourselves, our staff and our service generally.

Normally this control is vested in a committee representing those who provide the finance for the service. While librarians usually form part of the membership of the committee, they seldom have enough influence to determine singly the outcome of any deliberations. Their strength rests in relating actions (proposed or taken) to original objectives and presenting a sound case to show how the two relate. In many libraries the cost-effectiveness of an action is the most compelling argument for committee members.

What are these aims and objectives that form such an important part in the development of our service? Well, they vary greatly from place to place and from one type of library to another. Everyone working in a library ought to seek out and understand the precise aims and objectives of that particular library — usually the chief librarian will be able to produce them. There are, however, some generally agreed statements that can serve as introductory remarks regarding the aims and objectives of major types of libraries: public, national, academic, industrial/commercial and so on.

Public libraries
The aims of a public library can be said to be to contribute to the quality

of life, to promote the concept of a democratic society and to add to the sum total of people's happiness and awareness of themselves, others and their environment.

To fulfil these aims particular objectives that have been summarized as follows can be set:

1 Education. To foster and provide means for the development of the individual/group at all levels of educational ability.
2 Information. To give the user quick access to accurate information over the whole range of human knowledge.
3 Culture. To be a chief centre for cultural life and actively to promote participation and appreciation of all the arts.
4 Leisure and recreation. To play a positive part in encouraging an active use of leisure and recreational time.

The many services offered by our public libraries can be directly related to these aims and objectives, as can the selection of various materials and the organization of special events.

The history of the public library service dates back to before 1850. That date marks the first Act of Parliament relating to libraries. Other Acts, of 1919 and 1964, have assisted in developing the service and placing it firmly in the control of local authorities. In recent years, this has meant, chiefly, putting it into the hands of county and metropolitan councils.

These authorities all have subcommittees of the council to advise them on policy relating to the development of the library service. Titles vary: many are called library subcommittees, but in some places, they may be combined into leisure or educational committees. Membership of the committee is usually in three parts:

- Officers, e.g. librarian, architect etc.
- Elected members, i.e., local councillors.
- Co-opted members, usually members of the public who have special knowledge of or interest in the subject of the committee, e.g. local head teachers.

The officer members do not normally have voting rights, but, in conjunction with the chairman, prepare the agenda and any special reports for the consideration of members.

Items approved by the library committee often need to progress through other committees before reaching the full council — for example, staffing matters may go to a personnel committee, finance to a finance committee — each of which will comment on the suggestion being forwarded by the library committee.

Financial support for public libraries comes from the community charge (although this is to a large extent subsidized by central government via the charge support grant) and to this extent the will of the local community can determine the quality of the service. In most authorities you can obtain information showing how much, in percentage terms, is spent on libraries. Recent legislation (1989) has made legal the charging for some services offered by public libraries. Many now charge for the loan of recordings and special 'value-added' services, for example, electronic searches for information. However, a campaign by the library profession has had the effect of resisting charges for the loan of books. Money raised from charges should be spent upon improvements to the service.

Because of this local raising of money and the pressures that can be applied by residents on their councillors, the development of services could be influenced by pressure groups. It is to the credit of library committees and councils that this seldom happens and that a more structured approach is employed. The effect of local control of libraries has led to their providing different ranges of services and methods of accessing those services, according to local need.

In some authorities with a rural population the use of mobile libraries is an important way of delivering the service to the user. In towns large branch libraries are used; these may be in shopping areas or situated close to transport centres − whichever the local community finds most helpful.

All library services have a central 'headquarters' library that acts as their administrative centre and often also houses the main reference or information centre. Services for schools and the housebound, adult education and commercial information services will often be based upon this main library. Specialist staff may be attached to these units but will be available to service the needs of users calling into the branch or mobile library. The branches and mobile libraries will, of course, also have professional staff either based within them or serving as part of a team that travels around a group of service points.

Academic libraries

These range from the largest university libraries (some of which are virtually national libraries in that they obtain materials free of charge under the Copyright Acts) to the small school library. Each has a similar aim that may be expressed as 'to provide a service of reference and lending material appropriate to the needs of the staff and students of the institution'. These needs can be very closely identified in the case of most academic libraries in that they reflect the courses offered and the research undertaken within the institution. In this respect an academic library may be less universal in its subject coverage than a public library. General objectives may be listed as follows:

1 To serve the needs of the academic community (staff and students).
2 To provide reference materials at appropriate levels.
3 To provide study areas for users.
4 To provide a lending service appropriate to the different types of users.
5 To provide an active information service (this may extend beyond the institution to local industry and commerce).

The extent to which each of these objectives is carried out depends upon the size and nature of the institution. Obviously a school library will not function in as developed a way as a polytechnic library – but its general aims will be similar.

Leaving aside the school library for the moment, a recognizably similar structure operates for other academic libraries, that is, those of universities, polytechnics, institutions of higher education and further education colleges. Here the academic board (it may have different titles in different institutions) represents the equivalent of the council in a public library. It establishes the overall policy of the institution and monitors progress. Academic boards set up subcommittees to deal with major areas of concern; one of these may be a library committee. Alternatively, library matters may be dealt with as part of a larger group called 'resources' or 'learning resources'.

Senior members of the library staff are members of the relevant committee, as are other academics, who represent the 'users' of the service. The committee will operate much as the public library committee, referring matters to other committees and ultimately to the academic board or governing body. Presently higher education has two funding agencies, the UFC (University Funding Council) funds universities, while the PCFC (Polytechnic and Colleges Funding Council) funds polytechnics and those other colleges recently taken from local authority control and made independent corporations. Outside the higher education sector, detailed discussions subsequently take place with the local education authority which provides the money for the institutions and is necessarily involved in plans requiring buildings and other large items needing financial support.

The primary purpose of any educational library is to aid the learning, teaching and research that is the function of the institution. To do this, staff may be of various types. Some will be academic and they will aid users in the academic use of services, teach information skills and help plan courses. Professional librarians will be needed to perform all the usual tasks associated with any service: collection building, staff management, reader support and so on. Other staff will be needed to issue, process, repair and shelve material.

Users will expect the collection to match the contents of the courses and to relate to any research undertaken. Multiple copies will often be purchased to meet the needs of large numbers of students studying the same unit of work. Reference services will need to be of a high quality and supported by access to all the major online information hosts.

The design and layout of the library will be such as to provide good study spaces, tutorial rooms and ease of use for many of the new electronic aids in the information world, for example, CD-ROMs, computer terminals and personal computers.

School libraries differ significantly in that in many places they are provided as part of the county public library service and therefore control is not so directly vested in the school. In 1990 many schools will achieve local financial management (LFM) and the headteacher will be responsible to a governing body for the full range of financial controls. This could include the library, but the school may decide to contract the library service to the local public library. Decisions will vary around the country and you may like to discover what is happening in your area.

Many schools have their own 'councils' made up of staff and pupils who advise on the library and often select materials from visiting mobile libraries for inclusion in its stock. Larger schools may have a professional librarian, but all too often this work is undertaken as an extra duty by teachers. Frequently in schools the collection is broken up into classrooms rather than being contained in a central place. This is not unique to schools – many universities and colleges have subject department libraries as well as a main library.

Too many schools do not have a professional librarian and this can reduce the effectiveness of the service. Often the public library will help with advice and visits. In some local authorities moves are under way to provide a professional librarian in at least the secondary schools and sixth form colleges. This helps the library to become a focus for learning as in colleges and universities. A good school library is invaluable for project work and group study. The librarians will develop special collections to help teachers prepare for classes and pupils prepare for assessments.

Industrial and commercial libraries

The chief aim of an industrial or commercial library can be expressed as 'to save the parent organization both time and money'. The general objectives can be summarized as follows:

1   The production and distribution of bulletins containing information relevant to the product etc. of the company.
2   The circulation of original materials to key staff according to their subject interest.
3   The provision of a collection designed to enable 1 and 2 above to be accomplished and to provide a base for research.
4   To provide staff to conduct literature searches on behalf of the research teams and/or management.

Many industrial libraries are finding that they need to use computer-based information systems to search literature and patent sources, so great is the reliance of industry and commerce on up-to-the-minute information.

The place of the library within the organization is important if it is to be effective. Generally it is not associated with a particular department but is seen as part of the central provision, the librarian being responsible to the general manager, or to a director, for the provision of the service. Because of this direct relationship, decisions are often easier to arrive at in industrial libraries than in those previously discussed.

As detailed knowledge is required in this type of library, staffing may be of a different kind from that in other libraries. Often the professional staff of an industrial library will be a mix of professional scientists and librarians, and they are often called 'information officers' or 'scientists' rather than librarians.

Financing of the service will be seen as part of the total budget of the company and the librarian will have to submit estimates alongside other departments. It is at this stage that the cost of information is judged — is it cheaper to repeat research than to discover it has already been done and recorded? One well-known commercial company says: 'The cost of finding information is high, the cost of not finding it is higher still.'

The libraries falling into this group range from those serving major manufacturers, such as ICI or Marconi, to small subscription libraries, such as Lewis' Lending Library. In between there are a whole range of specialist services such as the specialist picture libraries used to supply photographs for books, television and publishing in general; and record libraries such as the comprehensive one operated by the BBC to support its radio and television programmes. Almost all of the government and trade-sponsored research associations offer a library and information service to their members, as do the major professional bodies such as the Library Association and trades unions. Many of these libraries also produce acquisitions lists which are circulated to members as part of their service.

National libraries

The focal point for the library service in the United Kingdom is the British Library which offers a comprehensive support service to libraries throughout the country. The Library is managed by the British Library Board. Policy is implemented by the Chief Executive and Directors of the Library's component parts.

At present the British Library is organized into Humanities and Social Sciences; Science, Technology and Industry; Research and Development and Central Administration. The Library is in the process of relocating those of its activities which need not be sited in London to Boston Spa in Yorkshire (see below) and there will then be an administrative reorganization into London Services and Yorkshire Services.

The British Library Humanities and Social Sciences comprises the former Department of Printed Books (one of the Copyright Libraries of the British Isles) which includes the British Library Newspaper Library at Colindale, the Department of Manuscripts and Department of Oriental Manuscripts and Printed Books. An admission pass is needed to consult material in these collections.

The British Library Science Technology and Industry is the country's premier research library for the natural sciences, engineering, technology and industrial property. No admission pass is needed to use the London reading rooms at Southampton Buildings off Chancery Lane (known as the Holborn Reading Room) which specializes in United Kingdom patents, physical sciences, technology and the Business Information Service; Chancery House (also in Southampton Buildings) for foreign patents and the reading room in Kean Street, Aldwych which specializes in the life sciences and technologies, earth and space sciences and mathematics.

The British Library Science Technology and Industry also contains the Document Supply Centre (BLDSC), which acts as the nation's main interlending agency. The BLDSC at Boston Spa in Yorkshire adds many thousands of items each year to its stock by purchase and international exchange. Its range of journals is one of the most comprehensive of any library in the world. Libraries may use the service through the medium of prepaid vouchers which cover the cost of handling and dispatch (or, at the discretion of the British Library, photocopying or microfilming the document requested). In 1990 the cost of the voucher was £3 for United Kingdom users, £4.50 for those overseas.

The National Bibliographic Service (NBS) is responsible for the *British national bibliography (BNB)* which is available in machine-readable cataloguing (MARC) format, online via the Library's BLAISE-LINE database, or in printed form, microfiche or on CD-ROM (Compact Disc

Read Only Memory). The *BNB* lists most British publications and offers the Dewey classification and other detailed information for cataloguers. Many libraries subscribe to the computer tape and transfer the information relating to books they buy directly into their computer catalogue system.

The Research and Development Department provides an important focus for research in topics related to all aspects of libraries and librarianship. It publishes many research reports each year which help the profession to keep up to date.

The Board Secretariat covers planning, Press and Public Relations. Central Administration supports the work of the rest of the Library by providing personnel, training, administrative, accommodation and other services.

Funding for the British Library comes in a variety of ways: by grant-in-aid from the Office of Arts and Libraries and other sources including revenue raised from the sale of British Library publications and artefacts; the *BNB*, online services, charges for use of the interlibrary loan service and sales of research publications.

The British Library is one of six Copyright (i.e. legal deposit) libraries in the British Isles. Publishers in the UK and Republic of Ireland are required to deposit one copy of each of their publications at the Library within a month of publication. (The British Library is entitled to have copies automatically; the other five may request particular titles required).

Between 1993 and 1996 most of the British Library's London operations will be transferred to its new building next to St Pancras Station. This project has been described as one of the largest public construction projects ever undertaken in the UK, and should result in vastly improved storage conditions for the stock and services for users and public. There is a question mark, however, about whether the new building will be capable of housing the entire stock of the British Library's London operations. It is possible that some outstorage will still be necessary.

The British Library is, of course, only one of the national libraries within the United Kingdom. It tends to take pride of place because of the very large range of services it offers, but there are also national libraries in the other countries.

Scotland has its library, the National Library of Scotland, in Edinburgh. As well as offering research facilities, it also publishes a bibliography of Scotland. It is entitled to material through the legal deposit scheme. These it gets by writing to publishers − some send direct but others await a request.

The National Library of Wales is based in Aberystwyth. It specializes in materials relating to aspects of Welsh and Celtic culture, language and life. It publishes a bibliography of Wales. The National Library of Wales has a special collection of non-book materials related to the political and cultural heritage of Wales; these are sound, video and film. Like the National Library of Scotland, the National Library of Wales has rights under the legal deposit scheme.

Outside the United Kingdom, many other nations have national libraries on a similar model to the British Library. Perhaps the most famous is the Library of Congress in Washington, USA. It was established to be the library of the Congress but it has developed to become the major library service in the country. It maintains the MARC database for the USA and adds classification and cataloguing details as the British Library does. It is responsible in the USA for the Library of Congress classification and Dewey classification schemes. Naturally, it has reading rooms and offers a number of specialized services.

Information and advice centres
In recent years there has been an explosion of specialist information services, some funded by government (local or national), others by voluntary donations. Each has been set up to provide services to a particular client group. Some of the more widely available are as follows.

Legal Advice Centres
These provide advice and legal support to those who cannot afford the usual legal services. The staff are often professional solicitors (many on a voluntary basis), social service staff, college lecturers and so on. They are mostly found in inner cities.

Citizens Advice Bureaux
These are in every town in the nation. They offer impartial advice to those having problems in many fields; they help with consumer, family, financial and social services matters, among other concerns. The staff are mostly volunteers but all are trained in the use of the centrally provided information service. They cooperate with professionals to offer more detailed support including representation at tribunals and so on. Funding comes from central government grants, local government grants and donations.

Tourist Information Centres
Usually locally funded, they provide local information for visitors. They often maintain a register of hotels and lodgings. They stock leaflets about tourist centres and events and offer advice about tours. Many offer a

booking service for local theatres. The larger ones are linked to the various national and regional tourist boards.

General finance of libraries

We have indicated above where many libraries obtain their financial support. In doing their budgets they have to consider some basic headings that are common to all. These are:

1   Salaries. In services that are operated by paid staff, almost half of the total expenditure will go on salaries. Associated with this heading may be travel and staff development costs.
2   Materials. The second major cost for most libraries is the purchase of the basic materials, books, journals, videos etc. Binding and processing costs may also be covered in this total.
3   Loan charges. Repayments for buildings, equipment leasing and similar charges.
4   Standard business charges and rents. Payable by all types of libraries, although in the public sector it may not be so clear in every case.
5   Energy costs. Heating, lighting etc.
6   General expenses. The normal office costs of printing, paper, equipment, furniture etc. will need to be looked at. In many budgets these could be separate headings.

Assignments

1   Visit a library different from your own and write a report of its structure and services.

2   Look at your own library's aims and objectives and assess how well you think the services offered fit them.

3   Which of the following statements are correct?

(a) The legal deposit scheme provides a free copy of all books for every library;

(b) The legal deposit scheme provides a free copy of books published in the UK for the copyright deposit libraries;

(c) Copyright deposit libraries can have anything a publisher thinks he will send them.

Bibliography

Line, Maurice, *National libraries*, London, Aslib, 1979.
British Library, *Structure and functions*, London, nd (1989?).

Chapter Two

Organization, management and training of staff

The effectiveness of any library service depends to a large extent upon the manner in which the staff and their duties are organized. Few librarians ever have the opportunity of starting a brand-new service in new buildings with new staff, so most of them are faced with the continual modification of an existing structure. 'Existing structure' is an impersonal way of saying we are dealing with people − members of staff − who have a perception of their role and place in the structure and will often feel under threat when changes are being considered. The sensitive manager, therefore, will take great trouble to discuss changes with staff and keep them fully informed about how they personally will be affected should the changes ultimately be approved. In conducting changes, the manager will soon become aware that in most organizations there are two types of structure operating simultaneously. There is the formal structure, as represented by an organization chart, that forms the basis of the hierarchy and interrelationships of the system, and the informal structure which represents how people actually relate to one another. It is seldom that the two correlate very closely. It can happen, therefore, that changes in the formal organization chart that appear not to affect an individual may in fact affect him or her in an important way because they can be thought to damage his or her informal relationships.

Organization charts

Formal structures are represented in a hierarchical fashion on an organization chart and are defined more closely in individual job descriptions. Typical examples of organization charts are given in Figures 1 and 2.

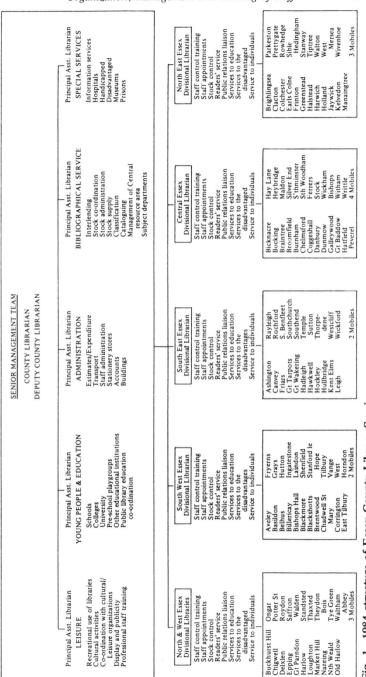

SENIOR MANAGEMENT TEAM
COUNTY LIBRARIAN
DEPUTY COUNTY LIBRARIAN

Principal Asst. Librarian
LEISURE

Recreational use of libraries
Cultural activities
Co-ordination with cultural/
Leisure organizations
Display and publicity
Professional staff training

Principal Asst. Librarian
YOUNG PEOPLE & EDUCATION

Schools
Colleges
University
Pre-school playgroups
Other educational institutions
Public library education
co-ordination

Principal Asst. Librarian
ADMINISTRATION

Estimates/Expenditure
Transport
Staff administration
Stationery stores
Accounts
Buildings

Principal Asst. Librarian
BIBLIOGRAPHICAL SERVICE

Interlending
Stock co-ordination
Stock administration
Stock supply
Classification
Cataloguing
Management of Central
resource area
Subject departments

Principal Asst. Librarian
SPECIAL SERVICES

Information services
Hospitals
Handicapped
Disadvantaged
Museums
Prisons

North & West Essex
Divisional Libraries

Staff control training
Staff appointments
Stock control
Readers' service
Public relations liaison
Services to education
Services to the
disadvantaged
Service to individuals

Buckhurst Hill	Ongar
Chigwell	Potter St
Debden	Roydon
Epping	Saffron
Gt Parndon	Walden
Harlow	Standsted
Loughton	Thaxted
Market Hill	Theydon
Nazeing	Bois
Nth Weald	Tye Green
Old Harlow	Waltham
	Abbey
	3 Mobiles

South West Essex
Divisional Libraries

Staff control training
Staff appointments
Stock control
Readers' service
Public relations liaison
Services to education
Services to the
disadvantages
Service to individuals

Aveley	Fryerns
Basildon	Grays
Belhus	Hutton
Billericay	Ingatestone
Bishops Hall	Laindon
Blackmore	Shenfield
Blackshots	Stanford le
Brentwood	Hope
Chadwell St	Tilbury
Mary	Vange
Corringham	West
East Tilbury	Horndon
	2 Mobiles

South East Essex
Divisional Librarian

Staff control training
Staff appointments
Stock control
Readers' service
Public relations liaison
Services to education
Services to individuals

Ashington	Rayleigh
Canvey	Rochford
Friars	S. Benfleet
Gt Wakering	Southchurch
Hadleigh	Southend
Hawkwell	Temple
Hockley	Sutton
Hullbridge	Thorpe-
Kent Elms	dene
Leigh	Westcliff
	Wickford
	2 Mobiles

Central Essex
Divisional Librarian

Staff control training
Staff appointments
Stock control
Readers' service
Public relations liaison
Services to education
Service to individuals

Bicknacre	Hay Lane
Bocking	Heybridge
Braintree	Maldon
Broomfield	Silver End
Burnham	S'thminster
Chelmsford	Sth Woodham
Coggeshall	Ferrers
Danbury	Stock
Dunmow	Wickham
Galleywood	Bishops
Gt Baddow	Witham
Hatfield	Writtle
Peverel	4 Mobiles

North East Essex
Divisional Librarian

Staff control training
Staff appointments
Stock control
Readers' service
Public relations liaison
Services to education
Services to the
disadvantaged
Service to individuals

Brightlingsea	Parkeston
Clacton	Prettygate
Colchester	Rowhedge
Earls Colne	Sible
Frinton	Hedingham
Greenstead	Stanway
Halstead	Tiptree
Harwich	Walton
Holland	West
Jaywick	Mersea
Kelvedon	Wivenhoe
Manningtree	3 Mobiles

Fig. 1 1984 structure of Essex County Library Service

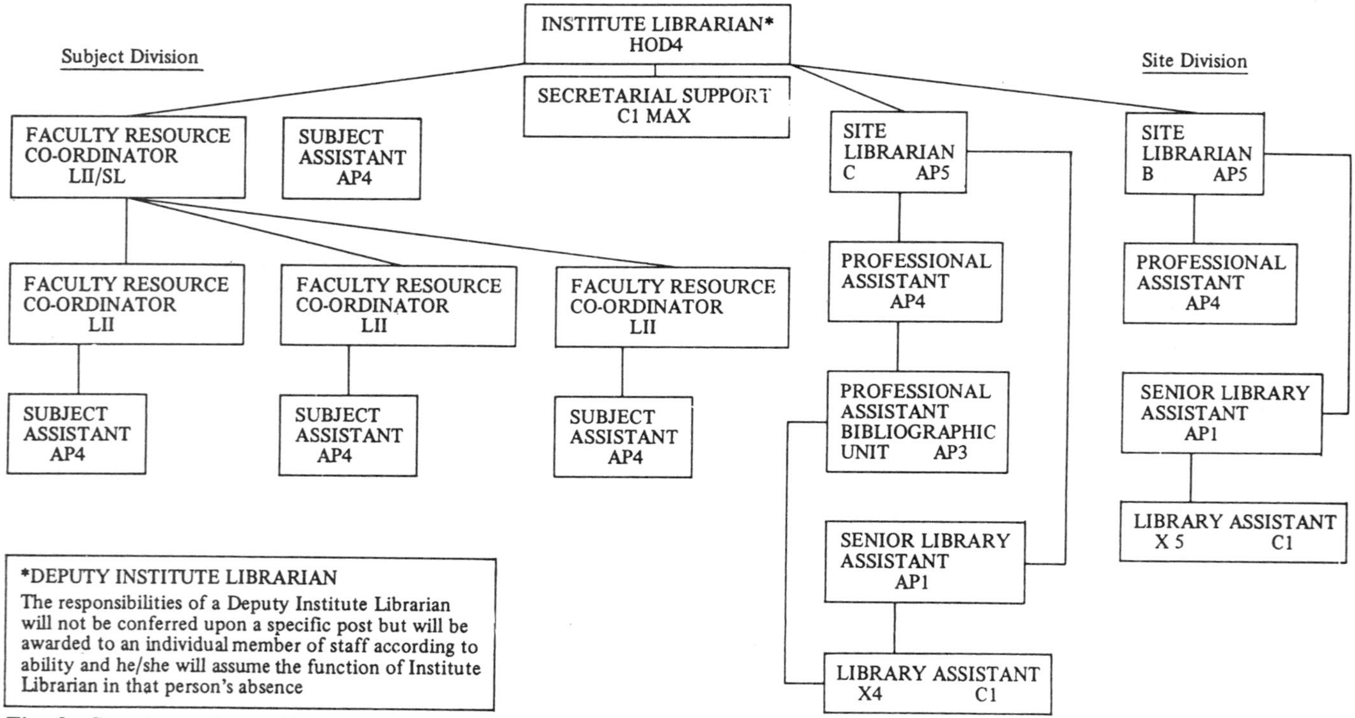

The basics of librarianship

Subject Division

Site Division

INSTITUTE LIBRARIAN*
HOD4

SECRETARIAL SUPPORT
C1 MAX

FACULTY RESOURCE
CO-ORDINATOR
LII/SL

SUBJECT
ASSISTANT
AP4

FACULTY RESOURCE
CO-ORDINATOR
LII

SUBJECT
ASSISTANT
AP4

FACULTY RESOURCE
CO-ORDINATOR
LII

SUBJECT
ASSISTANT
AP4

FACULTY RESOURCE
CO-ORDINATOR
LII

SUBJECT
ASSISTANT
AP4

SITE
LIBRARIAN
C   AP5

PROFESSIONAL
ASSISTANT
AP4

PROFESSIONAL
ASSISTANT
BIBLIOGRAPHIC
UNIT   AP3

SENIOR LIBRARY
ASSISTANT
AP1

LIBRARY ASSISTANT
X4   C1

SITE
LIBRARIAN
B   AP5

PROFESSIONAL
ASSISTANT
AP4

SENIOR LIBRARY
ASSISTANT
AP1

LIBRARY ASSISTANT
X 5   C1

*DEPUTY INSTITUTE LIBRARIAN
The responsibilities of a Deputy Institute Librarian
will not be conferred upon a specific post but will be
awarded to an individual member of staff according to
ability and he/she will assume the function of Institute
Librarian in that person's absence

Fig. 2 Structure of a medium-sized academic library

The first represents the structure of one of the largest county library services in the country while the second represents a typical medium-sized academic library. The charts can show the number of staff and the salary grades of the posts and the relationships between the different levels of management and employees. The production of one of these formal charts is a prerequisite to an understanding of the operation of a system. Many commercial organizations conduct searches among their employees to discover to whom those employees actually report in practice and with whom they have written or verbal communication as a regular part of their duties. By comparing the informal communication network with the formal organization chart, one can see how close the fit between actuality and theory is. Provided that key people are not being circumvented by the informal structure, a certain looseness of fit is quite acceptable.

The next stage in this process of looking at the structure of the organization is to define the actual duties allocated to each individual and to ensure that as far as is practical the group of duties allocated to each person is a fair quantity of work for him or her to perform.

Job description

What is a job description? It is a detailed list of duties attached to a particular post and it shows to whom the post-holder is directly responsible. Often the job description is combined with a personnel specification. This is an attempt to describe the sort of person who could adequately perform the duties given in the job description. The factors that one would take into account in producing a personnel specification would be:

1 Physical ability. For example, the job may require long periods of standing.
2 Age. Is there any reason to limit people applying for the post to a particular age range?
3 Qualifications. What qualifications are actually needed in order to perform the duties? Could you justify asking for a specific qualification for the work given in the job description?

The factors listed above are examples of the things that one would wish to consider when drawing up a personnel specification.

It is clear that the job description and the personnel specification are closely related and they are often produced as a single document which is sent to applicants to help them to assess their suitability for the post. In many cases, because of the similar nature of the duties, a job description is prepared for a particular group of posts, for example, senior library assistants or general library assistants. Depending upon the size and nature of the library service, the personnel specification may vary for people applying for posts within the same group. An example of a job description for a general library assistant is given in Figure 3. You will notice that some 32 tasks are identified as being appropriate

---

GENERAL LIBRARY ASSISTANT

Non-professional staff may be required to undertake any of the following activities. In general, however, some activities are allocated specifically to a particular member of staff.

1 *Issuing and renewals* Charging all material borrowed by members of the public. Amending loan records and recording renewals.

2 *Discharging material* Discharging material on loan.

3 *Issue maintenance* Moving up, filing and counting issue.

4 *Cancellation of issue* Cancellation of any written issue record.

5 *Sorting returned material* All sorting of material between return and shelving, e.g. for repairs and shelving.

6 *Shelving* Taking returned material to shelves and filing away. Moving stock to enable shelving to take place.

7 *Shelf tidying* Putting material in order on shelves and straightening.

8 *Maintaining readers' records* Registration and re-registration of borrowers. Making out tickets. Maintenance of membership records.

9 *Overdues* Preparation of issue records prior to overdue writing. Extraction of data from issue records. Writing overdues including accounts, instructions to book recovery officers, overdues to other libraries. Checking shelves and stock records before writing or despatch of overdues. Monitoring computer printouts as necessary.

10 *Reservations* Receipt of handling of reservations. Catalogue, shelf and issue checking. Routine bibliographical checking. Listing of reservations. Checking returned material against lists. All inter-library loan procedures including requesting material by telex, checking circulated reservation lists, etc.

11 *Ordering stock* Pre-ordering routines, e.g. checking bibliographical details, stock holdings, etc. Clerical aspects of ordering and follow-up procedures.

12 *Processing stock* Preparing material for addition to stock. Sorting stock records preparatory to filing. Inserting security triggers.

13 *Periodicals* Recording receipt. Display and filing. Maintaining records of holdings. Preparation for binding. Circulation procedures.

14 *Stock editing* Clerical procedures connected with stock editing.

15 *Repairs* Physical upkeep including cleaning, replacement of issue stationery and class marks, general repairs, insertion of triggers.

16 *Re-binding* Clerical procedures connected with binding, e.g. compiling records of material sent to binding; packing and unpacking; checking returned material and completion of processing. Amendment of stock records.

17 *Typing and duplicating* of handouts and catalogue records and correspondence.

18 *Film ordering service.*

19 *Withdrawals* Removal and amendment of stock records. Offering selected material to other locations. Disposal of withdrawn material.

20 *Stocktaking* Comparison of stock records with stock and issue.

21 *Inquiries* Directional inquiries and other routine inquiries which can properly be resolved by non-professional staff.

22 *Telephone.*

23 *Displays and extension activities* Putting up notices. Preparation and mounting of displays. Assisting with story hours and class visits.

24 *General administration* Statistics, accounts and cash handling, timetables, mail. General administration of service point.

25 *Information file maintenance* Updating information files.

26 *Filing pamphlet material,* e.g. standards, printed catalogues, prospectuses.

27 *Photocopying* Includes making photocopies, dealing with declaration forms and payments. Control of photocopier and similar machinery. Sales of tokens to operate machines.

28 *Amendments* Transferring information received from amending services to appropriate publications. Updating reference material from current sources.

29 *Office Supplies*

30 *Security system* Operation of system, including checking bags, etc. as necessary.

31 *Education training* Attendance at in-service training courses and general education as appropriate to the post.

32 Duties of the post may be varied, and or changed, from time to time as required.

Fig. 3 Example of a job description

to this post. In a small library the one or two members of staff falling into this group might need to be trained in all of these. In a large county library service there may be sufficient work in any grouping of two or three to keep staff fully occupied. Therefore, in drawing up the personnel description the abilities and qualifications that one is seeking will be directly related to the particular duties being advertised at that time. A practical example of this could be the grouping together of the following areas of work shown in Figure 3: 17, 18, 22, 25 and 29. For this group of tasks one would be seeking an applicant who had office/clerical qualifications, who had a pleasant voice for the telephone and perhaps a proven record of competence in the filing and handling of materials. However, if you group tasks 5, 6 and 7 you would be looking for somebody who is physically fit, who is numerate and literate and perhaps has a high boredom threshold. An example of a combined job and personnel description for a more senior post in an academic library is given in Figure 4.

JOB DESCRIPTION
A FACULTY RESOURCES CO-ORDINATOR

The person occupying this post will be responsible directly to the Institute Librarian for the performance of the following duties:

1 To know the detailed structure and educational goals of the courses in the Faculty, including the way they are administered, the methods of teaching and learning employed on the courses, and the relevant characteristics and problems of their students. To know the courses' entry requirements, validation process and assessment methods.

2 To obtain after appointment such subject knowledge of the topics covered by the courses as to make possible an understanding of the syllabus's content, range and emphasis and in particular to obtain detailed knowledge of [to be specified] courses.

3 To obtain after appointment some understanding of current developments in educational thought and practice.

4 To possess a high degree of competence in professional academic librarianship.

5 To have some familiarity with non-print material and with media equipment, and to gain after appointment some experience of media production.

6 To serve on the relevant course boards, committees and working parties in order to:
   (a) understand the courses' resource needs and to evaluate these in qualitative, quantitative and financial terms;
   (b) draw attention to the range of resources and facilities provided by the Institute's Library resources;
   (c) support and encourage within the courses the development of new approaches to teaching and learning;
   (d) convey information about course developments and needs to both academic staff and the appropriate Library staff.

7 In the study of [to be specified] to be aware of all significant works and sources of information for the courses, so as to be able to select and provide bibliographic records of stock, and to develop the collection to its maximum level of effectiveness; and to ensure that the collection contains all relevant formats of material, both print and non-print.

8 To apply the techniques of a professional librarian to ensure that resources are exploited fully, such exploitation to include:
   (a) the selective dissemination of information;
   (b) the critical analysis of library materials for information retrieval purposes;
   (c) the introduction of staff and students to the range and depth of resources available both within the Institute and elsewhere; formal and information instruction in the use of Library resources;
   (d) to provide an information desk service within the Libraries.

9 To provide academic leadership under the overall direction of the Institute Librarian to those members of the Library staff offering specific services into the Faculty of [to be specified]. To advise the Institute Librarian on the general developments and in particular needs of the courses within the Faculty so that adequate financial provision can be made for further growth and to ensure that the Library service develops its provision in accordance with the needs of staff and students within that Faculty.

Fig. 4 Combined job and personnel description

Work studies

Now we can turn to the day-to-day monitoring of how the work system operates. No organization can remain static, and as changes occur these will affect, sometimes dramatically, the loading of each individual task. A regular review of what is involved in each task must be undertaken to ensure a continued fair distribution of work. It is often considered to be the role of the senior library assistant to monitor this on a day-to-day basis and report any inequalities to a superior as soon as changes are needed. Routine supervision of people working is the usual way of monitoring problems. In some libraries this is supported by the application of simple work study techniques devised both to monitor work rates and to enable workers to suggest improvements in routines. By observing the work rate of reliable assistants or even by asking them to keep a record of how long certain tasks take, it is possible to calculate an average time to perform these duties. This information can be used to monitor work-loads. It is important to explain to the staff exactly what you are doing and why you are doing it, and to make it clear that if they have any doubts or concerns regarding the practice they should consult their work-place representative or union official. Major work study is best left to professionals and these are usually available within each county, metropolitan or business organization. A major national report, the LAMSAC (Local Authorities Management Services and Computer Committee) Report, concerned itself with the study of the staffing of public libraries. This lengthy document is of considerable use to librarians in all sorts of libraries and is worthy of study.

Some of the various factors which you will wish to take account of in any assessment of staffing levels following an organization and methods (O & M) survey are as follows:

1   The number of hours the library is open and the number of people required on duty for each hour.
2   The number of separate service points to be manned.
3   Enquiry desks − level of manning required during each part of the day.
4   Volume of processing work to be accomplished.
5   Book ordering and invoice checking, etc. − number of staff necessary to ensure that delays do not occur.
6   Cataloguing and classification.
7   Professional support services in terms of book lists, reading lists etc.
8   Staff training time − it is normal to make an allowance so that staff can be trained internally and can be released for education on outside courses.

9 Sickness cover — in many libraries there is a central pool of staff to offer sickness relief to branches and central departments.

10 Extension activities — these often make great demands on staff, particularly in public libraries where personnel may be involved in the organization of exhibitions or series of lectures.

11 Committees, working parties, staff development duties — although this work will normally be undertaken by senior staff as part of their duties, where there are a large number of internal working parties the time used in attending these should be taken into account.

Interviewing

The object of the interview is to enable the two parties to assess each other so that when an appointment is made an employer selects as an employee a candidate who actually wants to do the job. To achieve this desirable end, the method of interview has to be structured to overcome the totally artificial atmosphere that can so easily be induced. This is not to say that the formal interview across a table has no place in selection procedures since the stress it normally occasions is often replicated in real life when things go wrong. Requiring the interviewee to operate under some degree of pressure is in reality a fair test of ability. The following methods can be employed to give candidates a balanced interview and also to involve more of the library staff in the procedure.

Tour of workplace

The object of this is to enable candidates to look at the physical surroundings in which they would be working and to give them a chance to talk informally with members of staff performing functions similar to those covered by the job for which they are applying. It is helpful to involve senior library assistants, who can talk with candidates informally, either in a group or individually, and who will often form useful impressions of their suitability. These views should be passed to any later interviewing panel to form part of the overall assessment of an applicant's suitability for the post.

Testing

In too few cases do librarians seek any practical evidence that applicants are capable of performing the jobs for which they are applying. It is neither unfair nor unreasonable to expect candidates to be willing to undertake a limited range of practical tests such as putting a shelf of books in order, typing a page of text, putting plastic jackets on books and so on. This is also helpful for the candidate since it gives him or her, perhaps for the first time, a chance to appreciate what he or she may be spending many hours in doing in future.

Formal interviews

The formal interview in which the candidate is faced by a panel often composed of the librarian, the personnel officer and a few other individuals is the traditional method. All too often the size of the interviewing panel is out of all proportion to the salary being offered for the job advertised, and while it may be appropriate to have half a dozen people interviewing for a senior professional post, two or three are more than adequate for more junior posts. In conducting these interviews, the chairman should always allow a settling-in period so that the candidate can answer relatively simple, general questions before the session focuses on the more germane issues. In formulating questions to ask the candidate, the interviewers have three basic tools to assist them: they have the applicant's own application form, the job description and the personnel description. By seeing how closely the applicant's history, qualifications, age and so on, match up to the personnel description, areas that need to be explored normally become evident. The technique of questioning at these interviews is that you start with a general or 'open-ended' question to get the candidate talking. An example of this might be: 'What particular jobs do you enjoy most in your present post?' Once the candidate has answered this general question you might well follow it up with a question probing the areas that he or she did not like, such as: 'What in particular did you not enjoy about shelving books?' In this way your first general question does not give away too much of your own attitudes or expectations and therefore the candidate will find it easier to answer the questions truthfully than to provide an answer that he or she thinks you expect. Towards the end of the time available for the interview, one should always allow a period when the candidate can ask questions of the panel. Often these questions will be related to salaries, conditions of service, starting dates and so on, but they will occasionally produce more interesting questions, and these may well give an insight into the character of the applicant.

The expert interviewer will make notes on his or her feelings about each applicant in relation to individual areas of questioning so that by the end of a session of interviewing he or she has sufficient notes to allow a fair assessment of the candidates who appeared early on the list.

Group interviews

While this technique would normally only be used for higher professional posts, it is occasionally used for posts at all levels. Here the candidates are brought together and given the opportunity of joining in a general discussion with members of the interviewing panel. Often this is extended over a luncheon period so that the social skills of the candidates can also be measured. This can be an extremely helpful technique when used in appropriate circumstances.

Professional and non-professional duties

With the spread of O & M studies into the library world over the last 20 years, it has become increasingly the case that the work of people in libraries has been categorized into professional and non-professional duties. While there have always been professional and non-professional duties in libraries, it used often to be difficult, particularly in small libraries, to distinguish clearly the boundary between the two areas. This was simply because there was often only one member of staff on duty and he or she performed all of the jobs without any need for demarcation. In the modern world, since professional status and salary levels are often determined by the way the post is created, in O & M studies it has become increasingly important to identify tasks which are the chief prerogative of the professionally qualified librarian and those which can be performed by suitably trained library assistants. Referring back to Figure 3, you will see that all of the tasks on this list are of a non-professional nature. When preparing job descriptions it is important to take into account the nature of the duties to ensure that you are not asking professional staff to perform too wide a range of non-professional duties and, perhaps more importantly, vice versa. The Library Association can provide guidance on professional and non-professional duties. It has also approved a body of professional knowledge that underpins the education and training of professional librarians and it is from this that we can get a clear picture of the skills and duties of a professional librarian or information worker.

From the body of knowledge it is possible to extract concepts that give us a clear picture of the professional. They will be able to:

- analyse the information requirements of the service users,
- select and organize material to meet those requirements,
- select and manage staff for the purpose,
- devise and operate appropriate storage and dissemination systems,
- be aware of changing technology applicable to the service,
- prepare policy and financial statements and implement them,
- lead the team involved in training and developing the service,
- represent the service at management and policy board level.

The full body of professional knowledge should be read in some detail to ensure a proper understanding of the boundaries between the two areas of responsibility. What follows is that section of the LA document *Procedures for the accreditation of courses* that contains the body of knowledge. Like all policy documents it is subject to on-going revision and changes will be reported in the *Library Association record* from time to time.

'The development of analytical and management skills which can be applied to the acquisition and deployment of resources and the promotion of library and information services within a given organisation

The analysis of a situation, the handling of committees, practical control of staff and understanding human motivations need to be tested as part of the course. This may involve a combination of group and individual work. It will need to ensure that all students understand what being a 'professional' in the information community entails and that they aware of codes of conduct.

In practical terms it may encompass design of service points and the ergonomic layout of information centres. It may cover the costing of new services and their promotion and marketing to senior management. It may deal with staff interview for promotion and annual assessment and for staff development. It can cover analysis of comparative costs of printed versus electronic information services.

It could contain the consideration of information services to particular nations, groups or companies and the production and 'implementation' of a development plan.

However, in any or all of these the aim must be to develop self-critical assessment, professionalism, and an analytical approach to tasks in hand.

The library and information needs of society

A study of the social role of information in society and a consideration of the services to particular groups within society. It might consider topics such as multi-cultural provision, censorship, special needs provision, mass communication, class and gender, cultural values and information values. Themes such as the scope of the information economy, how information supply can be controlled, impact of technology on the supply of and access to information. Issues such as free or fee, location of public libraries within a community, services to industry and business could be considered. The study of a foreign language is an approprite part of the course. This would need to be related to the provision of a library and information service.

The role, function and value of library and information services

An opportunity to investigate particular types of library and information service and the clients they serve. This will allow for detailed study of particular types of service, eg. that to young people, academic libraries, industrial information services, public libraries, and for comparative relationships to be made between them. Cost effectiveness of services both to individuals, groups and nations can be researched. The range of appropriate services required within particular organisations can be discussed and the resource costs evaluated. Concepts of consultancy services, user groups, co-operatives, role of librarians as intermediaries in information provision, the place of publishing, book production, information production in any format and dissemination of information can be covered.

The organisation, management and promotion of library and information services

This must encompass the study of management skills, supervisory skills and training skills. It can deal with financial controls, budgeting and accounting practice. Students can investigate marketing of services, development planning, decision making, communication systems (both human and machine), staff recruitment and retention policies and the theory of organisations.

Design and production of information materials can be covered in any format. Display and extra curricular activities can be covered.

The acquisition, production, organization and dissemination of information

This will cover all aspects of bibliographical control and sources, their use and application in stock selection and maintenance. The selection, management and preservation of stock, in any form, will be considered. The application of information technology in all its forms will be dealt with and students will have access to computer systems and on-line services as well as library management systems.

They can consider databases and their design and construction, and the infrastructure of telecommunications networks. Computer languages, special applications packages and programming can be introduced. All of the above can be applied to special types of service, eg. archives, bookshops, printing industry, computer services, advice services, leisure services.

The evaluation, assessment and re-packaging of information for third party use will be considered.

Central matters such as cataloguing and classification, reference sources and materials, indexing, abstracts and indexes and their application into particular library and information services will be covered. Their application via particular schemes and an understanding of those schemes will need to be demonstrated.'

In October 1990 the Library Association Council approved a new statement on the role of the professional librarian. It focuses upon the chartered librarian and gives details of the range of professional skills and duties that an employer can expect from such a person. The publication, *Professional librarians: a brief guide for employers*, is available from The Library Association's Employment and Resources Department. Librarians seeking further advice should contact this Department.

It very much follows on from the text above from the LA's *Procedures for the accreditation of courses*, but puts that information clearly into the context of the employer and the job function.

In the opening section it makes the important point that,

'To function effectively all organisations need efficient access to information and ideas. It is the prime responsibility of the Librarian to assess the information needs of the organisation and to manage a service which effectively meets those requirements.

The importance of libraries and information units can be measured only by their contribution to the overall aims and objectives of the organisation or community of which they are a part. These, of course, vary enormously, but, for instance, in business and commercial firms it is the contribution that an effective information service makes to the competitive position and profitability of the company which is important. Similarly in education it is the support given to the learning process within the institution concerned.'

It defines a professional librarian as someone who can 'formulate, plan, direct and deliver library and information services by identifying the needs and demands of actual and potential users; collecting, retrieving and organising knowledge and ideas in a variety of forms, from books and manuscripts to computerised databases; and disseminating and marketing library and information services to clients'.

Clearly from these two short extracts you can see that the two policy documents from the Association mutually support and develop the themes of each other.

The first is aimed at the education and training market place, and provides a very broad list of concepts that the modern professional will need to practise; the second takes that a stage further into the workplace, and describes to the non-librarian employer the benefits that will accrue from having a fully developed library or information service available to the workforce.

While neither statement is concerned to list actual tasks, as did a previous statement of professional and non-professional duties, they do provide a very clear picture of the type of work that is professional and requires the knowledge and training that comes with being a chartered librarian.

In the preparation of job descriptions it is very important that one considers the factors given in the two documents above. When deciding whether a job is professional or not one should check the various items that make up the profile of the task against the concepts of what a professional librarian should be doing. Clearly at the margins or in a small library it will be difficult to keep the tasks so clear cut since some posts will have to combine both professional and non-professional work. However, the skill of the personnel officer is to keep these posts to the absolute minimum. It may well be that by looking at the duties of several posts the duties can be so organized that it is easier to delineate the duties.

Often the title of the post can help clear the mind. Reference Librarian, Readers Services Librarian, Chief Cataloguer or subject specialists all give you the clear starting point of a professional post. Problems arise in lower level posts where some of the tasks may sound, or in fact be, similar. The cut off point between a professional cataloguer and an assistant who checks databases for records, or updates basic records is more complex and could, depending on other duties, fall either side of the divide.

The middle ground is filled by staff who have taken courses like the City and Guilds Library Assistants Certificate or the BTEC Double Library Module. These are the sort of staff who will be filling the new LA 'Affiliate' grade of member and are the link staff in the library structure. Some of these qualifications are obtainable by distance learning methods, for example, the City and Guilds course is offered by Telford College in Edinburgh.

Normally a degree in librarianship or its equivalent is required for professional posts, while non-professional posts will be filled by staff having satisfactory qualifications in GCSE or A-level, the City and Guilds Library Assistants Certificate or the BTEC National Examination with the special library studies module. Success in the latter examination will probably be considered the appropriate standard for promotion to posts of senior library assistant in public and other libraries. The National Council for Vocational Qualification (NCVQ) are, 1990, setting up a lead body for library and information work to develop a series of vocational standard tests related to outcomes of training. These will, in time, provide another route for non-professional qualification.

Induction and training

An essential requirement for all non-professional posts (and many professional posts) is appropriate induction into the service whereby new staff meet colleagues and see how each department relates to the others. The induction course will give all the necessary employment details and conditions of service in relation to such matters as the amount of leave entitlement, the contract of employment, insurance stoppages, what to do in case of sickness and how to inform senior colleagues of inability to attend for duty. Equally important, it will provide a background to the social structure of the library − the staff guild, any clubs or unions that operate within the library, discount schemes, car parking facilities, arrangements for meals and so on.

This early opportunity should also be used to impress upon the new entrant the importance of right attitudes to work and to the public. Much of this information is best reinforced by issuing a staff notebook that can be given to every new entrant. The notebook should contain a list of staff and an explanation of departmental structures so that relationships can be learned easily and the right people can be contacted from the outset. The induction procedure must occur immediately after joining; otherwise bad habits will be formed and will be difficult to eradicate.

Training is a more structured and long-term project. Initial training will probably take place in the individual department or library where the entrant works, and he or she will be guided and instructed by responsible assistants in learning the background to the total service. It is often helpful to formalize this training procedure by the use of some simple form that enables the new assistant to check which tasks he or she has been trained to do and by whom the training has been done, and it should also allow either party to make comments about the training given. A simple example of this is given in Figure 5. In this case the duty numbers relate to the duties listed in Figure 3. The new assistant should be allowed to keep a copy for personal use while the carbon copy can be kept in his or her personal file as a permanent record of the training. This basic in-service training should always be supplemented by a staff manual of practice to which any member of staff can refer to refresh his or her memory about particular methods of operation or the library's basic policy decisions.

Once the initial in-service training has been completed, more extended training may well be considered advisable. In large library systems this may involve attendance on short courses run by the library training officer. In some cases it could mean attendance on courses at colleges in the area or it might take the form of attendance at meetings of local

TRAINING SCHEDULE

DUTY	INSTRUCTED BY	DATE	COMMENTS	SIGNED AS HAVING RECEIVED INSTRUCTION
1				
2				
3				
4				
5				
6				
7				
8				
9				
10				
11				
12				
13				

Fig. 5   Training schedule

groups of librarians. Membership of the Library Association brings staff into contact with people in their region who are employed in their particular type of library service. These meetings are valuable since they allow an exchange of views and techniques between colleagues at all levels.

Extended training is perhaps better described as a mixture of training and education, since the term 'training' is normally applied to practical skills acquisition rather than to the broader philosophical problems which the courses we have just been talking about would consider. Finance for training/education courses can often be obtained from the local education authority, particularly where attendance on recognized courses is involved, from the local government training board or one of the other industrial training boards. Many employers will also allow staff to take time off work to attend courses.

The object of this training is to enable the assistant to perform his or her duties satisfactorily, to enable him or her to see how the work fits into the total service, to give job satisfaction and, finally, to widen education in library matters so that he or she begins to appreciate the role of the service regionally and nationally.

In most authorities the new entrant will be employed for a probationary period, the length of which may vary. The reason for it is to enable the employer and the employee to assess one another. Obviously if the employee is dissatisfied with the job he or she will look for another post. If the employer is dissatisfied with the way the assistant is responding to training, he or she may wish to consider invoking the probation clause in the letter of appointment. If this is to be done, it is important that adequate warnings are given to the employee throughout the period of probation. These should include written warnings indicating very clearly the areas where dissatisfaction is being identified. It is equally important that additional training is given to allow the assistant an opportunity to improve his or her performance. Copies of all correspondence must be included in the individual's personal file. Attention must be paid to the Contracts of Employment Act of 1972 and to the National Joint Council's scheme of conditions of service (the 'purple book') and other nationally agreed schemes relating to the conditions of employment in particular areas.

Supervisory duties

The supervisor needs at least a little understanding of motivation and behaviour. Reference should be made to Chapter 10 of G. E. Evans's *Management techniques for librarians.* Perhaps we could summarize the situation by pointing out the importance of the recognition that every employee has 'needs'. These will vary, not only from person to person, but from time to time for each person. According to A. H. Maslow's theory of human motivation, there are five levels of need, which are:

1 Physical needs – these are often associated with bodily comfort. It is therefore important for the supervisor to take into account room temperatures, both hot and cold; the freshness of the air and the adequacy of ventilation; levels of lighting; decoration; canteen facilities etc.
2 Security needs – a basic need of most people since this applies to security both regarding employment and home life. From the supervisor's point of view it is worth bearing in mind that to exercise disciplinary control through threats may well be self-defeating since these threats will attack this basic need.
3 Social needs – this covers such things as acceptance by fellow-workers and integration into the formal structures of the organization.
4 Esteem needs – this covers not only how individuals see their own role but also their perception of how others see them. This need can be influenced by offering criticism only in private but by giving praise in public.
5 Self-actualization or the need to realize one's potential – training, education and promotion all play their parts in this need.

A basic understanding of what motivates each individual helps a supervisor plan the right approach. Generally it is sound to assume competence, to involve people in decision making, to take opinions into account – this all helps to create an atmosphere of trust, harmony and cooperation. Where problems do arise, it is sensible to check out the training programme before blaming the assistant for poor performance of duties. However, if after full investigation it is clear that the assistant has been trained properly and is capable of performing the duties accurately but is just not performing them satisfactorily, it is essential for the supervisor to take the assistant aside, attempt to discover the reason for the problems and try to overcome them. It can sometimes be of help to use the services of welfare or personnel officers since often people will talk to outsiders rather more easily than to their immediate superiors.

Supervisors do have an important responsibility to the organization. In spite of all this care and attention there may still be staff who are causing problems because they were selected for the wrong job, they feel some sense of grievance and are therefore being obstructive or they are just not able to handle certain tasks. If so, the supervisor has a clear responsibility to give adequate warnings as to future conduct, to ensure complete training is given, to follow this up with written warnings and, if necessary, to make contact with union representatives.

Personal record

From all of the foregoing the need to keep clear, confidential records will be apparent. Accuracy of information is vital and particular care must be taken to record joining dates, changes of post, salary levels and so on quickly and correctly. Only appropriate staff will be allowed access to these files, since they contain very sensitive information. Staff who do have access must be selected for their discretion and must never use their knowledge except in the performance of their duties. Increasingly, libraries are moving to computerized personnel systems and the requirements of the Data Protection Act 1984 are such that accuracy and confidentiality are even more important than hitherto since employees can take legal action if records that are not fully up to date are used for promotion, reference and so on. Under the Act employees have the right to see data held on them and ask for it to be corrected. Failure to do this could lead to a fine if the matter is taken to court.

Because of this some libraries prefer to keep to paper records which are not at present covered by the Act. These paper records can be in two forms. The first is a simple card which contains the 'core' details of each employee; an example is given in Figure 6. This is supported by an individual file which contains copies of all documents regarding the individual from the time he or she first applied for a post. The file

Department ....

SURNAME .... Christian names ....

Single name .... Date of Birth ....
(If married woman)

Private Address ....

Post .... Grading ....

Qualifications ....

Date of Appointment .... Superann. IN/OUT Telephone no. ....

Date of resignation ....

National Insurance Number / / / / Vice-

Date	Salary	Reason for Change	Courses attended and results	Remarks

Fig. 6 Employee's record card

will start with the job description and personnel description and will contain copies of the advertisement, the completed application form, references taken up, comments made during interview and the letter of appointment. Once the new member is in post, copies of letters relating to changes in conditions of employment and letters of commendation or warnings as to future conduct and so on would be placed in the file. The file would obviously conclude with a letter of resignation.

After resignation the file is usually kept in store for several years, after which time it may be microcopied and the original destroyed. The reason for keeping the file in its original state for a few years after the member of staff has left is that quite often he or she will give the former employer's name as a reference. Copies of any references given should be added to the file.

Computerized record systems are in some cases linked to a microfilm store; in other cases edge-punched card systems are used. Obviously this use of automation extends the usefulness of staff records since by careful encoding of information personnel officers can make useful statistical comparisons, for instance, they can identify all the staff who have a certain qualification.

Welfare
This can be considered in two parts, statutory and social.

Statutory
There are Acts of Parliament that lay down basic conditions of work and safety regulations that affect every employee. The Offices, Shops and Railway Premises Act 1963 and the Health and Safety at Work Act 1974 are the major pieces of legislation that must be considered. These Acts make it clear that certain basic requirements must be met before staff can be expected to work. Such things as the minimum room temperature within one hour of starting work, the adequacy of light and ventilation, toilet provision, fire regulations and exits and the safety of electrical appliances are all covered in considerable detail.

While every member of staff has a duty under the Acts to be observant where safety is concerned, it is inevitable that the chief responsibility must rest with the various levels of management. Staff showing signs of illness or injury should be sent to the medical centre and any necessary accident or safety forms must be completed. It is essential that once they have been completed these forms are acted upon and not just filed away. In cases where there is any doubt about how to comply with the Acts, professional help can often be obtained from safety officers or inspectors who can be contacted through local councils.

Social

Many large libraries have staff associations. These provide such services as entertainment, discount trading arrangements with local firms and a forum to discuss matters relating to working conditions or the development of the service. In some library authorities, these associations are highly developed and form a positive bridge between junior staff and senior management.

All libraries will have a majority of their staff belonging to trades unions. To some extent local authorities take a corporate attitude about how freely they allow the union or its representatives to operate within their departments, and this general attitude will cover the library. Generally, staff are allowed to attend meetings provided the service is not disrupted, and in some places staff are allowed time off from their normal duties to act as work-place representatives or to hold other official positions representing the union interests of workers. It is helpful to management to keep the appropriate union representative informed of changes of policy that affect his or her members. The staff association should also be kept informed so that non-union members are not discriminated against. This course of action can lead to both unions and staff associations providing positive help in the implementation of changes.

In larger library systems there will be a welfare or personnel officer who can assist staff with personal problems relating to home life or their employment. The sympathetic supervisor will be on the look-out for signs that staff require this type of assistance and will act in a positive way to encourage staff to make use of all the counselling facilities available to them, not only within the library service but also within the council or firm as a whole.

Communications

Libraries are often large and complex organizations and it is essential but difficult to keep all staff up to date with regard to policy, technical changes, training dates and the whole host of information that a member of staff needs to be confident in performing his or her tasks. The position is complicated by the need to keep the service open for long periods of time. This makes it difficult for all the staff to meet together to pass information round. Therefore it is essential that some way is found to keep staff informed of current library news.

Updates to the staff manual, circular memos, notice boards and so on are all used and each of these is helpful. However, the main need of staff is often to talk to someone. This does not have to be the chief librarian on every occasion; the line manager is often the best person.

In many libraries the technique of team briefings has been found to be useful in aiding communication. In these, information is passed both up and down the organization via small group meetings. The leader of each group is briefed at a 'higher' meeting and quickly passes news to the group he or she leads, then on down to the next level and so on. By using this approach, all staff can be informed quickly and the service can be kept running. Problems and suggestions for change can go up the line in the same way.

Assignments

1   Produce an organization chart for the library in which you work. Visit a different type of library and see if you can produce an organization chart for it.

2   Using the charts from (1) above, look for differences in the structure, and account for them in terms of aims and objectives and job functions.

3   Design a staff record card and write notes on why the information it would contain would be needed.

4   Describe the relationship between the staff in your library and the union(s).

5   Show how communications flow up and down the 'tree' in your library.

6   Devise an in-service training course for a new junior member of staff.

Bibliography

Baker, David, *Guidelines for training in libraries* (Part 6, Training library assistants), London, Library Association, 1986.

Department of Education and Science, *The staffing of public libraries*, 3 vols., London, HMSO, 1976 (LAMSAC Report).

Edwards, R. J., *In-service training in British libraries*, London, Library Association, 1976.

Evans, G. E., *Management techniques for librarians*, London, Academic Press, 1976, 163–86.

Harrison, C. T., *Communication in library management*, Association of Assistant Librarians (South East Division), 1979.

Library Association, *Procedures for the accreditation of courses*, London, Library Association, 1990.

Library Association, *Professional librarians: a brief guide for employers*, London, Library Association, 1990.

Chapter Three

Acquisition of basic library materials

The modern library stocks a wide range of materials with which to satisfy the needs of its clients. The acquisition of these materials is a skilful job demanding the sort of dedication that is required in running a home. In spite of the fact that books are controlled as far as their price is concerned and cannot be sold to the general public at less than the cover price imposed by the publisher under the terms of the Net Book Agreement, there are many ways in which librarians can obtain value for money when purchasing books and other materials. Almost all public libraries and many academic libraries apply to the Publishers Association for a library licence. In its application the library authority will list the names of designated suppliers. The Publishers Association will then contact these suppliers and, provided their agreement is obtained, will issue a licence which will allow the suppliers to offer a discount of 10% off net books. There will be some books — imported or non-net books — on which the full cover price may be charged but these form a small proportion of the purchases of most libraries. This discount is not available to industrial and commercial libraries since the basis upon which the licence is granted is that the library is open to the general public. Booksellers are usually very happy to agree to the issue of licences because they know they can anticipate a substantial volume of trade with the libraries concerned.

Books, while forming the major part of a library's stock, do not comprise the whole picture, and increasingly librarians are dealing with suppliers who are not on their library licence in order to obtain audio-visual materials, and in some cases are dealing with galleries for the purchase of photographs and works of art. It is unusual these days to find even the smallest library dealing with a single supplier for all its acquisitions. Consequently, the skill of shopping around and assessing the cost-effectiveness of a supplier's goods and services is important for the librarian to develop. For example, some major booksellers will process books at a nominal charge so that they arrive at the library complete with issue stationery, plastic jacket and spine label. This reduces the library's own staffing costs and therefore effectively is a reduction in the purchase price of new materials.

Stock selection

Stock must be selected to fulfil the aims and objectives of the particular library and so a strategy of stock acquisition is followed. It is done on a planned and logical basis, not on the whim or personal preference of the individual librarian. The library's senior management team will be aware of the needs and interests of people living, working or studying in their catchment area. They will also keep abreast of current affairs and matters of topical interest so that they can anticipate fluctuating demands. Librarians will endeavour to keep a balanced stock of fiction and non-fiction to match the anticipated needs of their present clients. That balance will therefore vary from library to library depending on its geographical location. For example, the town centre library may attract business and professional people as well as shoppers. If there is a college nearby, the library will also number students and tutors among its clients. On the other hand, the library in a large housing estate will attract mothers and toddlers, elderly residents and local schoolchildren. The reading needs and interests of these varied groups will be different from those of users of the town centre library and will be met by a correspondingly different range of books, periodicals and audiovisual materials. Each library member will also have needs related to education, information, leisure and culture, and these needs will vary at different times in the individual's life. Unfortunately, no library has sufficient funding to match all these demands, but the librarian will endeavour by a wise and carefully planned policy of stock selection to keep most of the customers happy for most of the time.

Some stock will be purchased as a direct result of specific and known demands. For example, readers will request or reserve specific books and the volume of demand will determine, to a large extent, the number of copies ordered. There is always a delay built into this kind of reactive purchasing, however, and some clients become rather impatient. The librarian will therefore try to anticipate demand, and if stock is being underused he or she will also try to stimulate demand by promotional activities such as displays or book-talks. The library may also have a member of staff called a stock editor whose task it is to continually peruse the shelves looking for obvious gaps in coverage or out-of-date or shabby items of stock which need to be replaced.

Obviously the best and safest way of selecting stock for purchase is to look at the books for oneself. In a large county library system the staff may have an 'on approval' arrangement with one or more major booksellers. A limited number of copies of every published work, or specified categories of publication, are forwarded to the library's headquarters. Larger branch libraries then review the current 'on approval' collection on a rota basis so that staff can examine the books and make their own selection.

Where time allows, a team of staff may make a more thorough evaluation of the books by reading them or perusing them sufficiently to be able to complete an evaluation slip or discuss their relative merits and demerits at a book review/book selection meeting attended by participating staff.

Staffing limitations may make this method of stock selection impossible for some libraries. Sometimes it is possible to allow a staff member to make an occasional visit to the stockrooms of a major bookseller where he or she can spend a very busy but enjoyable day browsing among the laden bookshelves and filling trolleys or trugs with selected items which will be forwarded when listed and processed. Obviously arrangements for the visit will have been confirmed in advance and the librarian will have done some homework so that the general areas of demand are known. The librarian must therefore have a very good knowledge of the library's existing stock and be aware of its shortcomings.

If it is not possible for the librarian to see and handle the prospective purchases, then the judgement of others may be considered as a reliable guide. Librarians will read reviews of new publications which appear in the better-class daily and Sunday newspapers and in periodicals such as the *Times literary supplement*, *British book news* and *Books* (formerly *Books and bookmen*). Other journals − such as the *Times educational supplement*, *NATFHE journal*, *Musical times*, *Library Association record* − cover specialist fields.

Probably all librarians concerned with stock selection will also scan each issue of the *British national bibliography* and the *Bookseller* to discover what books have been published recently or are forthcoming. Major booksellers will also supply their current stock lists and regularly send batches of slips or cards announcing recent publications. Publishers' catalogues are also useful sources of information but publishers are naturally keen to promote and sell their own publications, so librarians will read their promotional literature with a rather guarded attitude. Nevertheless, over the years librarians become very knowledgeable about the merits of authors and series and know which publishers are reputable.

There are also sources of information about recently produced gramophone records, compact discs, cassettes, videos and computer software — all of which have a place in the modern library and pose an even greater selection problem for the librarian than do books and journals. Again, previewing is the most foolproof method of selection but it is very time-consuming and therefore not always practicable.

Computerized ordering

Libraries which are computerized put their order records into the computer database. The system in use at the Anglia Higher Education College will serve as a case study. The Adlib — 2 Library Management System (now known as 'Equilibrium') displays the following main menu options on the computer screen.

```
          ADLIB – 2 LIBRARY MANAGEMENT SYSTEM

   Technical services            Acquisitions
   2  Cataloguer                 16 Head of acquisitions
   3  Authority file manager     17 Orders clerk
   4  Thesaurus manager
   Reference work                Serials control
   7  Reference librarian        20 Subscriptions librarian
   8  Information officer        21 Serials receipts clerk
   Reader services               22 Serials stock control clerk
   11 Reader services librarian  24 Management information
   12 Issue desk
   Use space bar, arrow keys, or type number to make selection.
   Enter 'h' for help or 'b' for bye.
```

The member of staff responsible for ordering stock will have received requests for orders from the subject specialists or resource coordinators employed at the various site libraries. The requests bear the appropriate signature to show that they are authorized. These staff members will already have checked the computer to ascertain that the items are not already in stock or previously ordered. To enter the order record on the computer, option 17, 'Orders clerk', is selected by keying in the appropriate digits on the keyboard terminal and depressing the 'Return' key. The Order clerk menu options then appear on the screen.

```
                         ORDER CLERK
    Control of requests              Control of invoices and credits
    2  Add/amend a request           16 Enter invoices
    3  List authorised requests      17 Enter credits
                                     18 Close invoices/credit notes
    Ordering                         19 List details of invoices/
                                        credit notes
    6  Enter orders and line details
    7  Close orders                  Supplier details
    8  Print orders                  22 Add/amend suppliers
    9  List details of open orders   23 List suppliers
    10 List details of closed orders Generate claims
    11 List order/invoice totals     26 List claimable orders
    Receipt of item                  27 Set next claim date
    14 Check in of item              28 Claims menu
    Use space bar, arrow keys, or type number to make selection.
    Enter 'h' for help, 'p' or 'm' for previous or main menu, 'b' for bye.
```

Depressing 6 on the keyboard brings up the option, 'Enter orders and line details'. Brief details of the order number and the supplier are entered at this stage. A second screen is then called up which allows the user to enter further details of the item to be ordered.

```
    Order number   Create a new catalogue item   Catalogue number
    Lead title  :              Title
    ISBN        :
    Edition     :                      Material type    :
    Pub. date   :                      Date entered     :
    Publisher   :                      Catalogue status :
    Author      :
    Corp author :
    -----------------------------------------------------------------
    1  Add a catalogue record or Query to retrieve existing one
    2  9F to assign an author or 8F for a corporate author
    3  Query an author name and Update or Add an author
    4  1F to create a new order, 2F to attach to an existing one.
```

'Lead title' refers to the definite or indefinite article which may precede the main title, i.e. The, A or An. In the 'Material type' box, the order clerk would indicate whether the item is a book or AV (audiovisual material). When the relevant details have all been entered, the computer generates a catalogue number which will be permanently attached to the item and allow the cataloguer to make use of existing details already in the computer once the item is received and at the cataloguing stage. The details of the order record will also appear on the online public access catalogue, so any library member will be alerted to items on order but not yet in stock.

Yet another screen allows details of the cost of the item and the cost centre to be added to the record. Each department in the college is allocated a proportion of the library's annual book/materials fund and given a cost centre code. This is always entered on the order record so that a tally can be kept of the total expenditure per department and a stop put on further orders once the limit is reached. If a particular tutor has generated the request, the tutor's name is also entered on screen so that he or she can be notified when the item is received and ready for loan.

When all necessary details have been entered into the computer, option 7 on the Order clerk menu will be selected (see above) and the order record closed. Following that, option 8 then allows a printout of the orders to be produced, one copy of which is attached to an order form and posted to the supplier and a second copy kept by the library.

Manual system of ordering

To simplify ordering procedures most libraries have devised order forms (see Figures 1 and 2).

Often these forms are produced in NCR (no carbon required) sets so that they can be split up for ordering and recording. You will see that there are spaces for each of the important items of information, and spaces to show allocation of funds, expenditure code, site or branch allocation and who wants the item if reserved.

Order forms are usually batched on a daily or weekly basis and subjected to a number of routine checks before being dispatched to the supplier. These checks include the following:

1 The library's catalogue − librarians cannot rely on memory when ordering. They will check to ensure that the item concerned is not already in stock, or if it is an additional copy of an existing stock item that it is actually required.
2 Bibliographies − the information on the order form, particularly the ISBN, will be checked for accuracy. As paperback and hardback versions of the same title have different ISBNs, it is essential that the correct one is shown.
3 On-order file − this is checked to ensure that the item concerned is not already on order.

Author	Buy	Loan
	Class No.	
Title	Acc. No(s).	

Publisher	Price	Date of Publication	SBN/ISSN/BNB
Reports/Bureau	Ordered From: – Date	Rota Date Sent	

PSL 1058

CHELMER INSTITUTE OF HIGHER EDUCATION

BORROWER DETAIL

Name ______

Address ______

Department ______

Staff ☐ Student Year ☐

Date request made

CHECK THE CATALOGUE!

Last date item of use

BIBLIOGRAPHICAL DETAIL

BNB ______

BBIP ______

CBI ______

BKS ______

Other – Please specify

USE BALLPOINT PEN – PRESS FIRMLY

J F M A M J J A S O N D

ISBN / / /	Acc. No.
AUTHOR	
TITLE	PUBR.
	Edn / Year

O. No.	Price	Dept.	Bkslr.	Rpt.	Price paid
Date Ordered	Date Received			Res'n	
No. of Copies	Other Copies	00	COM	Card	

	ML	RH	Dd.	Replacement (previous accn. no(s).)
L				
R				

Thames Polytechnic LIBRARY
On Order/Received
This book has been added to stock

Class No.

Figs. 1 and 2 Sample order forms

4 Orders-received file – a limited number of books will be in the library workroom awaiting processing, classification or cataloguing. The new order will be checked against the list of these items.

Expenditure checks

On completion of all these checks, the order form should be passed to the ordering department, who may need to allocate expenditure. For example, separate accounts may be kept for:

1 Adult non-fiction
2 Adult fiction
3 Children's non-fiction
4 Children's fiction
5 Reference/local history
6 Audiovisual materials of various kinds.

In academic libraries, individual faculties or departments usually have cost codes allocated to them so that the book fund expenditure can be monitored. The cost code is shown on the order form and a running total is kept of the library's expenditure for each department. These figures allow the librarian to put a stop on further orders once the budgeted sum has been reached. The statistics also allow a judgement to be made of the cost-effectiveness of the present book fund policy as, at a later date, expenditure can be compared with the use of various categories of stock.

Once costed, an official order is made out to a particular supplier and copies of the order forms are attached. The package is then posted to the supplier and the library awaits receipt of the goods. A duplicate copy of the order form will be kept in the on-order file so that the library has a record of orders. This copy will have the supplier's name and the date of order added to it. In some libraries an official order number will also be added. Normally, the supplier returns the order form inside the book to which it relates, as well as submitting a list of all books supplied in the form of an invoice.

Various special types of order may be created, for example, urgent, on approval, confirmatory. These are clearly identified on the printed form. Deferred orders may also be created and held until required, or until the necessary funds become available.

Discrete fund records are held. When an order is created, the estimated total expenditure (number of copies times price per copy) is calculated, added to the total committed expenditure and deducted from the remaining allocation for the appropriate fund.

Chasing

Reputable suppliers will normally send reports to the library if an item cannot be forwarded within a reasonable span of time. The item may be temporarily out of stock or temporarily out of print. This information should be clearly marked on the library's order record. Occasionally, however, booksellers have to be chased because no report has been received about long-standing orders.

Receipt of materials

When boxes of books/materials are received from the suppliers, a number of procedures have to be followed.

1 The order records must be retrieved from the on-order file and matched with the items received.

2 The supplier's invoice must also be checked against the items received to ensure there are no discrepancies. In particular, the price per item as it appears on the invoice must be checked against the price shown on the item itself and that stated on the order form. Discount would be accounted for, if applicable.

3 The book/material must be checked to see that it is not faulty. Years ago, librarians would meticulously check every item, but now the checking is more cursory. It is now considered to be a non-productive use of the librarian's time and, in any case, the first borrower will usually report any fault. Suppliers do not make a fuss if the item is returned a few weeks later, complete with the library's ownership stamp and issue stationery. The faulty item could not be resold in any case.

4 The order records would be dated with the date of receipt and re-filed in a 'newly received' file until the materials have been catalogued and put on the library shelves.

5 The invoice is passed for payment if all details are correct. Statistics of actual expenditure are kept by the library as well as the finance office

6 The books/materials themselves are placed on the appropriate shelves in the staff workroom so that they can be made ready for use. With computer-ordering systems which generate catalogue numbers, it is essential to write the catalogue number on the item before it progresses to processing.

Processing

The amount of work that most libraries carry out on an item before it is in a suitable condition to be made available to the reader is substantial. The basic elements are as follows:

1 Accessioning. This involves giving the item a unique number so that if it is lost the cost can be easily discovered. Remember that very often in libraries several copies of the same title may be purchased at various prices over a number of years, so to know the cost of one particular item is important. Traditionally this was achieved by the use of an accession number which was a sequential number. In more recent years the accession number has been arrived at by adding a library copy

number to the ISBN/ISSN.

2   Stamping. Most libraries employ some form of stamping to denote their ownership of the item. This used to involve rubber stamping the top edge of the book, the title page, the reverse of the title page and every plate, or any other combination of pages dreamed up by the ingenious librarian. Sometimes a very heavy die-stamp was used as well. Increasingly, however, the amount of stamping is being reduced owing to the high staff costs involved and many librarians are settling for a stamp across the outer edges of the pages and somewhere on the reverse of the title page.

3   Insertion of issue stationery. Major booksellers will often provide this service at a nominal extra charge. However, if the book/material is received in an unprocessed state, the library staff will have to ensure that the necessary issue stationery is pasted in. The stationery varies in accordance with the issuing system in use. For libraries which are computerized, it will involve the fixing of a date label and bar code label to one of the endpapers. The Browne issuing system necessitates the use of date label, pocket and book card. The practice of pasting in book-plates has now been abandoned except in cases of special donations.

To ensure that the issuing of books is done smoothly and quickly, the library will have an agreed policy as to the location of the issue stationery in the book, that is, whether it should be fixed to the front endpapers or the back.

4   Jacketing. Most libraries now use plastic sleeves to protect the paper dust-jackets on hardback books, and they either laminate paperbacks or use one of the slip-on plastic jackets specially designed for paperbacks. Experience has shown that this not only enhances the appearance of the library stock but also adds to its life. Some booksellers will include this service in their nominal processing charge.

5   Security devices. Increasingly, librarians are using library security devices (see Chapter Seven) and therefore the insertion of the trigger is a further addition to the list of processing tasks.

6   Spine labelling. In the case of fiction books, a label showing the first three letters of the author's surname is fixed to the spine to assist in shelving and shelf tidying. Some libraries also categorize their fiction and put additional symbols on the spines of books to denote which category they fall into, e.g. crime, historical novels, romances and so on.

Non-fiction books must be classified before the spine labelling is done as it is the class-mark which is shown on the spine. Usually the first three letters of the author's surname appear under the classification symbol to make shelving more precise.

The use of the electric stylus, which used to be common in most libraries, has now been abandoned in favour of written or typed characters on self-adhesive labels which may then be protected against peeling by the addition of a strip of transparent self-adhesive tape.

The height of the label from the bottom of the spine will be predetermined and adhered to as far as possible so that the books on the shelves present a neat and uniform appearance.

Uniformity of procedure
Instructions for processing will form part of the staff manual, which can be consulted by all members of staff as an *aide-mémoire*. It helps to ensure uniformity of practice and upkeep of standards.

Periodicals − ordering, receipt and processing
The cost of periodicals has escalated in recent years and their acquisition accounts for a large proportion of most libraries' annual expenditure. However, journal articles provide up-to-date information on matters of current concern so their importance must not be overlooked. Academic and special libraries probably spend a higher proportion of their funds on journals than public libraries do, but nevertheless great care must be taken with their selection. Satisfying clients' needs is the first criterion, so librarians will monitor the usage of journals very closely. Current awareness services whereby specific clients are alerted about the contents of relevant journals can assist in promoting maximum usage.

Ordering
Daily and local newspapers are normally ordered through a newsagent in the vicinity of the library. Some journals may be supplied direct by the publisher, using the normal postal service. However, larger libraries usually order their periodicals through a major supplier such as Blackwells of Oxford, who will act as an intermediary. This simplifies procedures for the library as there is only one supplier to chase if items do not arrive and one organization to correspond with when dealing with invoices.

Receipt of periodicals
Accurate records must be kept so that missing items can be chased and invoices checked for accuracy. Manual systems of record-keeping may involve the use of a ledger, or specially designed record cards filed in boxes or drawers, or Kardex files in which larger cards are filed flat but overlapping in narrow drawers in a metal cabinet. The details of each journal will include title, frequency of publication, supplier and cost (annual subscription or cost per issue). As each issue is received

the appropriate card is marked up with the volume and/or issue number and date of receipt. A record is also kept of any separate index received. An example of a record card is shown below.

JOURNAL BACK COPIES									LOCATION				
Year	Vol.	Jan.	Feb.	Mar.	Apr.	May	Jun.	Jly.	Aug.	Sept.	Oct.	Nov.	Dec.

Increasingly, as libraries become fully computerized, the checking in of periodicals is done on the computer. It may be helpful to look at the system in use in the libraries of the Anglia Higher Education College as a case study.

The main menu looks like this:

```
        ADLIB – 2  LIBRARY MANAGEMENT SYSTEM
 Technical services              Acquisitions
 2  Cataloguer                   16 Head of acquisitions
 3  Authority file manager       17 Orders clerk
 4  Thesaurus manager
 Reference work                  Serials control
 7  Reference librarian          20 Subscriptions librarian
 8  Information officer          21 Serials receipts clerk
 Reader services                22 Serials stock control clerk
 11 Reader services librarian    24 Management information
 12 Issue desk
 Use space bar, arrow keys, or type number to make selection.
 Enter 'h' for help, or 'b' for bye.
```

Following the commands at the foot of the menu screen, the librarian would key in the number 21, or use the arrow keys or space bar to move around the menu options in order to highlight option 21, 'Serials receipts clerk'. Pressing the 'Return' key then brings up on screen the Serials receipts clerk menu which looks like this:

SERIALS RECEIPTS CLERK

Check in and claims
2 Check in items
3 List claimable items
4 List damaged items
5 Generate claims

Maintain suppliers
8 Add & remove a supplier
9 List suppliers
10 Supplier performance report

INFORMER search utilities
13 Display part details
14 Display copy details

Circulation control
16 Add & remove readers from lists
17 Print circulation slips
18 Print lists by reader
19 Print lists by title
Maintain readers file
22 Add & remove a reader
23 List readers by name or number

Choose another job
26 Subscriptions librarian
27 Serials stock control clerk

Use space bar, arrow keys, or type number to make selection.
Enter 'h' for help, 'p' or 'm' for previous or main menu, 'b' for bye.

The cursor automatically reverts to option 2, 'Check in items', as this is the most frequently sought function, so depressing the 'Return' key on the keyboard will call up the following screen:

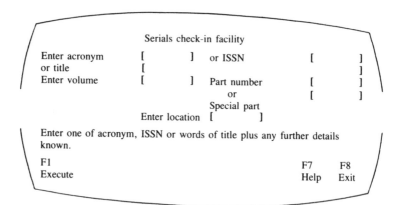

Serials check-in facility
Enter acronym   [   ] or ISSN   [   ]
or title   [   ]
Enter volume   [   ] Part number   [   ]
                                or   [   ]
                             Special part
              Enter location [   ]

Enter one of acronym, ISSN or words of title plus any further details known.

F1   F7   F8
Execute   Help   Exit

At the outset, each journal title is fed into the computer and each is given an acronym of no more than ten digits. For example, *Industrial relations journal* has the acronym INDRELJ. Keying in those seven digits brings up further details of full title and ISSN. If the journal is taken by more than one site library, the correct one will need to be selected from a list displayed on screen. Two sites subscribe to the journal in question so the screen looks like this:

```
This serial has more than one subscription — please choose one

Title:        Industrial Relations Journal
Acronym   INDRELJ                    ISSN: 0019 — 8692
Sub. No.   Site    Supplier No.      Supplier Name
21395567  DAN    S1                 Blackwells
21391987  LAW    S1                 Blackwells
    Use arrow keys to move up and down; F1 to make selection
F1                                   F7        F8
Select                               Help      Abort
```

The appropriate subscription, either that for the Danbury site library or the college's law library would be highlighted and then selected by depressing the F1 key.

The computer then searches the database and produces a further screen showing volume numbers and part numbers of copies already received and others expected. The appropriate volume and part number of the issue being checked in is highlighted by moving the cursor with the arrow keys, and then selected by depressing the F1 key. On screen it looks like this:

```
                    Serials check-in facility
   Title:      Industrial Relations Journal
   Acronym:    INDRELJ      ISSN: 0019 – 8692    Subscription: 21395567
   Volume      Part         Date due             No. due and rec'd
   20          1            [01/03/89]           [ 1 ]              [ 1 ]
   20          2            [01/06/89]           [ 1 ]              [ 1 ]
   20          3            [01/09/89]           [ 1 ]              [ 1 ]
   20          4            [01/12/89]           [ 1 ]              [ 1 ]
   21          1            [01/03/90]           [ 1 ]              [ 0 ]
   21          2            [01/06/90]           [ 1 ]              [ 0 ]
   21          3            [01/09/90]           [ 1 ]              [ 0 ]
   21          . 4          [01/12/90]           [ 1 ]              [ 0 ]
   F1          F3           F6                   F7                    F8
   Select      Pagedown     Specials             Help                  Abort
```

The screen above shows that the four issues published in 1989 have been received and that the first issue of volume 21 is not expected until 1 March 1990. When that is received the arrow key will be used to highlight Volume 21 Part 1 and then the F1 key depressed to select it.

The final screen in the process is thereby called up and the following information shown:

```
                    Serials check-in facility
   Title:      Industrial Relations Journal
   Acronym:    INDRELJ      ISSN: 0019 – 8962       Subscription: 21395567
   Volume:     21           Part 1                  Date due: 01/03/90
   Location    Date rec'd   First claim   Next claim   Claims Status Circ.
   DAN         00/00/00     00/00/00      15/03/90        0
   No. of copies expected   [ 1 ]        No. of copies arrived    [ 1 ]
   To be circulated         [   ]        Actually circulated      [   ]
   Shelfmark                [   ]
```

When checking in the journal, a flashing cursor will appear over the digit 1 in the No. of copies arrived field. To tell the computer that the copy has actually been received, the F1 key is depressed. The information is then stored in the system and the instruction at the bottom left corner changes from F1 Execute to F1 Next, allowing the first of the screens to be called up and the acronym of the next journal to be keyed in.

Checking in journals in Anglia Higher Education College's computer system is tedious and time-consuming as four screens have to be called up in turn and there is a delay in getting from one screen to the next. There is no doubt that manual checking in on cards is faster. However, the advantages of the computer system are seen in the chasing of late or missing items and in the control of invoice payments and budgets. The computer can print out all manner of reports at a moment's notice.

Processing of periodicals

Periodicals require very little processing apart from rubber stamping with the library name, and perhaps adding a stamp or label which says 'Do not remove' or 'Reference only' if it is the policy of the library to restrict the use of journals in that way. Specific articles of particular relevance may be catalogued in the same way as books are catalogued, and contents lists may be photocopied and sent to library members who have requested that service. These procedures are mainly pursued in academic and industrial libraries where clients have more specialized information needs rather than in public libraries which subscribe to journals of more general interest.

Audiovisual materials – ordering, receipt and processing

Librarians will order audiovisual materials from specialist suppliers. That may entail dealing with quite a large number of commercial outlets in order to purchase computer software, videocassettes, gramophone records, compact discs, audio cassettes, wallcharts and so forth. Careful records must be kept of which items have been ordered, and when and from whom.

Receipt of audiovisual materials

The same meticulous checking is entailed as with the receipt of books. The order record must be checked to see that the right materials have been received and the invoice details checked to ascertain that they are correct. It would be too time consuming to preview items such as videos or listen to audio materials; a cursory check is usually as much as can be managed.

Processing of audiovisual materials

Audiovisual materials need to be prepared for use in a similar way to that for books but additional routines may be followed for specific types of material. Each library will have its own policy about the integration of non-book materials with the book stock. Where there is a preference for shelving non-book materials alongside the books, librarians will probably resort to the use of specially designed storage boxes. The exterior of the box, to all intents and purposes, looks like a book in that it has a spine and covers to which the spine label and issue stationery can be attached. Inside, however, each box is designed to house one or more specific types of audiovisual material such as filmstrips, slides or audio cassettes. The relevant details, such as the accession number and class-mark, must appear on the audiovisual material itself as well as on the storage box.

Gramophone records are rarely kept on open access because of their susceptibility to damage. Normally each record sleeve is given the protection of an added transparent plastic sleeve which can be wiped clean, and then it is displayed with others in browser bins. The gramophone record itself is protected by a plain cardboard sleeve to keep it dust-free and then shelved behind the issue desk or in some other non-public area. Again details of accession number and class number, if appropriate, must appear on the record itself and on the display sleeve so that the two can be married up prior to issue.

Computer software poses particular problems for librarians because inexperienced computer users may corrupt the information on the disc. For this reason, librarians may take the precaution of making a back-up copy for clients' use while keeping the original under lock and key. Computer software may also be affected by the electronic security devices used in many libraries. For this reason, computer software is never fitted with triggers even if the book stock is triggered. The same would apply to video cassettes and any other materials susceptible to electronic security systems.

Some materials may be laminated at the processing stage. These may include maps and wallcharts which are thereby protected by a wipeable transparent adhesive cover.

It is evident that the processing of audiovisual materials can be very time consuming, and that because of the fragility of materials and the resultant need for care the task cannot be rushed. Nevertheless, the time expended is amply rewarded by a lengthening of the life, and the attractiveness, of the library's stock.

Assignments

Practical

1 Find out, in your public library, how many requests there are each year for:

   (a) fiction,

   (b) adult non-fiction,

   (c) non-book materials.

Can you discover, approximately, how much of the fund is spent on requests as opposed to stock building?

2 Stock selection is done by many people, some not librarians. Make enquiries to discover what categories of library staff and library members are involved in stock selection in:

   (a) a public library,

   (b) an academic library.

3 Follow through one order in your own library system from selection to receipt and produce your own checklist of how it is done.

4 Visit a library which operates a computer-ordering system and ask to see it demonstrated. Compare the procedure with any manual system known to you.

5 Consider the advantages and disadvantages of the system in use in your library for checking in periodicals.

6 Discover how much processing is done by your library's suppliers and how much is done by library staff.

7 Visit two libraries in your locality. Look at the books and other materials on the shelves and assess the spine labelling for clarity and neatness. Also, make a comparison of the issue stationery.

Written

1 List four types of library materials and explain how your library orders them. Are different methods and suppliers used?

2 Outline, sequentially, each stage a book passes through in your library from the moment it arrives until it is on the library shelf.

3 Redesign your library's current ordering procedures and explain how the changes could be beneficial.

4 List the available ways of obtaining materials at reduced price. Comment on those used by your library.

5 Discuss the advantages and disadvantages of:

   (a) computerized methods of ordering stock or

   (b) computerized methods of checking in periodicals.

Highlight specifically any benefits which are not obvious in manual systems.

Bibliography

Advances in library administration and organization, Vols. 1 − 4, 7 − 8, London, Jai Press, 1982 − 9.

Burkett, J., *Library practice: a manual and textbook*, Huntingdon, Elm Publications, 1977.

Chirgwin, F. John and Oldfield, Phyllis, *The library assistant's manual*, 3rd ed., London, Bingley, 1988.

Grieder, Ted, *Acquisitions*, London, Greenwood Press, 1978.

Kumar, Krishnan, *Library administration and management*, Vikas, 1987. Distributed by Sangam, London.

— *Library organization*, Vikas, 1987. Distributed by Sangam, London.

Neal, K. W., *Introduction to library administration*, Wilmslow, Neal, 1975.

Ritchie, Sheila (ed.), *Modern library practice*, Buckden, Elm Publications, 1982.

Chapter Four

Classification

The basic concept of classification
Many people stand in awe of classification, believing it to be a skill completely beyond their capabilities. The truth is that every one of us is involved in the process of classification as part of our day-to-day lives and often it is a subconscious activity.

The process begins when we are toddlers acquiring a vocabulary. Try to imagine yourself as a 2½-year-old, out walking in the park with your mum, when across your path pads a little animal. You note that it is furry, and has four legs and a tail. Your mother informs you, 'It's a dog.' Some days later, you are again out with mum but this time at the local shopping precinct. Right across your path strides a little furry animal with four legs and a tail. You proudly say 'dog', but mother says, 'No, dear! That's a cat.' At that point your brain has to wrestle with a problem, 'What is it that distinguishes the cat from the dog?'

Children very quickly learn to differentiate and categorize so that they can correctly name what they see. The noting of similarities and differences becomes almost automatic so that there is instantaneous recognition, and it is not long before the child identifies a Pekinese as a dog and an Alsatian as a dog. Now he is classifying not only by species but by breed within the species. This is what classification is all about. It is the identification of similarities and differences, enabling one to group together things which are similar, and separate them from things which are dissimilar.

As has been said, all of us are involved in categorization or classification as part of our daily lives and it is automatic. However, some people are involved in classification as part of their daily work and it is for them a conscious and precise activity.

Consider, for example, the work of the shoe shop manager. Take a few minutes to think about the way he or she arranges the stock of shoes. The first thing the shoe shop manager will do is to separate the stock into men's shoes, women's shoes and children's shoes. Indeed, a large shop will have a separate department or area for each category. He or she will then arrange the shoes by style, size and colour.

Why does the shoe shop manager go to the trouble of classifying the stock in this way? Because customers ask for shoes in that manner. 'I'd like a pair of men's slip-on shoes, black leather, size 10, please.' On hearing that request, the assistant's aim will be to get the shoes to the customer in the quickest possible time.

Imagine what would ensue if the stock were not classified. It would be chaotic. The shop assistant would take ages to find the right shoes. The customer would become irate and would eventually walk out in disgust, and for the shop manager that would be very bad business.

Classification in libraries

The principle is much the same in libraries. The object of classifying the stock is to get the book to the reader, or the reader to the book, in the quickest possible time. The librarian has to consider the needs of the library users and the way they frame their requests. The latter usually depends on whether the reader is wanting fiction or non-fiction. When a library member asks for a work of fiction the request is usually framed in this way: 'I have just read a book by P. D. James. Have you another by the same author, please?' The best way to arrange the fiction stock is therefore alphabetically by authors' surnames. However, some readers frame their fiction requests differently and may say, 'I like to read detective novels. Can you show me where to find them, please?' In libraries where many readers frame their fiction requests in this way, the librarians may categorize their fiction and group novels of a certain type together, e.g. all the love stories, all the westerns, all the detective stories, all the historical novels; but there is always a residue of fiction which cannot be categorized in this way. Other librarians solve the problem by arranging all the fiction alphabetically by author but put easily identifiable symbols on the spines to indicate the type of novel.

Classification of non-fiction stock

When readers request non-fiction books they usually frame their questions in this way: 'Have you any books on stamp-collecting?' In other words, they ask for non-fiction books by subject, so the most convenient way to organize the non-fiction stock is by subject. Books on the same subject are shelved together, and books on related subjects are alongside.

When a factual book is added to the library's stock, the librarian has to peruse it in order to discover what its subject is. Sometimes this is an easy task but sometimes it is quite difficult. The librarian will look at the book's title, subtitle, preface, contents list and so on in order to determine the subject-matter. Sometimes a dictionary, encyclopaedia or other reference work has to be consulted in order to shed light on unfamiliar terminology.

Imagine, however, that the book is a straightforward one about physics. The librarian could put a label which says 'PHYSICS' on the spine and the book could be shelved alongside other books on physics. However, some subjects have very lengthy names – for example, electromagnetism – and sometimes subjects cannot be expressed by a word but need a phrase. Also, how would one manage to keep books on related sciences such as chemistry and mathematics nearby?

What is needed is a logical arrangement of subjects accompanied by a system of symbols which represent the subjects. Librarians call these symbols a notation. Many people have devised such classification systems – Bliss, Brown and Ranganathan to name only three – but the one who is most widely known is Melvil Dewey (1851–1931). Dewey lived and worked in New York, where he first produced his Dewey Decimal Classification scheme in 1876.

Dewey set himself some constraints when he launched out on his life's work. First, he wanted to restrict himself to ten main classes, and then to subdivide by ten, and by ten again until he reached the degree of division required. Secondly, he wanted to use numbers only for his symbols, introducing a decimal point after the third digit.

Imagine yourself setting out on this task. In front of you, figuratively speaking, is the whole of human knowledge and you have to divide it logically into ten separate subject areas. One of the easiest ways to envisage this is to consider the subjects which are taught in school. The same principle applies – a body of knowledge has to be transmitted but to make this easier and more methodical it is divided into subject areas with departments and subject specialists concerned with each area. Find some scrap paper and jot down the subject areas taught in schools. Now compare your list with Dewey's list (below) and note the similarities and differences.

It is doubtful whether your list will match that of Dewey, primarily because teachers see a close link between certain subject areas that Dewey apparently did not see, or chose to ignore. For example, language and literature go hand-in-hand in the school curriculum but Dewey separates the two. Similarly, social sciences and history are interrelated in teaching but widely separated in Dewey. This wide separation of related subject areas is one of the major reasons for criticism of the Dewey scheme.

PHILOSOPHY and PSYCHOLOGY
RELIGION
SOCIAL SCIENCES
LANGUAGE
NATURAL SCIENCES and MATHEMATICS
TECHNOLOGY (Applied sciences)
THE ARTS
LITERATURE and RHETORIC
GEOGRAPHY
HISTORY

Dewey wanted only ten main classes and he achieved that in his list above. However, Dewey was concerned not only with abstract knowledge but with knowledge as it was contained in books, and some books pose problems for the classifier. For example, could you fit into the above list of subjects the following books?

1 *Encyclopaedia Britannica*
2 *Six famous lives*

A general encyclopaedia encompasses all of the subject fields listed so it cannot be slotted into one of them. A special place has to be provided for general encyclopaedias and all books of general knowledge, so Dewey added at the top of his list a class called GENERALITIES (formerly GENERALIA). A collected biography may include the life-stories of a scientist, an engineer, a musician, a philosopher and so on. Again, there is no provision in Dewey's main list of ten classes for collected biography, so he added BIOGRAPHY at the end of his list. Now the list comprises 12 items, not 10.

Undeterred, Dewey allocated his numerical symbols and the list of ten main classes ended up like this:

000 GENERALITIES
100 PHILOSOPHY and PSYCHOLOGY
200 RELIGION
300 SOCIAL SCIENCES
400 LANGUAGE
500 NATURAL SCIENCES and MATHEMATICS
600 TECHNOLOGY (Applied sciences)
700 THE ARTS
800 LITERATURE AND RHETORIC
900 GEOGRAPHY, HISTORY and auxiliary disciplines (including BIOGRAPHY)

Each of the above main classes is subdivided by 10, e.g.:

500	NATURAL SCIENCES and MATHEMATICS
510	Mathematics
520	Astronomy and allied sciences
530	Physics
540	Chemistry and allied sciences
550	Earth sciences
560	Paleontology Paleozoology
570	Life sciences
580	Botanical sciences
590	Zoological sciences

Each of these in turn divides by 10, and then by 10 again in the following way:

530	Physics
539	Modern physics
539.7	Atomic and nuclear physics
539.72	Particle physics; ionizing radiations
539.722	Ionizing radiations
529.7222	x and gamma rays

The rule to remember is:

The broader the subject, the shorter the class number.
The more specific the subject, the longer the class number.

It is quite fascinating to study the way in which Dewey identified similarities and differences and logically built up his classification numbers. Consider the chain of thought involved in classifying books on soccer at 796.334:

700	THE ARTS
790	Recreational and performing arts
796	Athletic and outdoor sports and games
796.3	Ball games
796.33	(Sports involving an) inflated ball driven by foot
796.334	Soccer (Association football)

The Dewey Decimal Classification scheme is now in its twentieth full edition and an abridged edition and a schools edition are also available. Its popularity is due in part to the timing of its appearance. Libraries were looking for a suitable classification scheme at that time and, having once adopted a scheme, it is very rare that a library will abandon it and turn to another scheme owing to the enormity of the task of re-classifying.

The universality of its numerical symbols also adds to its appeal, and of course the scheme itself has merits which make it suitable for many types of library, particularly public libraries which have a wide-ranging stock rather than an in-depth stock in a limited subject field. Some libraries such as school libraries and smaller public libraries choose not to use very lengthy class numbers because the size of the stock and the needs of their readers do not warrant this. If you consult the classified sequence of *British national bibliography* you will observe that the lengthy Dewey numbers which are given have apostrophes indicating where the number can be shortened.

Advantages and disadvantages of the Dewey scheme

Advantages

1   It has a simple, pure notation.
2   Arabic numbers are used internationally.
3   The class numbers are easy to write, type and remember − at least to hold in one's mind long enough to get from a library's catalogue to the shelves.
4   Mnemonic devices (memory aids) are widely used. Normally these occur where numbers retain the same meaning in more than one part of the schedules.
5   The classification scheme allows for expansion so that new subjects can be included. This facility is known as 'hospitality'.
6   Alternative placings are provided for many subjects so that different libraries can cater for the needs of their own clientele.
7   The scheme allows for close classification (lengthy numbers for specific subjects) or broad classification (shorter numbers where less detail is required).
8   The scheme is hierarchical, like a family tree, showing the relationship of specific subjects to the parent subject.
9   The scheme has an excellent relative index.
10 The schedules are comparatively inexpensive.
11 The scheme is being constantly revised, and therefore is up to date.

Disadvantages

1   The provision of only ten main classes means that the base is too short, resulting in lengthy classification numbers.
2   The limitation of division and subdivision to only ten places leads to the squeezing of subjects into a conglomerate last division called 'others'.

3 The arrangement of classes has been criticized, especially the separation of language from literature, social sciences from history and psychology from medicine.
4 There is a tendency to bias the scheme towards the needs of libraries in the West, and particularly in the USA. This is reflected in the amount of detail allocated to subjects on which libraries in the West would have large stocks, e.g. American history in comparison with that of other countries and the Christian religion as opposed to other religions.

Other classification schemes

The Bliss Bibliographic Classification scheme
The Bliss classification scheme has been widely praised, mainly because of its very logical arrangement. The provision for its revision was not comparable with that of Dewey so it became outdated, but a second edition began to appear in 1977 and had reached class T by 1987. Its notation consists mainly of letters of the alphabet, with both upper case (capitals) and lower case (small letters) employed. Numerals are used in the Generalia class.

History of the Scheme
The bibliographic classification was developed by Henry Evelyn Bliss (1870–1955), an American librarian employed from 1891 until 1941 in New York College Library. Classification fascinated him and he devoted his entire life to its study. He conceived the scheme as long ago as 1908 but it was not until 1935 that a condensed version was published and 1940–53 that the full edition appeared in print.

Structure of the scheme
1 Bliss claimed that a group of subject specialists will generally agree on an arrangement and order of topics, based on the way that subject is taught or used (i.e. educational and scientific consensus). This order is relatively stable and does not alter greatly.
2 He believed in the subordination of topics – from the general to the specific.
3 He brought related topics together (collocation).
4 He provided alternative locations.
5 He provided auxiliary tables for compound subjects.

Order of main classes — following evolutionary order

A	— Philosophy and logic (including mathematics and science)	
B	— Physics (including physics-based technologies, e.g. radio)	PHYSICAL SCIENCES
C	— Chemistry (including chemical technology)	
D	— Astronomy and space sciences	
E	— Biological sciences	
F	— Botany (including bacteriology)	BIOLOGICAL SCIENCES
G	— Zoology	
H	— Human sciences and studies (including human biology, physical anthropology, health and medicine)	
I	— Psychology (including psychiatry)	HUMAN SCIENCES
J	— Education	
K	— Society (including customs, folklore and mythology)	
LA	— Area studies	
LB	— Geography	
LC	— Travel and description	
M	— (Favoured country)	
N	— Other countries	
O	— Local history ... biography	HUMAN STUDIES
P	— Religion, occult, morals and ethics	
Q	— Social welfare and administration	
R	— Political science ... public administration	
S	— Law	
T	— Economics	
U/V	— Technology and useful arts, including recreative arts, leisure arts	
W	— Art(s), fine arts	ARTS
X	— Philology, language and literature	
Z	— Favoured language, e.g. English	

Points to note

1 Each main class is subdivided by capital letters, e.g.:

    T   –   Economics
    TL –   Labour economics
    TN –   National economy

2 Blanks are left for the inclusion of new subjects.
3 Each subdivision can be further subdivided by the addition of a third capital letter, e.g. TLC Industrial relations.
4 Auxiliary schedules

    (a) Auxiliary Schedule 1 – common subdivisions, corresponding to Table 1 of Dewey. Bliss uses a combination of numbers and upper case letters, e.g. 3A – encyclopaedias.
    (b) Auxiliary Schedule 2 is for places, corresponding to Dewey's Areas Table, and for this he uses upper case letters, e.g.
        E   –   British Isles
        EF   –   Eastern England, East Anglia
        EFD –   Essex
        EFER –   Chelmsford.
    (c) There are also auxiliary schedules for language and ethnic groups and chronology.

Advantages of the Bliss Bibliographic Classification Scheme

1 The order of main classes is generally praised because of its logical progression, e.g. Class A ends at AZ – General physical science, leading naturally into Class B – Physics.
2 The placing of a technology alongside the science to which it relates is sensible, e.g. C – Chemistry CT – Chemical technology.
3 Bliss proportioned the scheme to match the stocks of most libraries.
4 The scheme is a practical one as well as logical:

    (a) It was first used in the New York City College Library.
    (b) Help was sought from librarians in specialist libraries (e.g. medicine).
    (c) Practical criticism from librarians was welcomed, considered and acted upon.

5 Classification symbols are kept short, because Bliss used a wide base of 26 letters. Most class-marks are limited to two or three places, although in zoology and botany they extend to four places.

Television – BO (Bliss)   621.388 (Dewey)
Aviation   – BT (Bliss)   387.7   (Dewey).

6 Bliss provides simple form divisions, again maintaining short class-marks, e.g.:

5V – Bibliographies   BT5V – Bibliography of aviation
3A – Periodicals   C3A   – Periodical on chemistry.

7 Bliss provides alternative locations for many subjects so that his scheme can be adopted by different kinds of libraries, e.g. three alternatives for the treatment of biography:

(a) classified under subject, with the addition of No. 4 from Schedule 1, e.g. B4 – biography of a physicist;
(b) all biography at L9 but subdivided in classified order, e.g. L9B – biography of a physicist;
(c) all biography at L9 but subdivided alphabetically by the name of the biographee.

Religion can be classified at P in a class of its own or at AJ as a subdivision of philosophy, or may be transferred to class K.

8 The scheme uses literal mnemonics but never at the expense of logical order, e.g. AL – logic; AM – mathematics.
It uses some constant mnemonics as form divisions:

1 – Reference books (dictionaries, encyclopaedias)
2 – Bibliographies
6 – Periodicals.

9 The scheme has a very full relative index, which includes many personal and place names.

10 Revision is carried out via the Bliss Classification Association and their annual bulletin. The second edition is still in the process of production. The Bliss classification scheme is now detailed and relatively up to date, comparing favourably with any other scheme available.

Faults of the scheme

1 Confusion can be caused by the use of the same letters to indicate totally different things, e.g.:

GXED   – Divers (birds)
GXEDA – Birds of London.

2 There is verbal difficulty in referring to some class-marks, e.g.

GWXD, and also the unfortunate pronunciation of certain combinations of letters, e.g. GUT.

3 Too many alternative locations can cause confusion and prevent consistency between one library and another.
4 Facilities for revision do not compare with Dewey. Twenty years passed without a comprehensive revision.
5 The scheme appeared too late. Most libraries had already adopted Dewey or Library of Congress, and would not undertake the difficult task of reclassifying their entire stock.

General evaluation of the scheme
Bliss is the most scholarly of all the classification schemes. It is estimated that about 90 libraries use the scheme, most of which are in the British Commonwealth and very few in the USA. The users are mainly academic, learned, government and special libraries. An abridged edition of the scheme for school use was published in 1967 by the School Library Association and a revised full edition (the second) commenced publication in 1978.

The Library of Congress classification scheme
This classification scheme derives its name from the library for which it was devised, namely the library of the United States Congress in Washington DC. The scheme was designed by the Library of Congress staff and was tailor-made for their own library with its immense and rapidly growing stock and with its bias towards law and the social sciences. Each main class was published separately, commencing in 1902, and each has its individual structure and its own index. The schedules are continually updated and cumulations of additions and changes are published.

The notation employed by the Library of Congress scheme is based on letters of the alphabet, 21 of which have been used and 5 kept in reserve for further expansion.

The following is a list of main classes:

A General works
B Philosophy, psychology, religion
C Auxiliary sciences of history
D History: general and old world
E United States (history)
F United States (local)
G Geography, anthropology, recreation
H Social sciences

J   Political sciences
K   Law
L   Education
M   Music
N   Fine arts
P   Language and literature
Q   Science
R   Medicine
S   Agriculture
T   Technology
U   Military science
V   Naval science
Z   Bibliography, library science

The main subdivisions employ an additional letter, e.g.:

P   Language and literature
PR   English literature

Further subdivision is then effected by using arabic numerals, in arithmetical sequence from one digit to four digits in length, e.g.:

PN 6511   Oriental proverbs

To achieve very specific classification, the class-mark can be lengthened further by adding decimal points or full stops followed by additional letters and numbers, e.g.:

PN 6519.C5   Chinese proverbs

The arrangement of stock within the Library of Congress is made even more precise by using call numbers. A call number is a symbol combining the class-mark and an author symbol. The latter is usually the initial letter of the author's surname followed by one or two numerals. Despite the fact that the Library of Congress Classification scheme was designed for one particular library, it has been adopted by many libraries, particularly in the United States but also some in the United Kingdom.

Specialized classification schemes

There are many classification schemes in use, several designed specifically for special libraries which have an extensive stock but a limited subject field. General schemes such as Dewey do not give the minuteness of detail necessary for such libraries. Two examples are:

1   Universal Decimal Classification — commonly referred to as UDC and in use in many industrial libraries. It is based on Dewey, but

is a faceted scheme incorporating letters of the alphabet and full stops or decimal points. This is what the notation looks like:

TD 189.5.N4 Environmental pollution in New Zealand.

2   Sfb (Samarbetskommittén för Byggnådsfragor) — a scheme devised for literature concerned with the construction industry. It is a faceted scheme with different parts of the symbol appearing in a four-part grid. The notation incorporates numbers, letters and parentheses. Here is an example of Sfb notation:

41	(74)	Xg3	–

fireclay sanitary fixtures for hospitals

Features common to classification schemes

To be of maximum benefit to the classifier, classification schemes need to include the following features:

1   Schedules
2   An index
3   Notation
4   Tables including (a) standard subdivisions (form divisions); (b) an areas table
5   A form class
6   A generalities class

1   Schedules. The term 'schedules' is used to describe the printed list of all the main classes, divisions and subdivisions of the classification scheme. The schedules provide a logical arrangement of all the subjects encompassed by the classification scheme, this arrangement usually being hierarchical, showing the relationship of specific subjects to their parent subject. The relevant classification symbol is shown against each subject.

2   Index. The index to the classification scheme is an alphabetical list of all the subjects encompassed by the scheme, with the relevant class-mark shown against each subject. There are two types of index:

(a)   A relative index includes broad topics in its alphabetical arrangement, but indented below the broad subject heading is a list of all the aspects of the subject. The Dewey Decimal Classification scheme has an excellent relative index, e.g.:

Flight
  guides
    aeronautics   629.13254
  instrumentation
    aircraft eng.   629.1352

                    into Egypt
                        Christian doctrines   232.926

(b) A specific index lists specific subjects in a precise alphabetical
     sequence. It does not indent lists of related topics under broad
     subject headings. Brown's Subject Classification scheme has a
     specific index.

3 Notation. The notation is the system of symbols used to represent
the terms encompassed by the classification scheme. The notation can
be 'pure' − using one type of symbol only − or 'mixed' − using more
than one kind of symbol. A pure notation would normally involve only
letters of the alphabet or only numerals. A mixed notation would normally
utilize both letters and numerals. Some notations also involve the use
of grammatical signs or mathematical symbols.

The notation usually appears on the spines of library books to facilitate
shelving and to ensure that each book is in its correct place. The notation
is also shown on catalogue entries to help the staff and public to retrieve
books quickly. It therefore serves as:

(a) a link between the index and the schedules of a classification
     scheme, and
(b) a link between the library catalogues and the shelves.

4 Tables. The tables of a classification scheme are additional to the
schedules and provide lists of symbols which can be added to class-marks
to make them more specific and precise. Probably the more important
of the tables are:

(a) Table of standard subdivisions or form divisions which lists
     symbols which can be added to class-marks to denote the form
     of arrangement cr method of treatment of a book's subject. The
     following is an abbreviated list of standard subdivisions from the
     Dewey Decimal Classification scheme, twentieth full edition:

          01 Philosophy and theory
          02 Miscellany
          03 Dictionaries, encyclopedias, concordances
          04 Special topics
          05 Serial publications
          06 Organizations and management
          07 Education, research, related topics
          08 History and description with respect to kinds of persons
          09 Historical, geographical, persons treatment.

The rule to remember is that a book must first be given a class-mark which represents its subject content and then the appropriate symbol from the table of standard subdivisions is added to that class-mark to denote the form or treatment of that subject, e.g.:

| Medicine | 610 |
| Medical dictionary | 610.3 (i.e. base number 61 + 03) |

(b) Areas table: this lists symbols which can be added to class-marks to indicate the particular geographical area − e.g. continent, country, state, county etc. − to which a book's subject is restricted. Again, a book would be classified first by subject and then by area. Examples from the Dewey scheme would be:

Cricket	796.358
Historical and geographical treatment	09
Essex (from areas table)	4267
Cricket in Essex	796.358094267

The other tables in the Dewey scheme are:

Table 3 − Subdivisions for individual literatures, for specific literary forms.
Table 4 − Subdivisions of individual languages.
Table 5 − Racial, ethnic, national groups.
Table 6 − Languages.
Table 7 − Groups of persons.

5 Form class. A form class makes provision for those books where form is of greater importance than subject. Most books of this kind are literary works − fiction, poetry and plays, for example. Poetry is primarily read for its own sake and not because the poems may be about animals or trees or whatever. Dewey's literature class is an example of a form class except that the class is divided first by language and then by form:

800 Literature
820 English literature
821 English poetry
822 English drama
823 English fiction
    etc.

6 A generalities class. This class caters primarily for books of general knowledge which could not be allocated to any particular subject class

because of their pervasive subject coverage. In some respects, a generalities class is also a form class because general bibliographies, general encyclopaedias, general periodicals and so on would be encompassed in it. Class 000 of Dewey is a generalities class.

The arrangement of stock in libraries

A library will arrange its stock according to the classification scheme in use in that library. If a library is using the Dewey scheme, its stock will be arranged on the shelves in a numerical sequence from 000 to 999 and its decimal placings. However, libraries may introduce modifications to this arrangement.

    1   Broken order. This term is applied when a library deviates from the arrangement of its chosen classification scheme. For example, Dewey provides a place in the literature class for current English fiction (823.91). Many libraries elect not to use that classification but to arrange the fiction stock quite separately from the non-fiction and in alphabetical rather than classified order. Libraries may also choose to modify the specified arrangements when dealing with biography or special collections.

    2   Parallel arrangement. A library will sometimes have more than one sequence of non-fiction stock. The reference books are normally left separate from the lending stock and the oversize books may be shelved separately from the normal-sized stock. However, the books will be classified in the usual manner but will form two additional and parallel sequences to the main stock. Symbols will preface the class-marks on the spine and catalogue entries to make this apparent to the library user. Reference books are usually identifiable by the letter 'R' or abbreviation 'Ref', and oversize books by the letters 'q' for quarto or 'f' for folio.

A retrospective view

Fixed location

Before bibliographic (book) classification schemes such as Dewey became available, libraries had to use some other method of arranging stock. Some of the very early libraries did attempt a crude form of categorization but it was not systematic. The first public libraries operated a system known as 'fixed location' whereby each book as it was added to stock was allocated a specific place on a particular shelf and was given a location symbol. The symbol related to the shelf and bookcase and had nothing at all to do with the book's subject. It was really akin to arrangement by accession number and not classification at all.

Closed access

Allied to fixed location was a system known as 'closed access' whereby the reader was allowed to approach the library counter but prevented from going to the bookshelves. He or she had to request what was wanted and the library staff had to search the shelves for it.

Obviously, there were drawbacks to the closed access system and we can drawn an analogy from the world of commerce in order to understand them. Imagine you are shopping in the village grocer's shop. You stand behind the counter with your shopping list, and, item by item, you tell the assistant what you want. He or she retrieves the goods from the shelves and you put them in your basket and pay for them. However, you decide next time to go to the supermarket for your week's groceries. You collect a trolley on the way in and off you go round the laden shelves. You may still have your shopping list as a reminder but as you wheel your trolley along you see a new product in very attractive packaging. 'I'll try that', you say to yourself, and into the trolley it goes. You see another item and begin to wonder whether you have any in the cupboard at home. 'I'd better take a tin, just in case', and it, too, goes into the trolley. When you arrive at the check-out desk you have a laden trolley and many more items than on your shopping list.

The situation in libraries was and is much the same. Under the old 'closed access' system, only a limited number of books were ever borrowed. Some of the most worthwhile books sat on the shelves gathering dust. What a waste of resources and public money! When open access was introduced and people were allowed to browse and select their own books they, too, borrowed more than the particular book they had on their reading list. As they made a bee-line for their favourite section their eye was attracted by books on other subjects and by different authors. The readers benefited because their horizons were widened and they read more. The library benefited also because issue statistics went up. However, fixed location could not survive when open access was introduced. It became imperative that books were arranged to make it easy for the readers to find what they wanted. If they were interested in gardening books, they would want to see them all in one place, not scattered all over the library. This is what made classification so important.

Assignments

Practical

1 Visit your local public library and locate:

    (a)   the fiction stock,
    (b)   the non-fiction lending stock,
    (c)   the reference books,
    (d)   the oversize stock.

2 Did you find it easy or difficult to locate the various types of stock? What improvements could be made, in your opinion?

Written

1 Prepare a written guide for a new library member which explains the arrangement of stock in the library in which you work or of which you are a member.

2 Compile a list, from memory, of the ten main classes of the Dewey Decimal Classification scheme.

3 What is the purpose of classification? What schemes are available to the public librarian? Evaluate one scheme for use in a large municipal library.

4 What principles and/or features have most bibliographical classification schemes in common?

5 What steps should be taken to ensure that the arrangement of books in a children's library is clear to users?

6 Compare and contrast the following pairs of terms:

    (a)   specific index and relative index,
    (b)   form class and form divisions (i.e. common subdivisions).

Bibliography

Bakewell, K. G. B., *Classification and indexing practice*, London, Bingley, 1978.

Bliss, H. E., *Bliss bibliographic classification, Class I*, 2nd ed., London, Butterworth, 1978; *Class H*, 2nd rev. ed., London, Butterworth, 1980; *Class K*, 2nd ed., London, Butterworth, 1984; *Class T*, 2nd ed., London, Butterworth, 1987.

Dewey decimal classification and relative index, 12th abridged ed., Albany, NY, Forest Press, 1990; 20th ed., Albany, NY, Forest Press, 1989. Available in the UK from OCLC Europe, Birmingham.

Hunter, Eric J., *Classification made simple*, Aldershot, Gower, 1988.

Maltby, A. annd Gill, Lindy, *The case for Bliss*, London, Bingley, 1979.

— *Sayers' manual of classification*, 5th ed., London, Deutsch, 1975.

South, Mary L., *Dewey decimal classification for school libraries*, Albany, NY, Forest Press, 1986.

Chapter Five

Cataloguing and indexing: traditional methods

In the previous chapter, it was shown that user needs determine the most effective way to arrange the stock of a library. Similarly, the information required by library members and staff determines the type of catalogue provided, the number and kinds of catalogue entries included, and the amount of information in each entry.

Typical questions posed by readers include the following:

Does the library have any books by a given author? Which books are they? Where are they shelved?

Does the library have a particular book of which the author and/or the title is known?

Does the library have any books on a specified subject? Which books are they and where are they shelved?

The library staff cannot rely on memory to answer these questions. A tool must be provided which can supply the answers accurately and quickly, and that tool is the library catalogue.

The advent of computer cataloguing has revolutionized the theory and practice of cataloguing and many traditional practices have become outmoded. However, an understanding of the history and development of library cataloguing is still of value.

Types of catalogue
Traditionally the two main types of library catalogue were:

1 a classified catalogue
2 a dictionary catalogue.

Classified catalogue
A classified catalogue consists of three sequences:

1 Subject index. An alphabetical list of subjects covered by the

library's stock. Against each subject is shown the appropriate classification symbol. A typical example from a library which uses the Dewey system might be:

Physics   530

The subject index gives no information about particular titles or authors, nor how many books the library has on a given topic. To glean that information, one must consult the classified sequence.

2 Classified sequence. This follows the same arrangement as the classification scheme in use in the library and the classification symbol usually appears at the top of the entry to make filing and consultation easier. If the stock is classified by Dewey, the classified sequence of the catalogue will be in numerical order with entries running from the 000s to the 999s. As the catalogue represents a library's own stock, it follows that there will be gaps in the classified sequence where the library does not have any books on particular subjects. Also, there will be as many entries bearing the same class-marks as there are books on that subject in the library's stock, except that multiple copies of the same book are normally represented by a single entry which may or may not show the accession number of each copy or otherwise indicate the number of copies available. If Dewey is used in the library, a typical entry may look like this:

530
JARDINE, James Turnbull
 Physics through applications/by Jim Jardine.
 O.U.P., 1989.
 256p.: ill. (Oxford standard grade science)

3 Author index. The third sequence of the classified catalogue is:

 (a) an author index, or
 (b) a name index, or
 (c) an alphabetical sequence.

The author index (a) is arranged alphabetically by authors' surnames, and contains a separate entry for each of the books by each author represented in the library's stock. It used to be common practice to give only brief details of the book in the author entry as this saved the cataloguer's time. Full information could be found, if required, in the main entry in the classified sequence. An example of a simplified author entry might look like this:

JARDINE, James Turnbull
Physics through applications
O.U.P., 1989
530

However, the availability of mechanical methods of document copying popularized the unit form of entry. With this method, one master entry is produced in the form of a full author entry and then identical copies of the master are produced which, with the addition of the appropriate headings, can be filed in different parts of the catalogue.

A name index or name catalogue (b) is one which contains entries for works about persons, corporate bodies and/or places as well as author entries.

Alphabetical sequence (c): some librarians file several types of added entry in this part of the catalogue in addition to the author entries. These could include entries under title, series, translator and illustrator. When this happens, the name 'alphabetical sequence' is more accurate than author index or name index.

Dictionary catalogue

A dictionary catalogue, as its name implies, is one which is arranged like a dictionary in a single, straightforward alphabetical sequence. Each subject entry has the name of the subject as the heading instead of a classification symbol and these entries are interfiled with the author entries and any added entries under title, series, translator and so on which the cataloguer deems fit to include. Dictionary catalogues are very popular in the United States but less common in the United Kingdom. A survey carried out in 1976−7 by E. J. Hunter and K. G. B. Bakewell showed that 270 libraries in the United Kingdom had classified catalogues and only 49 had dictionary catalogues.

One of the major problems in constructing a dictionary catalogue, and to a lesser extent in consulting one, is the selection of subject headings. The English language is complex. Words with identical spellings may have entirely different meanings and, conversely, a number of different words may have the same meaning. Also some subjects cannot be conveyed by a single word but need a phrase. To assist in the task of selecting subject headings, the cataloguer will normally use a printed list such as *Sears list of subject headings*. This also ensures a high degree of uniformity of headings in dictionary catalogues in different libraries. Such a printed list also gives assistance with the choice of 'see' and 'see also' references which are required to guide the catalogue user from one heading to another. A 'see' reference leads one from a heading which has not been chosen to the one which has, linking synonymous terms; for example:

> Ornithology
>   see
> Birds

A 'see also' reference guides the user from one used subject heading to other related subject headings which may be more precise; for example:

> Vertebrates
>   see also
> Birds

The need for references in a dictionary catalogue tends to make it more bulky than a classified catalogue and therefore slightly more expensive to construct.

Here are some examples of entries and references from a dictionary catalogue:

Author entry: (i.e. main entry)	JARDINE, James Turnbull
	   Physics through applications/
	   by Jim Jardine. O.U.P. 1989
	   256p.; ill. (Oxford standard grade
	   science)
	                                    530

Subject entry (i.e. added entry: unit entry format)	Physics
	JARDINE, James Turnbull
	   Physics through applications/
	   by Jim Jardine. O.U.P. 1989
	   256p.; ill. (Oxford standard grade
	   science)
	                                    530

References (see also)	Dynamics
	   see also
	Physics
	Science
	   see also
	Physics

Alphabetico-classed catalogue

A third type of catalogue is the alphabetico-classed catalogue in which entries under broad subject headings are arranged in alphabetical order but each broad heading is subdivided into more specific subject divisions which are also alphabetically arranged. It therefore has many sub-sequences within the main sequence.

Full catalogue entries

Information given in a typical full catalogue entry

Layout	Example
Author	IREDALE, David
Title, including any subtitle or alternative title/	Discovering your family tree: a pocket guide to tracing your ancestors and compiling your family history/by
Author statement	David Iredale and John Barrett.
Edition statement	4th ed.
Imprint	Princes Risborough: Shire, 1985
Collation	71p.: facsims, geneal. tables; 18cm.
(Series statement)	(Discovery series; no. 93)
Annotation	Bibliography: p.37−62 Includes index.
ISBN	0-85263-767-5
Class no.	929.10941

Analysis of items in a full catalogue entry

AACR2
Rule
number

1 *Author*
Surnames to be given first, in capitals, followed
by full Christian names (forenames), e.g.:

BEENHAM, Rosemary Elizabeth

2 *Title*   1.1B
Follow the exact wording of the title page, and adopt
normal practice with regard to capitalization, i.e. the
first word, and also proper nouns and adjectives formed
from proper nouns, would have a capital letter, e.g.:

History of the world in ten and a half chapters
Library automation in North America.

3 *Subtitle*   1.1B
The subtitle should be given immediately following the
title, separated from it by a colon. The first word of the
subtitle should be in lower case unless it is a proper
noun, e.g.:

Library alive : prompting reading and research
in the school library.

4 *Alternative title*   1.1B
Authors rarely give an alternative title but, when they
do, it is separated from the title on the title page by
the word 'or' or its equivalent. In cataloguing, the
alternative title is separated from the title first by a
comma, then the word 'or' followed by a comma. The
first word of the alternative title should start with a
capital letter, e.g.:

Twelfth night, or, What you will

5 *Author statement* (statement of responsibility).   1.1F
In full cataloguing the author's name followes the title
(or alternative title or subtitle, if there is one),
provided the information appears prominently in the
book, and should be separated from it by an oblique
line. Give the author's name as it appears on the title
page. If the author's name does not appear on the title
page it should be included in the author statement but
in square brackets, e.g.

Twelfth night, or, What you will/by William Shakespeare
Microcomputer communications/by Martin Gandy

5.1 *Author statement in cases of joint or shared authorship*
Name joint authors, collaborators or contributors up
to a maximum of three. When there are more than three,
mention the first named only, followed by the mark of
omission (. . .), followed by the words 'et al.' in parentheses.
The names of the others should be mentioned in the
annotation.
Note: only one author is to be mentioned in the heading,
he or she being the one mainly responsible for the authorship
of the work. When authors share equal responsibility, the
first named on the title page is the one to be shown in the
heading. When there are more than three collaborators
sharing equal responsibility for the work, then the heading
must be under title.

6 *Edition statement* (edition area)   1.2B
The edition is always stated if given in the book. In
practice, this means that the edition is stated if it is

the second edition or later, e.g. 2nd ed., rev. ed. When
a subsequent edition of an author's work has been edited
or revised by someone else, the name of the editor should
be given in the edition statement, e.g.:

BURDETT Geoffrey
The Newnes guide to home electrics.
2nd ed./revised by W. Turner

7 *Imprint* (publication, distribution, etc., area)   1.4
The imprint in a catalogue entry shows the place of
publication, the name of the publisher, and the date of
publication in that order, e.g. London: Harrap, 1989.
When a foreign publisher is named first, followed by
a British publisher, both are to be shown in that order, e.g.:

New York: Wiley; London: Chapman & Hall.

The name of the publisher is to be given in the briefest
form in which it can be clearly recognized, e.g. Pitman,
not Sir Isaac Pitman & Sons Ltd. The date to be given
is that of the edition in question, and should always be
given in arabic numerals even if shown in roman numerals
in the book itself. Where no date of publication is given in
the book, it is to be ascertained or estimated and given in
parentheses, e.g. (1981?) (198−).

8 *Collation* (physical description area)   1.5
This is a statement about the physical make-up of the
book − its pages, its illustrative material and its spine
height. A simple example might be:

321p : ill. (some col.); 23cm

9 *Series statement* (series area)   1.6
When a book is one of a series of publications issued
under a collective series title, a series statement is to be
given in parentheses after the collation. It consists of the
title of the series and the number within the series of the
book being catalogued, and it may also include the name
of the editor of the series when his or her name is not
that of the author of the individual work, e.g.:

(International geophysics series)
(Perspectives in mathematics series no. 9)
(Syntax and semantics series; edited by Stephen R. Anderson)

10   *Notes* (note area or annotation)   1.7
     Notes may be given to amplify or explain any of the
     items in the catalogue entry, especially where these
     may be ambiguous or misleading. Notes may give
     further information, therefore, about the title, author,
     edition, imprint, collation or series. Notes may also
     be given on the scope, language or form of the book,
     e.g.:

> Discusses the case for free trade
> Text in Punjabi
> Play in 3 acts

When the cataloguer presents notes in the form of a
quotation from the book or its jacket, quotation marks
must be used and the source of the quotation given, e.g.:

> 'A textbook for 6th form students' − Preface

10.1 *Contents note*
     Contents may be specified, either selectively or fully,
     in order to show individual items in a collected work,
     or to draw attention to material whose presence is not
     indicated by the title or to stress an item of particular
     interest, e.g.:

> CONTENTS : V.1. Plain tales from the hills. V2 etc.
> PARTIAL CONTENTS : The place of Japan in world
> trade/P H Tresize.
> Bibliography, p.859−910
> Includes bibliographies

11   *Standard number* (ISBN)   1.8
     The international standard book number should be
     shown as follows:

> ISBN 0-85157-370-3

12   *Class mark* (classification symbol)
     The class mark is to be given at the foot of the unit
     entry at either the left or right side, depending on the
     cataloguer's preference.

13   *Tracings*
     Tracings are shown on the main entry only. For the
     benefit of staff, they provide a guide to the added

entries which have been filed in the catalogue for the
same book. Precise headings for the added entries may
be shown, or the tracings may be in abbreviated form
and indicate only the types of added entry included for
the book, e.g. 'Ti' to indicate a title entry has been made,
'Sr' to indicate a series entry and so on. Tracings ensure
that all the entries relating to a particular book are
removed from the catalogue when the last copy is withdrawn
from stock.

Forms of catalogue

The term 'form' refers to the physical form of presentation of the
catalogue, whether it be in the form of a loose-leaf or bound book, sheaf
slips in binders, cards in cabinet drawers, computer printout, microfilm
or microfiche.

In selecting which form of catalogue to adopt, a librarian will consider
the following factors:

1 Ease of construction/ease of input of information.
2 Ease of consultation, including ability to 'guide', i.e. providing a
  means whereby the catalogue user can quickly locate the required
  information from the catalogue just as a thumb index helps the
  person consulting a reference book to locate the appropriate section
  or chapter.
3 Facility in updating, i.e. adding new entries, amending existing
  entries and extracting entries when stock is withdrawn.
4 Ease of reproduction of entries, and facility for compilation of bibliographies.
5 Cost of materials and labour.
6 Space required to house the catalogue.
7 Portability of the catalogue or parts of it.
8 Durability of the catalogue.

Printed catalogue

This form of catalogue used to be fairly common but is now very rare
owing to the expense of production and the difficulty in updating. It is
in book form and therefore users find it easy to consult. A single volume
can be taken to a nearby table to be used, thus freeing all the other
volumes of the catalogue for the use of others. However, its portability
can be a disadvantage as readers may remove a volume and fail to return
it to its proper place. Compilation of bibliographies is straightforward
as pages of the catalogue can be photocopied. The *British Museum*

catalogue of printed books is an example of a printed catalogue.

Guardbook catalogue

This is similar to a printed catalogue except that additional pages can be inserted and new entries can be pasted in. It is sometimes used in conjunction with a printed catalogue as the cataloguing staff's master catalogue in which deletions, amendments and additions can be shown prior to the printing of a supplement to or new edition of the printed catalogue.

Sheaf catalogue

The sheaf catalogue (Figure 1) contains entries on paper slips with holes or slots at one edge so that they can be fastened into binders. Each binder has a locking/releasing mechanism to allow the insertion of new entries when required yet ensure that slips remain securely in place when the catalogue is consulted. Because the entries are on thin paper, several copies can be produced by using a typewriter and carbons. Sheaf slips appear to be quite durable though much depends on the amount of use a catalogue has. Insertion of new entries is time consuming but amendments are easy and withdrawals easier still as slips may be torn out without the binder having to be opened. The sheaf catalogue is easy to consult, though not very easy to guide. It is portable and cheap and takes up a minimum of space.

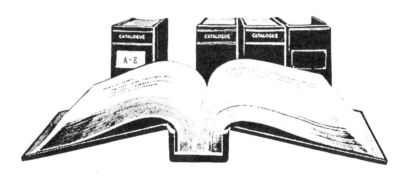

Fig. 1   Sheaf catalogue

Card catalogue

This used to be the most common form of catalogue in use but has now been superseded in popularity by computer catalogues. Entries are on cards filed in drawers in a catalogue cabinet. Internal guiding is achieved by inserting guide cards with tabs which protrude above the catalogue entries, and external guiding by labelling the outside of each drawer. Consequently the catalogue user can quickly find the required entries. Initial expenditure is required for the purchase of the cabinet but thereafter stationery costs are low. Most card catalogues are equipped with rods which lock the cards in place and prevent unauthorized removal of entries, but rods can be released to allow easy insertion of entries. Withdrawals do not even require the removal of the rod as cards can be torn out. Multiple copies of entries cannot be produced with carbons and a typewriter owing to the thickness of the card, but small duplicating machines and photocopiers can be utilized. Individual drawers can be carried to the shelves if necessary, perhaps for stocktaking, but normally a drawer-stop prevents the removal of a drawer by a reader. This does mean that a reader consulting one drawer can restrict access to several other drawers. Also the cabinet itself may be bulky and take up considerable floor space in the library.

Microfiche and microfilm catalogues

A microfiche catalogue has a considerable number of entries on each of a number of flat pieces of film which are slightly larger than catalogue cards. The information can be read only when a microfiche reader is used and the image enlarged and displayed on a screen. The great advantage of microfiche is that the maximum number of entries can be contained in a very limited space. It is costly and difficult to update, unless one also has the back-up of a computer, but this would add immensely to the cost. Some library members are still reticent about using technological innovations such as microfiche readers so it may be only library staff who use the catalogue.

Microfilm catalogues are similar except that entries are on a continuous length of film which is wound on to open spools or cassettes, and the appropriate type of 'reader' would have to be provided for their consultation.

Cooperative cataloguing systems

Cooperative cataloguing systems operate at local, regional, national and international levels.

Local systems

At local level, a large municipal library or a county library headquarters may do all the cataloguing for the smaller libraries over which they have control. This system is normally referred to as centralized cataloguing. When card or sheaf catalogues were in vogue, multiple copies of catalogue cards or sheaf slips would be produced and distributed to the smaller libraries to match these libraries' own stocks and to be filed in each library's own catalogue. The central or headquarters library would normally keep a master union catalogue showing the location of all books within the system's libraries and this master catalogue would be constantly updated. 'Union catalogue' is the term given to a catalogue which represents the stock of more than one library. The union catalogue maintained at a county library headquarters may include the holdings of college and other libraries within the county as well as its own branch libraries. Nowadays, the central library might produce and distribute several copies of a computer printout or microform catalogue or have an online computer system which covers the stocks of all the participating libraries, in which case locations would be shown against the catalogue entries to indicate which libraries have particular books in stock.

Regional systems

The regional library bureaux keep union catalogues covering the stocks of libraries within their own region. Their reliability depends on the cooperation of individual libraries within the region in notifying the bureau of additions to and withdrawals from stock. The London and South Eastern Regional Library Bureau − covering Greater London, Bedford-shire, Berkshire, Buckinghamshire, East Sussex, Essex, Hertfordshire, Kent, Surrey and West Sussex − produces microfiche catalogues arranged (1) by *British national bibliography (BNB)* numbers and (2) by ISBN numbers. Against each book number is shown a list of numbers which identify the particular libraries within the region which have copies in stock. Libraries can purchase their own copy of the annually updated LASER microfiche catalogue so they have immediate and direct access to the information. Online access to LASER's database is also available. A new initiative, code-named Viscount, has recently been started whereby all existing regional library bureaux share their records in a cooperative cataloguing project.

National systems

At national level, the British National Bibliographical Service produces *BNB*. This is a bibliography of new books/editions published in the United Kingdom which appears in the form of a printed, classified catalogue. It comes out weekly with interim cumulations culminating in an annual cumulation in microfiche format or in bound volumes. The bibliography cannot be used in lieu of a library's own catalogue as it would contain entries for many books not in a particular library's own stock. However, librarians can use it as a cataloguing tool when constructing their own library's catalogue. At the time of writing, the books listed in *BNB* are classified by the nineteenth full edition of Dewey and catalogued according to the second edition of the *Anglo-American cataloguing rules* (see below).

For almost a quarter of a century it was possible to purchase catalogue entries pre-prepared by a central agency. Until 1969 one could purchase pre-printed entries for a sheaf catalogue from *BNB*, and until 1978 *BNB* sold catalogue cards. The *BNB* numbers for new books added to stock could be traced by consulting copies of the *BNB* and these numbers could be used as the means of ordering the relevant catalogue entries. From 1978 the Birmingham Libraries Cooperative Mechanisation Project (BLCMP) provided a national and international catalogue service which included the sale of catalogue cards as well as machine-readable catalogue formats. It now offers an online service known as BOSS.

In 1966 the staff of *BNB* introduced MARC, and the system has been subsequently modified and developed. MARC is an acronym for machine-readable cataloguing. Participating libraries receive catalogue information on magnetic tapes from which they can produce card or microform catalogues using their own computing facilities, or, if preferred, they can have online access to the MARC computer records. Other countries also have national cooperative cataloguing systems. In the USA, for example, the Library of Congress and H. W. Wilson Company have both provided cataloguing services for American libraries, and there are now networks based on some of the larger universities and colleges.

International systems
There is considerable development in this field, but an example worthy of note is *Books in English*. It may be more accurate to call this a bibliography rather than a catalogue, but none the less it provides very useful information for the cataloguer on new books published in the English language in both the United Kingdom and the USA. The list is compiled from *BNB*'s MARC tapes and the Library of Congress accessions. The format of *Books in English* was ultrafiche, a type of microfiche which gave reduction/magnification of 150 times and which could cover up to 3000 A4 pages on a single piece of film 4 inches by 6 inches. Now the format is standard microfiche.

There are information retrieval banks for many specific subject areas.

Medlars is one example. This stands for Medical Literature Analysis and Retrieval System and it is operated from the National Library of Medicine in the USA. The British Library Lending Division acts as the UK centre for Medlars.

In the realm of cooperative and centralized cataloguing systems, acronyms abound. One could devote many pages to BLAISE, LOCAS, SWALCAP, SCOLCAP and the others but this basic introduction to the topic cannot offer such detail.

Cataloguing rules

Since the first decade of the twentieth century, published lists of cataloguing rules have been available to assist cataloguers in their task and to ensure a degree of uniformity of practice in libraries. British, American and Canadian committees have worked together to produce common codes of cataloguing practice, though, to provide for the differing needs of libraries in Britain and North America, separate editions known as *British text* and *North American text* have been published. Developments this century have included:

1   1908 Cataloguing Code incorporating a British text and a North American text.
2   An international conference on cataloguing principles in Paris in 1961.
3   Publication of *Anglo-American cataloguing rules* (AACR), 1967.
4   Formation of the Cataloguing and Indexing Group of the Library Association.
5   Formation of a cataloguing rules committee by the Library Association, and the establishment of an international committee on cataloguing under the auspices of the International Federation of Library Associations.
6   Introduction of computer-operated cataloguing systems which had repercussions on existing cataloguing rules.
7   Increasing stocks of non-book media in libraries which necessitated the publication of cataloguing rules for this material in 1973. Aslib (the Association of Special Libraries and Information Bureaux) and the National Council for Educational Technology participated in this venture.
8   Publication of a new edition of the *Anglo-American cataloguing rules* in 1978.
9   A concise edition of AACR was published by the Library Association in 1981. Cataloguing rules for the use of school libraries have been published. The first edition came out in 1957 and subsequent editions appeared in 1961, 1966, 1970, 1976 and 1984.

10   A revised version of the second edition of AACR was published in 1988 by the American, Canadian and British Library Associations.

Filing rules

There are several published codes of rules for filing catalogue entries and they include those produced by the American Library Association, the British Standards Institution and the Library of Congress. Some of the problems which occur in filing are concerned with (1) initials, (2) abbreviations, (3) numerals, (4) hyphenated words, (5) words with 'modified' letters and (6) words with different spellings. Listed below are the American Library Association (ALA) rules which deal with these problems:

1   Initials — where word-by-word filing is used, the problem arises as to where to place initials, including groups of initials separated by full stops. The ALA code (rule 5) decrees that initials precede words, e.g. AA, ALA, ASM, Abstracts. The exception is that acronyms (groups of initials which can be and are pronounced like a word, e.g. UNESCO, can be treated as words.

2   Abbreviations — the problem here is whether to file abbreviated words as they are written (e.g. Mr) or as they would appear if spelled out (e.g. Mister). The ALA code (rule 6) decrees that abbreviated words should be filed as if they were spelled out in full, with one exception, i.e. the abbreviation Mrs. St is therefore filed as if it were spelled Saint, and M' and Mc are filed as Mac.

3   Numerals — the filing problem is whether to file numerals in numerical order or to treat them as if spelled. The ALA code (rule 9) says that numerals should be treated as though spelled out, but in the language of the entry, e.g. 7 = seven (English) or sept (French), etc.

4   Hyphenated words — the question arises as to whether one should treat a hyphenated word as two separate words or as a single word. The ALA code (rule 11) treats a hyphenated word as two separate words, with the following exceptions:

   (a) When the first part of a hyphenated word cannot stand alone (e.g. anti-freeze, inter-university) that hyphenated word should be filed as if it were one complete word;

   (b) when a hyphenated word is sometimes written as one complete word and there is an entry in the catalogue under the complete form of the word, that form should be adhered to throughout, e.g. 'press-mark' filed as if it were 'pressmark'.

5   Words incorporating 'modified' letters — the problem here is how

to file words which include letters with accents or other modifications (e.g. the acute, grave or circumflex in French, or the umlaut in German). For example, should 'ö' be filed as if it were 'oe' or 'o'? The ALA rule decrees that all modifications should be ignored, i.e. 'ö' is to be filed as if it were 'o'.

6 Words with different spellings − some words can be spelled in two ways, in particular those words which are spelled differently in the USA from the way they are spelled in the UK, e.g. 'color' and 'colour'. The ALA code decrees that a uniform spelling be adopted for filing purposes, with a 'see' reference from the spelling shown on the title page when this differs. In practice, one should choose the form of spelling most likely to be sought by the catalogue users.

Some filing problems occur only when word-by-word alphabetization is used and do not apply to letter-by-letter arrangement. Some filing difficulties are peculiar to dictionary catalogues and would not occur in classified catalogues. For example, in a dictionary catalogue, one could have entries where the same word is used for the heading but the word relates to author, title and subject.

The ALA code states that author entries should come first, followed by a straightforward alphabetical arrangement of other entries, regardless of whether the heading is that of a title, a place or an object, e.g.:

MARK, Stephen	(author)	authors
MARK, Trevor	(author)	first
Mark and Sylvia	(title)	other
MARK (German coin)	(thing as subject)	entries
The Mark of Cain	(title)	follow
Mark, Saint	(person as subject)	alphabetically
Mark (Somerset, England)	(place as subject)	

Indexing

Indexes were mentioned in Chapter Four, where reference was made to the two types of index which might accompany the published schedules of a classification scheme. Examples were given of a specific index and of a relative index. It is important to note also that there are two methods of alphabetization − or two ways of arranging words in alphabetical sequence. One is known as the 'letter-by-letter' or 'all-through' method and the other as the 'word-by-word' or 'nothing before something' method. Compare the relative order of words in the following two lists:

Letter by letter	*Word by word*
Bookbinding	Book jacket
Bookcase	Book list
Booking hall	Book of hours
Book jacket	Book plate
Booklet	Book pocket
Book list	Book sale
Book of hours	Bookbinding
Book plate	Bookcase
Book pocket	Booking hall
Books	Booklet
Book sale	Books

With the letter-by-letter method, each letter is considered in turn whether or not there is a single word involved or two or more words. The gap between words is ignored.

The word-by-word method differs in that the gap between words is taken into account, therefore all items beginning with the simple word 'book' are dealt with first, and then the longer words such as 'bookbinding' follow.

Word-by-word is probably the more common system and is used in the most recent edition of the *Encyclopaedia Britannica*. It is also recommended in all major codes of filing rules. However, problems can occur and rules would have to be followed with regard to hyphenated words (whether they are treated as a single word or two separate words) and words which can be written either as one word or two, e.g. book card or bookcard.

The letter-by-letter method is less confusing in that hyphens and gaps between words are ignored and are therefore irrelevant. This method has been used in quite a number of reference books including some major encyclopaedias.

Chain indexing

This is a method introduced by S. R. Ranganathan for systematizing the compilation of an index and is intended to show the hierarchical relationship of a specific topic to its broader parent and grandparent. One of its applications would be in the construction of a subject index to a classified catalogue. Each of the lines of terms below would appear as a separate entry in the alphabetical subject index to a classified catalogue. The indexer works from the bottom to the top, that is from the specific to the broad.

The following is an example of chain indexing as applied to subject index entries for a classified catalogue. In a library using the Dewey classification scheme, a book on the subject of public libraries in England would be classified at 027.442. The index entries would therefore be:

ENGLAND − PUBLIC LIBRARIES	027.442
EUROPE − PUBLIC LIBRARIES	027.44
PUBLIC LIBRARIES	027.4
LIBRARIES	027
LIBRARY SCIENCE	020

Citation indexing

The earliest index of this type comes from the legal profession, where it is common practice to cite previous cases in order to substantiate a point. The principle has been applied to other information retrieval sources, notably in Science Citation Index and Social Sciences Citation Index. If someone doing research knows of a relevant periodical article on the topic, a citation index can be used to see which other authors have cited the author/title of that periodical article in their published work. It would then be known that these authors were also concerned with the same field of research and the researcher would be able to make use of their work. The citation index gives sufficient information about the source − that is, title of periodical, issue/volume number and year − for the researcher to trace it and hopefully, obtain it. These citation indexes can now be accessed via the DIALOG computer database.

Keyword indexing

Keyword indexing is used in some published bibliographies. The bibliography will normally index a book under author and under the first word of the title, excluding the definite or indefinite article, but in addition the indexer will pick out the most important words or keywords which appear in the title and include an index entry under each of these words. Normally the title will be inverted so that each keyword appears at the start, for example:

British town centre shopping schemes: a statistical digest (title entry)
Shopping schemes, British town centre: a statistical digest (keyword entry

Optical coincidence coordinate indexing

The optical coincidence coordinate indexing method, known as OCCI, has been used in offices and to a limited extent in libraries, particularly school library resource centres. In such a resource centre the stock is arranged by accession number and/or by form but not by any classification scheme which would bring together items on the same subject. The stock is listed numerically in an accessions ledger or card file so that if the accession number of an item is known one can consult the file, find details about the item and discover what its location is in the resource centre.

However, one must first be provided with a means of discovering the accession numbers of items relevant to one's subject of enquiry. To do this, the accession numbers must be punched on a number of feature cards which would together represent the subject covered. For example, if one added to stock a book about houses in London in the eighteenth century, one would need three feature cards: one filed under 'houses', one under 'London' and the third under 'eighteenth century'. The accession number would be punched on each of the feature cards.

If pupils wanted to discover what items the resource centre had on the subject of houses in London in the eighteenth century, they would have to retrieve the three cards from their storage box and hold them over a strong light source. A light box would be provided for this purpose so that the cards could be accurately stacked on top of each other to allow the light from the box to shine through any holes that the three cards had in common. This is why the term 'optical coincidence' is used – it signifies that light passes right through all the relevant cards at certain points because holes have been punched at the same places. In other words they have an accession number, or numbers, in common.

One can have feature cards filed under subjects, places, chronological periods and even under form. For example, one could have a card headed 'video cassettes' and all accession numbers of video cassettes in stock could be punched on that card.

Printed pre-numbered feature cards which can accommodate from 200 to 10,000 items can be purchased. (See Figure 2 for an illustration of an OCCI card). The supplier will also sell the necessary equipment such as storage units for the feature cards, a punch and a light box. Librarians using the OCCI system will usually compile their own feature list which acts as an authority file to remind them of feature card subject headings which relate to their own library's needs and stock. As with other traditional methods of cataloguing, the popularity of OCCI has waned with the advent of computerized systems.

Precis indexing

The acronym 'Precis' stands for preserved context index system. It is a systematized method of subject indexing designed to suit the requirements of computerized information retrieval systems. In some respects, it resembles keyword indexing but it is much more precise.

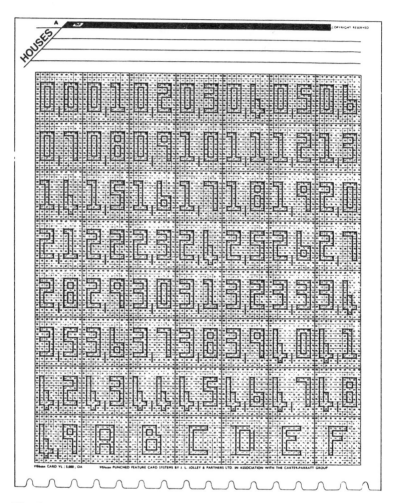

Fig. 2 An OCCI card

In Precis indexing, the subject of the book or other item must be expressed by a string of terms which together encompass the subject. All of the subject index entries would then be shown as a complete string of terms, but with each term being brought to the front of the string in turn. For example, a book concerned with the prevention of heat loss in houses by using thermoplastic insulation materials would require the following four subject index entries if the Precis method were used:

1 Houses
   Heat loss.   Insulation.   Thermoplastics
2 Heat loss.   Houses
   Insulation.   Thermoplastics
3 Insulation.   Heat loss.   Houses
   Thermoplastics
4 Thermoplastics.   Insulation.   Heat loss.   Houses

Each of the above entries displays the broader context of the more specific subject under which the entry is filed.

Other indexing methods are available, but they suit the requirements of office filing systems better than those of libraries. For example, edge-punched cards can be used whereby the information sought is found by manually inserting rods or needles through holes, suspending the pack and allowing the cards which have been punched at the required place to drop out. A variation of this method employs an electrically operated device which speeds up the location of the required punched cards.

In smaller libraries, traditional methods of classification and cataloguing are still proving effective. However, when these methods are allied to computerization the speed and efficiency of information retrieval is vastly enhanced, as the next chapter will seek to show.

Assignments

Practical
1 Visit your local public library and discover:

   (a) Whether the catalogue is readily accessible to the public. If not, why not?
   (b) What type of catalogue is provided (classifed or dictionary).
   (c) What form of catalogue is provided (card, microfiche etc.).
   (d) What information is given on catalogue entries.
   (e) If the catalogue is guided and how.
   (f) What instructions are provided to help catalogue users.
   (g) How easy or difficult it is to use the catalogue.

Written
1 Using the list of factors which librarians will consider when choosing the format of a library catalogue (see p.79), draw up a list of advantages and disadvantages of the following forms of catalogue:

   (a) card,
   (b) microfiche.

2   The following is a list of terms in random order. Arrange the list
in strict alphabetical order:

(a) By the word-by-word method.
(b) By the letter-by-letter method.

    Carp
    Carburettors
    Car port
    Cardiff
    Car maintenance
    Carpets
    Cars
    Carborundum
    Carpet tiles
    Car sales

Bibliography

Anglo-American cataloguing rules, 2nd rev. ed., London, Library
    Association, 1988.

Bakewell, K. G. B., 'The Precis indexing system', *Indexer*, **9** (4),
    October 1975, 160−4.

Diaz, A. J., *Microforms and library catalogs*, London, Meckler,
    1978.

Harrison, K. C., 'Elements of classification and cataloguing', *First
    steps in librarianship*, 5th ed., London, Deutsch, 1980.

Hunter, E. J., *An introduction to AACR2: a programmed guide to the
    second edition of Anglo American Cataloguing Rules 1988 revision*,
    London, Bingley, 1989.

Hunter, E. J. and Bakewell, K. G. B., *Cataloguing*, London, Bingley,
    1979; 2nd ed., London, Bingley, 1982. 3rd ed. in preparation for 1991.

Johnson, A. and Baker, K. J., 'Practical considerations in establishing
    and operating an optical coincidence card system', *Information
    scientist*, **1** (1), March 1970, 11−25.

Montgomery, A. C., *Acronyms and abbreviations in library and
    information work*, 4th ed., London, Library Association, 1990.

McGregor, J. W., 'In defence of the dictionary catalog', *Library
    resources and technical services*, **15** (1), Winter 1971, 29−33.

Rowley, J. E., 'Towards AACR3: a review of the implications of
    OPACs for cataloguing codes and practices', *Library review*, **38** (3),
    1989, 7−18.

Sears list of subject headings, 13th ed., New York, H. W. Wilson,
    1986.

School Libraries Association, Furlong, N. and Platt, P., *Cataloguing rules for books and other media in primary and secondary schools*, 6th ed., Swindon, School Libraries Association, 1984.

Chapter Six

Cataloguing and indexing: computerized methods

The advent of computers caused librarians to rethink the principles and practices of cataloguing. It was obvious that computers had great potential in the library world but the initial problems encountered were, first, the financial outlay required; secondly, the enormous size of the first generation of computers; thirdly, the limited information storage capacity and fourthly the enormity of the task of changing to a completely new and different system. Few libraries could afford to buy their own computer but some were fortunate enough to have the use of, or the possibility of buying time on, a computer owned by the local authority and housed in the civic centre.

The coming of the microchip reduced the size of the computer hardware and also facilitated an increase in the 'memory' or storage capacity. Computer wizards designed software packages suitable for a multitude of library operations, so that the traditional forms of catalogue began to disappear from many libraries and VDU screens appeared in their place. Nowadays, technology is advancing so rapidly that computers become outdated almost as soon as they are installed. However, the rising generation of library users is computer literate and they take to computer methods in libraries like ducks to a pond. For them the traditional methods of cataloguing must seem very old-hat.

Computer catalogues come in various guises. Those which are 'online' allow the catalogue user direct and immediate access to the data store, and the information appears on the screen of a computer terminal. Others involve the production of some form of intermediary between the catalogue user and the computer. This intermediary may be a computer printout or computer-produced microfiche.

A computer printout catalogue is usually presented in book form, but with pages bearing the typical appearance of computer-produced characters like the example shown in Figure 1.

```
FRONTIERS OF SCIENCE AND PHILOSOPHY
  SEE  COLODNY, ROBERT G.
FROMME, S. H;                        WHY TOMMY ISN'T LEARNING. TOM STACEY, 1070,    370.183
FROSSARD, ANDRE                      GOD EXISTS; I HAVE MET HIM; TR. BY MARJORIE    920 FROS
                                       VILLIERS. COLLINS, 1970.
FROST, BEDE                          ART OF MENTAL PRAYER. NEW ED. S.P.C.K. 1940    242
FROST, CONRAD                        ALICE ABOUT THE HOUSE THOMSON 1960            640
FROST, CONRAD                        AMATEUR COLOUR PRINTING. FOUNTAIN P. 1962     778.6
FROST, CONRAD                        TAKING AND PROCESSING AMATEUR COLOUR NEGATIVES 778.6
                                       FOUNTAIN P. 1965 95P.
FROST, DAVID                         MOTOR CYCLE CARE AND MAINTENANCE. APCO 1961   629.2275
FROST, DAVID LEONARD                 SCHOOL OF SHAKESPEARE THE INFLUENCE OF        822.09
                                       SHAKESPEARE ON ENG. DRAMA C.U.P.1968
FROST, DAVID, AND JAY                TO ENGLAND WITH LOVE HODDER 1967              942.085
FROST, DAVID, B.1929                 ALL BLACKS 1967 TOUR OF THE BRITISH ISLES AND 796.33374
                                       FRANCE WOLFE 1968
FROST, DAVID, B.1939                 AMERICANS. HEINEMANN, 1971.                   973.924
FROST, DAVID, B.1939                 TO ENGLAND WITH LOVE, BY DAVID FROST AND ANTONY 942.085
                                       JAY. HODDER 1967
FROST, J.H.                          HOW TO LISTEN TO THE WORLD   SEE   HOW TO
                                       LISTEN TO THE WORLD
FROST, M GILBERT                     TEACH YOURSELF MANAGEMENT E.U.P. 1951 (TEACH  650.01
                                       YOURSELF BOOKS)
FROST, M GILBERT                     TEACH YOURSELF MANAGEMENT REV. ED. E.U.P. 1962 650.01
FROST, ROBERT                        COMPLETE POEMS CAPE 1951                      811 FRO
FROST, ROBERT                        IN THE CLEARING HOLT, RINEHART & W. 1962      811 FRO
FROST, ROBERT                        INTERVIEWS WITH ROBERT FROST ED. BY EDWARD    920 FROS
                                       CONNERY LATHEM CAPE 1967
FROST, ROBERT                        POETRY OF ROBERT FROST; ED. BY EDWARD CONNERY 811 FRO
                                       LATHEM. CAPE, 1971.
FROST, ROBERT                        SELECTED LETTERS EDITED BY LAWRANCE THOMPSON  920 FROS
                                       CAPE 1965 645P.
FROST, ROBERT                        SELECTED POEMS; WITH AN INTRODUCTION BY C. DAY 811 FRO
                                       LEWIS. PENGUIN BOOKS 1955.
FROST, STELLA                        TRIBUTE TO EVIE HONE AND MAINIE JELLETT; ED. BY 709.415
                                       STELLA FROST. DUBLIN; BROWNE & NOLAN 1957
FROST, THOMAS W                      HYPNOSIS IN GENERAL DENTAL PRACTICE KIMPTON   617.6
                                       1959
FROST, W E, AND BROWN                TROUT COLLINS 1967                            597.55
FROSTICK, MICHAEL                    ADVERTISING AND THE MOTOR-CAR. LUND HUMPHRIES, 659.19629222
                                       1970.
FROSTICK, MICHAEL                    GRAND PRIX; ED. BY MICHAEL FROSTICK, PUBLISHED 796.7209
                                       FOR THE BRITISH RACING DRIVERS' CLUB BY PAUL
                                       HAMLYN 1969
FROSTICK, MICHAEL                    RETURN TO POWER THE GRAND PRIX OF 1966 AND 1967 796.72
                                       ALLEN & U. 1968
FROT, MAURICE                        NINEPGUE. GALLIMARD 1969                      843 FRO
FROUD, NINA                          COOKING THE CHINESE WAY SPRING BOOKS 1960 223P. 641.5251
FROUD, NINA                          HOME BOOK OF RUSSIAN COOKERY, BY NINA AND     641.5947
                                       GEORGE J. FROUD. FABER 1958
FROUD, NINA                          WORLD BOOK OF EGG AND CHEESE DISHES PELHAM    641.675
                                       BOOKS 1967
FROUD, NINA                          WORLD BOOK OF FISH DISHES PELHAM 1965 128P.   641.692
```

Fig. 1   From a computer printout catalogue

The computer may also act as a store of catalogue information from which magnetic tapes can be produced and these in turn can be processed into microfilm or microfiche. The abbreviation COM has become the accepted way of referring to such computer output microform.

These indirect, computer-produced systems used to be the norm but now many more librarians are offering their readers access to online computer catalogues.

Online computer catalogues

The input of cataloguing data

The term 'online' is applied to computer catalogues which give the library member direct access to the stored information. Sometimes the word OPAC, which is an abbreviation of Online Public Access Catalogue, is used. The catalogue user sits in front of a computer terminal and instigates a search by tapping the keys of a keyboard which resembles that of a typewriter. The information sought then appears on the screen or VDU.

Some libraries input all of their own data and to a lesser or greater degree design their own system to match the needs of their clients. Other libraries buy in an existing system and incorporate data produced by a central agency.

As systems differ from one library to another, it may be advisable to consider one library's system as a case study, bearing in mind that the basic principles will apply to all online computer catalogues but that there will also be differences in some of the more detailed aspects. The online system described below is the Adlib−2 system in operation in the libraries of the Anglia Higher Education College in Essex. At present the system operates on three sites but in four libraries. These are the main library on the Chelmsford site where all the maintenance and back-up of the system is concentrated, the law library which is also on the Chelmsford site, the library of the Brentwood site about 12 miles away and the library of the Danbury Park Management Centre about three miles outside Chelmsford. Following a recent merger with the Cambridge College of Arts and Technology, the online system will shortly be upgraded to include the library stock of the Cambridge campus.

The computer system is used for ordering and checking in stock, for checking in periodicals and for the issue and discharge of loan items as well as for cataloguing, so it is necessary to select the required process from the various options on the main menu. The diagram below shows the main menu as it would appear on the computer screen.

ADLIB − 2 LIBRARY MANAGEMENT SYSTEM

Technical services
2 Cataloguer
3 Authority file manager
4 Thesaurus manager

Reference work
7 Reference librarian
8 Information officer

Reader services
11 Reader services librarian
12 Issue desk

Acquisitions
16 Head of acquisitions
17 Orders clerk

Serials control
20 Subscriptions librarian
21 Serials receipts clerk
22 Serials stock control clerk

24 Management information

Use space bar, arrow keys, or type number to make selection. Enter 'h' for help or 'b' for bye.
Enter carriage return to execute selection.

Typing the number 2 causes the word 'Cataloguer' to be highlighted on the screen. Tapping the 'Return' key then activates the selection of the cataloguing option and the Cataloguer menu then appears on the screen. The options offered to the cataloguer are as follows:

CATALOGUER

Use the catalogue
2   Add/update a catalogue record
3   Retrieve by author
4   Retrieve by corporate author
5   Retrieve by subject term
6   Catalogue an article

List/print by material type
9   Search for any material
10 Search for papers
11 Search for patents
12 Search for reports
13 Search for A-V materials

Produce printed catalogues
16 Complete author catalogue
17 Subject catalogue
18 Classified catalogue

Maintain copy details
21 Add a copy
22 Amend copy details
23 Withdraw a copy

Choose another job
26 Authority file manager
27 Thesaurus manager
28 Run OPAC

Use space bar, arrow keys, or type number to make selection. Enter 'h' for help, 'p' or 'm' for previous or main menu, 'b' for bye. Enter carriage return to execute selection.

The system has been so programmed that option 2 is automatically highlighted because adding or updating a catalogue record is the function selected approximately 90% of the time. It makes for greater speed and efficiency merely to press the 'Return' key without having to select and key in the number as well.

Depressing the 'Return' key brings up the following simple menu:

Cataloguing system

Menu screen

Select option: A to Add a new catalogue record
                      U to Update an existing catalogue record
                      B for Bye from cataloguer system

When a book is ordered through the computer system, the order clerk will enter the book's details in a prescribed manner so that the information can form the basis of a simple catalogue entry. At the same time, the computer generates a catalogue number. On receipt of the book, the order record is updated and the catalogue number written on the reverse of the book's title page.

The cataloguer's first job is to check whether the book already has a catalogue number, and if it has then the Update option is selected by keying in the letter 'U'.

If no catalogue number appears on the book, as will happen, for example, for an item supplied annually on a standing order, then option 'A' is chosen and the details of the book are keyed in by the cataloguer. A unique catalogue number is then automatically generated by the computer and can be written on the reverse of the book's title page for future reference.

Let us follow the process through, screen by screen, for a book ordered via the computer system which has the catalogue number 20578 appearing on the verso of the title page. The letter 'U' is keyed in to activate the Update process and this brings up the first of a series of cataloguing screens which looks like this:

```
Number (RET) to update record, or (RET) to change prompt, DEL to abort
                        Cataloguing system
    Lead title      [    ]
    Title           [

                    [
    Sub title       [

                    [
    Edition         [    ]           Material  [                ]
    ISBN            [    ]           Catalogue No  [            ]

    Classification  [         ]           No of copies  [       ]
    Accession       [    ] [ ] [    ] [ ] [    ] [ ] [   ] [ ]
    & Location      [    ] [ ] [    ] [ ] [    ] [ ] [   ] [ ]
    Enter catalogue number for update: [20578]
```

Keying in the digits of the book's catalogue number, in this case 20578, brings up brief details such as those in the example shown below:

```
ESC ESC to Execute, DEL to abort
                        Cataloguing system
Lead title      [     ]
Title           [Small business and entrepreneurship
                [
Sub title       [
Edition         [     ]     Material     [book                    ]
ISBN            [0333420977]     Catalogue No     [  20578  ]
Classification  [               ]     No of copies   [          ]
Accession    [      ] [ ] [      ] [ ] [      ] [ ] [      ] [ ] [ ]
& Location   [      ] [ ] [      ] [ ] [      ] [ ] [      ] [ ] [ ]
```

The cataloguer would then key in information to fill in gaps in the record. 'Lead title' is where one would type in the definite or indefinite article, that is, 'A', 'An' or 'The', if there was one at the start of the title. In our chosen example the 'field' or space is left blank.

The title of the book has been correctly entered by the order clerk so it needs no amendment. The book has no subtitle, so that field is also left blank. The edition is stated only if it is a second or later edition. If the book is in the first edition, that is taken for granted and the information does not appear.

In the field named 'Material', it has already been stated that the item being catalogued is a book. If it were some kind of audiovisual material the abbreviation 'AV' would have to be entered in this space. The ISBN is always shown on the order record if it is known as this is essential information for the supplier. However, the cataloguer would quickly check whether the ISBN correctly matches that on the book being catalogued.

The book will already have been classified and the class number will have been written on the book and/or on its issue stationery. The cataloguer now enters that class number in the appropriate field. The three letters which follow the class number assist in the book's filing and location. If the book has a principal author, these letters would be the first three of the author's surname. However, if the book is written by more than three collaborators or is edited, then the first three letters of the book's title (excluding the article) would appear after the class number. In our chosen example, the class number would be shown as 658.022 SMA.

Following the commands at the top of the screen, the cataloguer will then press the 'Escape' key twice to execute the process and enter the information into the computer. Immediately on doing this, an enquiry appears at the foot of the screen — namely:

Do you wish to add any more accession numbers? Y or N

It says 'any more' even if there is none appearing at present. Obviously it is essential for the cataloguer to enter the accession number of each copy of the book being catalogued, so 'Y' is keyed in to indicate 'yes' and to take the cursor to the required field. When a college is on several sites, each with its own library, it is also necessary to show the site where each copy will be located.

An example would look like this

Accession   [ZZ019531]   [D]
and Location

The lengthy ZZ number is the accession number, or bar code label number, of the book, and 'D' indicates that it is in the Danbury site library. The screen as it stands shows enough boxes for up to eight copies of the book, but when all eight are filled, the computer automatically asks whether the cataloguer has further copies to add.

The information about the accession number(s) and location(s) is entered into the computer's memory as soon as the cataloguer executes the process by depressing the 'Escape' key twice. The computer automatically shows the number of copies in the appropriate field. This number is the total number of copies held at all site libraries.

This would complete the details required on the first screen, so the computer now displays the second screen. Once again, some information will already appear if it has been entered at the time of ordering. Normally this would consist of the name of the publisher and the date of publication. These details would be checked for accuracy by the cataloguer and amended if necessary, and then additional information would be keyed in, for example in the collation, series and notes fields. The completed screen for our chosen book would look like this:

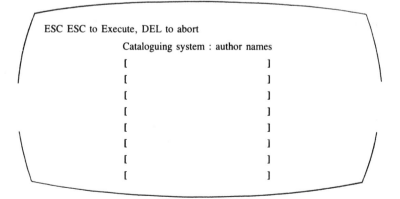

```
ESC ESC to execute DEL to abort
              Cataloguing system: books catalogue
                                    Cat. No    [20578    ]
Conference  [                                            ]
            [                                            ]
Publisher   [Macmillan                                   ]
Language    [           ]      Year of publication   [1989]
Collation   [xiii,(1),294p;ill                           ]
Series      [Macmillan small business series             ]
Notes       [Text intended for undergraduate and postgraduate  ]
            [students undertaking business studies courses     ]
```

The language field is left blank if the text is in English but completed if the book is written in a foreign language.

When the screen is completed and 'executed', a new option appears at the foot of the VDU which allows the cataloguer to choose one of three screens, that is:

Type: A for authors, C for corporate authors, S for subject terms, or B for bye.

Typing 'A' will therefore bring up the following screen:

```
ESC ESC to Execute, DEL to abort
              Cataloguing system : author names
              [                          ]
              [                          ]
              [                          ]
              [                          ]
              [                          ]
              [                          ]
              [                          ]
              [                          ]
```

Our chosen example has no authors but is edited by Paul Burns and Jim Dewhurst. With online computer catalogues it is not essential to stick rigidly to AACR 2. The cataloguer is at liberty to anticipate user needs and enter the names of authors and editors as he or she deems appropriate. The status of those named is not specified. Our example would merely show the two names on the screen as follows:

[BURNS, Paul   ]
[DEWHURST, Jim   ]

On depressing 'ESC' twice, the information is entered and the same options list as before appears at the foot of the screen, allowing one to move on to corporate authors or subjects. Sometimes there is value in recording the name of an organization even when there is a personal author or editor. At other times it is imperative to include a corporate author entry because there is no personal author and it is the name of the organization which would be remembered and sought. The screen for corporate authors is identical to that for authors except for the heading.

Subject entries are vital, of course, as the cataloguing of the book would not be complete without the input of relevant subject terms. This is probably the cataloguer's most difficult task because of the complexity of the English language and the problem of being logical, succinct and consistent in the choice of terms. It is essential for all cataloguers within the particular library system to come to a consensus of opinion about preferred terms and then to compile a thesaurus which each of them can consult when memory fails. This thesaurus can be computer produced in its entirety as a printout, but also can be accessed term by term online.

The subject terms for the example chosen would probably be:

[entrepreneurial activities
[entrepreneurship
[small businesses
[management
[managerial activities
[business enterprises
[marketing
[case studies

The cataloguer may even choose to highlight individual sections or chapters of the book by adding their specific subjects in the list of subject terms. The time factor and the memory available in the computer system will probably act as a brake on the cataloguer who aims to be a perfectionist.

All screens have now been completed for our sample book. The cataloguing details will be stored temporarily in a computer with limited memory which is housed in the college's main library at Chelmsford, but at regular intervals, usually weekly, the data is transferred to the main computer which is in the control of computer experts rather than library staff. The smaller computer is therefore released for the input of the following week's cataloguing.

As with all computer systems, human error can creep in to foul things up, and of course mechanical breakdown or power failure can occur from time to time, usually at the most inopportune moment.

Accessing information from the online computer catalogue: the library user's viewpoint

It is the duty of the library staff to see that the computer catalogue is up and running and ready for use. First thing in the morning, a librarian will switch on the OPAC terminals and type in the appropriate log-in command in order to activate the system. In 'user-friendly' systems the first screen shows a welcome message from which one would rapidly move to the main menu.

In the Anglia College's Adlib -2 system, the main menu screen looks like this:

```
          INFOBASE PUBLIC ACCESS SYSTEM
  Select items by their:

                    Free text search
          or    Title
          or    Author Name
          or    Organisation Name
          or    Subject Search.
  Press the up or down arrows to select your option, then press RETURN.
```

The commands associated with this computer catalogue are clear and simple, but library members would be given instruction in the use of the catalogue to make sure that the process was understood and they would be encouraged also to seek the help of a librarian if difficulties were experienced at a later date.

Let us examine in more detail each of the types of search offered by the menu.

Free text search

Having highlighted the Free text search option by using the appropriate arrow key, pressing the 'Return' key will bring up the following screen:

```
                    INFOBASE PUBLIC ACCESS SYSTEM
   Enter free text  [                                        ]

       In Freetext you may search using any of the following:
          AUTHOR SURNAME, SUBJECT TERM, KEY WORDS IN TITLE

   These may be in any order and may be truncated by * wherever required,
   e.g. Sm* will find Smith, Smart etc.

   After entering term(s) press return until cursor leaves box. Press F1 to view
   details of previous searches or enter a term and press F2 to browse through
   the free text terms list.
   F7 displays more help information and F8 returns to the menu.


   [ F1  History ]   [ F2  Pick a term ]   [ F7  Help ]   [ F8  Exit ]
```

As with any information retrieval exercise, feeding in a very broad term, for example, 'management', will throw up a great many records which the interrogator will then have to plough through page by page or screen by screen. Normally a message will appear on the computer screen which states that more than 50 records have been found. These may be scanned by pressing the 'Return' key and then using the arrow keys to move through all ten pages or screens each listing five books on the subject of management. The option is given to key in letter 'C' to continue the search and scan all the other management titles until the entire stock of management books has been covered. Obviously this is a tedious business, so it is preferable to be more precise with the keying in of search terms and thereby limit the search to texts which are especially relevant. Even the more specific term 'Library management' calls up more than 50 records. Typing in 'School libraries management' makes for a quicker search and calls up only four items, and these are numbered and listed on the screen. To discover more details of a particular book from that list, one keys in the appropriate number to highlight it and then presses the 'Return' key. A full catalogue entry then appears, as in the example shown below:

INFOBASE PUBLIC ACCESS SYSTEM

Catalogue no: 4608

Title	Developing a policy for a school library
Subtitle	
Author(s)	PAIN, Helen; LESQUEREUX, John
Corporate author	SCHOOL LIBRARIES GROUP
Publication details	School Libraries Group (1985)
Edition	
Collation	54p
Series	Studies in school library management
Type of material	book
Shelf location	Q027.8 PAI
Number of copies	1 In stock 1

| F1 Copies | F2 List | F3 New | F6 Terms | F7 Help |

A series of commands appears at the foot of the screen. Keying in F1 brings up the following information on another screen:

INFOBASE PUBLIC ACCESS SYSTEM

No of copies   1   Cat. no. 4608
Title   Shelf   Q027.8PAI
Developing a policy for a school library   Location
Book numbers   A15575
Book location   B
Key: In stock On loan Cancelled On circulation Damaged Missing
        Borrower number: [   ]

| F1 Return | F2 List | F3 New | F4 Reserve | F5 Locations | F7 Help |

The book number on the above screen is that copy's accession number, and the location symbol indicates that it is in the stock of the Brentwood site library. The number may be highlighted on screen to tie in with the highlighted words 'In stock' which appear lower down. This shows that the book is on the shelf at the time of searching and not on loan. Conversely, if the accession number is not highlighted, it indicates that the book is already on loan and the return date appears directly below the accession number. The option is then given to reserve the book by keying in F4 and typing in one's membership/borrower number.

The other commands listed at the bottom of the screen activate the following processes:

F1 Return — takes the catalogue user back to the previous screen showing full details of the book.

F2 List — takes the user back to the original list of four books on school library management.

F3 New — returns the enquirer back to the original free text search option so that he or she can initiate a new search.

F6 Terms — brings up a list of all the subject terms which the cataloguer entered when cataloguing that particular book.

F7 Help — brings up an explanatory list of all the command terms, any one of which can then be selected and activated.

Title search

The main menu, described earlier, allows one to search by title. It is not essential to type in the precise title in full. Any keywords from the title can be keyed in, in any order, to activate a title search. In other respects the procedure is similar to searching under free text.

Author search

To search by author, the enquirer has to type in the author's surname. If the initial of the first of the author's forenames is known, it is useful to type this in also as it limits and speeds up the search; for example, typing in 'PAIN, H*' will very rapidly bring up information about four books by Helen Pain. The effect of the asterisk is to truncate the forename. For some strange reason the Adlib−2 computer system will not find the information if one types in 'PAIN, Helen'. Most systems have quirks which one has to tolerate; alternatively one can try to persuade the computer programmers to rectify matters if possible.

The screens showing information about this author's books which are in the stock of the Anglia College's libraries are identical to those retrieved by free text search and described earlier.

Subject search

The final option on the main OPAC menu is a subject search. In fact this is really a way of browsing through the thesaurus of subject terms which the cataloguers have previously compiled and entered on the computer system. On activating the subject search, the first screen to appear looks like this:

INFOBASE PUBLIC ACCESS SYSTEM – THESAURUS BROWSE

Current term:

Class: [   ]   Code: [   ]

Relationships

Enter first term and press RETURN to find relationships, then press D to Display catalogue entries, S to Select new term or B for Bye. Use up and down arrows to indicate choice for Display and Select. When appropriate, N displays Next page of relationships, P displays Previous one.

The flashing cursor is in the box marked 'Current term' to indicate that the subject term sought should be typed in to instigate the search. For example, on keying in the subject 'marketing' and pressing the 'Return' key, the following information appears on the screen:

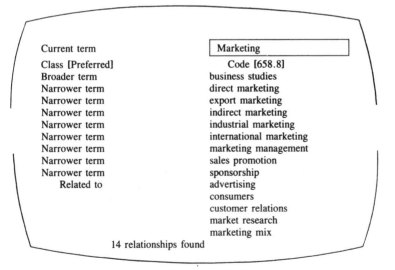

Current term	Marketing
Class [Preferred]	Code [658.8]
Broader term	business studies
Narrower term	direct marketing
Narrower term	export marketing
Narrower term	indirect marketing
Narrower term	industrial marketing
Narrower term	international marketing
Narrower term	marketing management
Narrower term	sales promotion
Narrower term	sponsorship
Related to	advertising
	consumers
	customer relations
	market research
	marketing mix

14 relationships found

By indicating that the term sought is 'preferred', the computer tells the enquirer that the subject term 'marketing' has been used by the cataloguer and that the associated class number is 658.8. Pressing D for 'Display' will call up a list of all the books on marketing in the Anglia College's libraries. However, the computer also lists 14 other subject terms which are in some way related to the subject of marketing. Most of these are narrower, more specific subjects, any one of which might be more appropriate to the enquirer's needs and which could be selected in preference to the more general term 'marketing'.

If the catalogue user keyed in a subject term which the cataloguer had not used, the computer would show 'non-preferred' in the appropriate field and would highlight the correct subject term under which to search. For example:

Current term	:	abused children
Class	:	[not preferred]
Relationships:	:	Use child abuse

In other words, the thesaurus browse facility is serving the same purpose as the subject index of a classified catalogue in linking the subject term sought with its class number, but it is also fulfilling the same function as 'see' and 'see also' references in a dictionary catalogue which link synonymous and related subject terms with the original sought term. The computer system therefore offers the best of both worlds, provided, of course, that the cataloguing staff have been diligent and constructed the thesaurus to a high standard in the first instance.

Having a thesaurus built into the computer's memory also enables the librarians to offer a selective dissemination of information (SDI) service to college staff whereby individual tutors notify the library of the subject areas of particular significance to themselves. At regular intervals the tutor is sent a computer printout of all new items added to stock in the named subject fields.

Advantages of online computer catalogues

1 Easy to construct once the cataloguers have mastered the technique.
2 Very easy and quick to access the stored information once the catalogue user has had a little instruction, and provided the system itself gives clear commands on screen.
3 Very comprehensive in its search facility. It can offer the best of both classified and dictionary catalogues.
4 The computer system, if linked to a computerized system for the issue and discharge of material, can tell the catalogue user whether the item sought is actually sitting on the shelf or is on loan. It can also offer the library member the option of immediately reserving

the item if all copies are on loan.

5   It makes the task of operating multi-site libraries much more viable in that the computer can access catalogue records for the stocks of all the site libraries.

Disadvantages of online computer catalogues

1   Expense – apart from the computer itself, each library must have sufficient terminals, otherwise people will be queuing to consult the catalogue. There is also a great deal of peripheral hardware behind the scenes, e.g. gandolphs etc.

2   Cataloguers, and, to a limited degree, catalogue users need key-boarding/typing skills. For this reason the system is more open to human error.

3   Computers have to be switched off while maintenance and regular tasks like back-up are undertaken.

4   The equipment is subject to breakdown and problems with the power supply. One can temporarily resort to manual methods for a computerized issue system but there is no replacement source available if the computer catalogue is not working.

5   As a library's stock increases, or the system is enlarged to include more and more site libraries, so the search time may be lengthened.

Assignments

Practical

1   If possible, visit a library which has an online computer catalogue. Try the system and assess its ease of use.

Written

1   Compare and contrast a computer-produced microfiche catalogue with an online public access catalogue. List the advantages and disadvantages of each.

Bibliography

Hildreth, Charles R. (ed.), *The online catalogue: developments and directions*, London, Library Association, 1989.

Hunter, Eric J., *Computerized cataloguing*, London, Clive Bingley, 1985.

Mitev, Nathalie N., *Designing an online public access catalogue*, London, British Library, 1985.

Rowley, Jennifer E., *Organising knowledge: an introduction to information retrieval*, Aldershot, Gower, 1987.

Chapter Seven

Basic library routines

Libraries offer a variety of services for the benefit of their clientele, the chief of which is the lending of books and other materials. However, libraries will not normally offer all of their services to all comers, principally because resources are limited.

A policy decision will have been taken at the outset by a library's senior management team about eligibility for membership of that library. Normally those who are deemed to be eligible are people who in some way or other are paying, either directly or indirectly, for the library's services. In a public library, the groups considered to be eligible are:

1 Those who live in the local authority's area and therefore contribute via the community charge. All the members of a household would be included, not just those who pay the community charge.
2 Those employed in the area, because the place of employment would be rated.
3 Those attending an academic institution in the area.

Some public libraries recognize the validity of library tickets issued by other libraries. Others will allow non-eligible groups access to the library's materials for reference purposes only but will not offer loan facilities to them.

In colleges and universities, the students' fees will include a sum of money to cover library use. Academic libraries will normally restrict membership to students and staff of the institution, though some may offer associate membership to certain categories of individuals, such as local schoolteachers. Other academic libraries open their doors to all comers for reference purposes only, considering it detrimental to the students if books on their reading lists are inaccessible because they are on loan to 'outsiders'.

Industrial firms may provide libraries for the benefit of employees. Even so, individual departments within an organization may be charged for the use they make of the library. In this world it appears increasingly that nothing is free.

Registration of library members
The procedure entailed in registering library members varies according to the type of library. In a school library, for example, pupils may not need to complete an application form for library membership because information about each pupil will already be held by the administrative staff. The fact that a child is a pupil at a particular school is sufficient entitlement for him or her to be issued with tickets for that school's library.

In other academic libraries some proof that the applicant really is a student at the institution will be required, and this may take the form of a receipt for course fees or a lecturer's signature.

Proof of identity of the applicant is usually required in a public library. This verification might be achieved by checking the voters' register, or examining the applicant's driving licence or some other documentation which will provide evidence. The application form would normally show the applicant's name and address, and in addition a signature would be required below a statement of intent to comply with the library's rules and regulations.

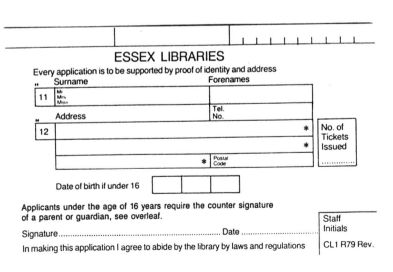

Fig. 1 Public library membership application form

On completion and acceptance of the membership application, the reader will be issued with a ticket or tickets. In libraries which are computerized, the names, addresses and other details of library members will be stored on computer. In other libraries, membership application forms may be filed, usually alphabetically by surname, in the register of borrowers. At this point, the new member is usually given some instruction in library use and may also be issued with a printed guide to the library and its services.

Charging methods (issuing systems)

As has been said, one of the principal services offered by libraries is the lending of books and other materials. Obviously, libraries need to keep some kind of record of such loan transactions and many methods have been devised to systematize this task. These methods are known as issuing systems or charging methods. The recording of the loan of the material is called 'charging' or 'issuing', the actual record of the loan is known as the 'charge' or the 'issue' and the cancellation of the record when the material is returned by the borrower is called 'discharging'. The charging method selected by a particular library depends to a large extent on the library's clientele, the size of stock and the need to restrict the number of items which a library member may have on loan, and on whether the library has peak periods for the lending and returning of material. The choice of method will also be affected by the amount and type of information the library staff require the issue to furnish. For example, the issue will be expected to answer the following basic questions:

1   Who has materials on loan? What are the names and addresses of the borrowers?
2   Which materials are on loan? What are the titles and who are the authors of the books which have been borrowed?
3   When are the materials due for return?

In addition, the library staff may require that the charging method facilitates the following tasks:

1   The keeping of issue statistics.
2   The operation of systems for renewing the loan period and for re-calling overdue materials.
3   The operation of a reservations system.
4   The monitoring of the popularity of specific materials, and some-times, in school libraries, the monitoring of an individual pupil's reading.

The charging method selected should be simple and speedy to operate for both staff and borrowers. If the system is complex and involves the borrower in a considerable amount of effort, such as laboriously filling in book and borrower details on forms or cards, the temptation will be for the borrower to bypass the issue desk and sneak out of the library with his or her chosen books.

The charging methods which involve the completion of forms or cards at the point of issue include NCR forms and the BIC system, which are explained below.

NCR (no carbon required) forms

With this method, the borrower or member of staff has to complete details of the book to be borrowed − for example, author, title, class-mark and accession number − along with the name and address of the borrower on the top copy of a set of NCR forms. The information appears also on the other copies of the set. The number of copies in a set of NCR forms is determined by the library's own requirements. It ranges from two to six copies. If the NCR forms are in a pad, a metal or cardboard plate has to be inserted below the set of copies to be produced to prevent transfer of information to the next set of forms. If two copies are produced, it is usual to file one under date/author and one under borrower's name. The book borrowed has its date label stamped with the date due, and when the book is returned both copies of the loan record have to be retrieved from the files. This method is popular in some college libraries where students are encouraged to serve themselves at the issue point and where they do not have to wait at the discharge point because the staff dispose of the completed NCR forms once they have been retrieved from the loan files. Such colleges do not normally restrict the number of books which a student may borrow and do not charge fines on overdue books.

An industrial library known to the authors employs six copies in each set of NCR forms. One copy is filed under author, one under the borrower's name, two are filed together under date to serve as overdue notices if necessary, one copy is put into the book in lieu of a date label, and the last copy is sent to the borrower's departmental manager because the library receives payment for each loan transaction. The forms in a set are colour coded to assist in filing. Obviously, the discharging of loan material involves the retrieval of forms from three different sequences so it is a time-consuming business for the library staff. Therefore, the method is feasible only in a small library with a very limited daily issue.

BOOK		Copy No.	Writtle Agricultural College Library
Author			
Title			
JOURNAL			
Title			
Vol:	Pt:	Date:	
STUDENT	DATE BORROWED		
COURSE			
PSL 385			

Fig. 2   An NCR form (Note that this system is no longer in use at Writtle Agricultural College)

Book Issue Card (BIC) system

This method has been devised principally to meet the needs of school libraries and there are two variations of it, both of which employ 75mm (3 in) by 125mm (5 in) cards.

1   The card used in the first of the two variations is pre-printed with the words 'author' and 'title' at the top and this information would be typed or written on the card by the librarian to match the book into which the card is inserted. The card would stay in a pocket inside the book while it remained on the library shelves but would be removed at the time of issue. Also pre-printed on the card are the words 'date' and 'name' so that the card can be stamped with the date of return and the borrower's name can be written alongside. A date label in the book would also be stamped so that the borrower has a record of the date of return. The BIC card is then filed, usually by date and then by author, as the loan record, and retrieved and returned to the book when it is brought back by the reader. The method requires a minimum of effort by librarian and borrower and it does not restrict the number of items which can be borrowed by a library member.

2   The second variation of the BIC system employs a card with the words 'name' and 'form' pre-printed at the top which would be completed by the school librarian to show a pupil's name and class. Underneath are pre-printed the words 'date' and 'book' ready for completion at the time of issue by date stamping and writing in the title of the book

to be borrowed. The purpose of this variation of the BIC system is to maintain a record of an individual pupil's reading.

AUTHOR	
TITLE	
Date	Name
....	....
....	....
....	....
....	....
....	....
....	....
....	....
....	....
....	....
....	....
....	....
....	....
LIBREX 35X	....

Fig. 3   A BIC card

The Browne system

For many, many years the most commonly used charging method was the Browne system. However, as libraries became busier, the daily issues increased and the task of filing became more onerous. Libraries which had to cope with peak periods of borrowing faced the embarrassing prospect of queues of irate readers waiting at the discharge side of the issue desk while frantic assistants fell over each other's feet trying to retrieve tickets from the rows and rows of issue trays. Such libraries had to abandon the Browne system in favour of mechanized or computerized methods which offered greater speed of charging and discharging and dispensed with manual filing. However, in some smaller libraries the Browne system is still going strong, and it operates as follows:

1 *Stationery/equipment required*

   (a) Date label in each book   } [(a) and (b) can be combined]
   (b) Book pocket in each book   }
   (c) Book card in each book
   (d) Reader's ticket (one per book)
   (e) Issue trays
   (f) Date guides (or other guides used in issue trays).

2 *Method*
   Having filled in a membership application form, the reader is given a number of tickets bearing his or her name and address. The reader presents the books to be borrowed at the issue desk, along with a reader's ticket for each book. The date label in each book is stamped with the date of return; the book card is removed from each book and inserted into the reader's tickets (one book card per ticket).
   Therefore the 'charge' is one book card inserted into one ticket.
   The charges can be counted for statistical purposes and then filed behind date guides in issue trays by accession number, author or class number (in the case of non-fiction). Whatever is chosen as the 'filing medium' should appear at the *top* of the book card.
   When a book is returned the assistant will look inside it to ascertain from the date label, or pocket, the accession number/author/class number as well as the date due. The appropriate charge must then be removed from the issue, the book card replaced in the book pocket and the ticket returned to the reader.

3 *Advantages*

   (a) Simple
   (b) Economical
   (c) Can locate any book on loan at any time
   (d) Can locate and send overdues
   (e) Facilitates reservations (if filed correctly)
   (f) Number of books issued to each reader controlled
   (g) No delay in returning books to circulation after return
   (h) Possession of reader's ticket provides proof of return of material.

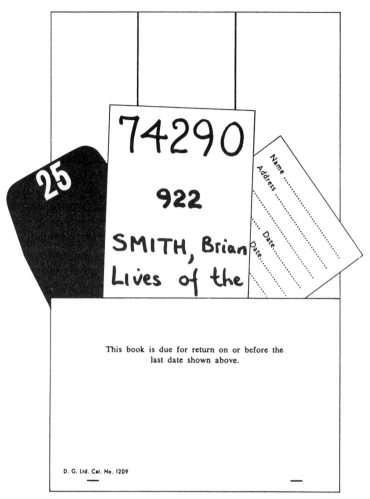

This book is due for return on or before the last date shown above.

D. G. Ltd. Cat. No. 1209

Fig. 4 **Stationery for the Browne issuing system**

4 *Disadvantages*

(a) Time consuming because of manual filing
(b) Errors can occur in filing and discharge
(c) Necessity for large issue desk to house rows of issue trays plus number of staff required to man the desk
(d) Possibility of upsetting issue trays
(e) Discharge is a lengthy process, therefore queues form at peak periods.

The Islington system (a variation of Browne)

1 *Stationery/equipment required*

    (a) Embossing machine
    (b) Plastic cards (one per reader)
    (c) Small printing machine(s)
    (d) Supply of paper slips
    (e) Date label in each book
    (f) Pocket in each book
    (g) Book card in each book
    (h) Issue trays
    (i) Date guides.

2 *Method*

Each reader is given *one* plastic ticket on which is *embossed* his or her name and address. The stationery inside the library books is the same as in the Browne system. However, the difference lies in the fact that the reader must print an address slip (using the embossed ticket) for each book he or she wishes to borrow.

Therefore, the 'charge' is a book card plus a paper address slip inside a blank ticket.

3 *Advantages*

    (a) Fairly easy to operate
    (b) Can locate any book on loan
    (c) Can locate and send overdues
    (d) Facilitates reservations
    (e) Obviates queuing to return books. One can operate 'delayed discharge' at peak periods.

4 *Disadvantages*

As Browne system (a)−(d).

    (f) Fairly expensive
    (g) Needs reader participation in printing address slips
    (h) Reader may lose or forget to bring the embossed ticket
    (i) No real control over the number of books borrowed by each reader.

Ticket book or cheque book charging

1 *Stationery/equipment required*

    (a) Register of borrowers in number order
    (b) Book of tickets for each reader, each ticket showing that reader's number
    (c) Date label

(d) Book pocket
(e) Plain pocket (inside book pocket)
(f) Book card (inside plain pocket).

The 'charge' is a plain pocket inside which are the book card and one numbered ticket slip.

2 *Method*
Each book has a book pocket permanently fixed inside the cover on which details of the book are given. Within this book pocket is a plain pocket, inside which is a book card bearing details of the book. The reader need only insert one of his or her ticket slips into this plain pocket and present the book for date stamping. The assistant removes the 'charge' and it is subsequently filed. The issue trays are usually kept in a separate 'discharge room' and not at the issue desk. There is a reception desk where books are returned, the actual discharging being done later in the 'discharging room' when the charge is removed from the issue, the reader's ticket destroyed and the plain pocket and book card returned to the book. An additional 'cheque book' is issued to the reader whenever the previous one is used up.

3 *Advantages*

(a) Simple to operate
(b) Rapid charging
(c) Rapid discharging
(d) Complete record of the whereabouts of books
(e) Reserved books easily traced
(f) Inexpensive
(g) Can deploy junior staff in discharging room, and discharge books at less busy periods.

4 *Disadvantages*

(a) Filing of charge is time consuming
(b) Overdue notices take longer − no name and address on ticket slip
(c) No real control of number of books borrowed
(d) Reader may lose or forget ticket book
(e) Extra expense and effort in supplying additional 'cheque books'.

Token charging

1 *Stationery/equipment required*

(a) Membership card for each reader − valid for one year only
(b) Number of tokens equivalent to number of books a reader may borrow

(c) Date label in each book.

2 *Method*

The book's date label is stamped in the usual way, and the reader must surrender one token for each book being issued. On returning books the reader merely receives the appropriate number of tokens in exchange. At the end of each year the reader must be able to produce the full complement of tokens or pay a replacement cost for any which have been lost. A visible index (i.e. a list of reserved books which must be checked whenever books are returned) is used for reservations.

SOUTHEND
ON
SEA
PUBLIC
LIBRARIES
TOKEN

Fig. 5   Token as used some years ago

3 *Advantages*

(a) Simple to operate
(b) Very quick charging and discharging − no queues
(c) Economical on staffing.

4 *Disadvantages*

(a) No record of which books are on loan
(b) No record of which books are in the possession of a borrower, therefore overdue notices cannot be sent
(c) Scheme lends itself to dishonesty.

Punched card charging

1 *Stationery/equipment required*

   (a) Computer or other mechanical sorter
   (b) Automatic key punch machine
   (c) Plastic membership cards — one per reader
   (d) Punched cards — two for each book issued
   (e) Book pocket in each book.

2 *Method*
   Charging. When a book is borrowed, the assistant takes two punched cards, pre-dated with date due for return (both date punched and date stamped), places the two punched cards in an automatic key punch machine and punches on both cards the reader's number and the book's accession number and class number. One card is then retained as the library's record of loans; the other card is inserted in the book pocket with the date of return clearly visible.
   Discharging. The punched cards are removed from returned books, sorted into accession number order by machine, and then matched by machine with the duplicate cards kept as the library's record of loans. Unmatched cards represent books still out on loan and these can be refiled mechanically, this time in date order, to reveal overdues. A list of overdues can then be produced by a tabulator showing the reader's membership number and the book's accession number. From this list, overdue notices can be sent.

3 *Advantages*

   (a) Provides a record of loans similar to the Browne system
   (b) Discharging is speedy, therefore no queues
   (c) Facilitates reservations
   (d) Facilitates sending of overdues.

4 *Disadvantages*

   (a) Expensive equipment and stationery
   (b) Charging is a fairly lengthy process
   (c) Open to errors in operating key punch machine — really requires trained operators
   (d) Sending overdues is a lengthy process — must look up members' register to match reader's name and address with reader's number as shown on punched card.

Photocharging

1 *Stationery/equipment required*

   (a) Photocharging machine(s)
   (b) Computer
   (c) Microfilm reader
   (d) Membership tickets − one per reader
   (e) Transaction cards − several colour coded sets
   (f) Pocket in each book
   (g) Label in each book − showing accession number, author, title
       (but not a date label).

2 *Method*
   Charging. The reader presents the books to be borrowed at the issue
   desk, and hands over his or her reader's ticket. Each book is opened
   to reveal its label, and placed on the platen of the photocopying
   machine. Alongside the book is a stack of transaction cards which
   are in numerical order − lowest number at the top and highest number
   at the bottom. These transaction cards have already been date stamped
   with the date of return. The reader's ticket is placed alongside the
   stack of transaction cards and a button is depressed to activate the
   camera in the photocharger. A photograph is taken of all *three* items
   side by side. Then the top transaction card is placed inside the pocket
   of the book with which it has been photographed. When all of the
   borrower's books have been dealt with in this way, the membership
   ticket is returned and the borrower goes off with the books.
        The 'charge' is a photographic record of book details and
   transaction card and reader's ticket. When the film is 'full' it must
   be removed from the photocharger and sent off to be processed. A
   new film is put into the photocharger.
   Discharging. If no fines are charged, the reader just leaves the
   returned books on the library counter and goes straight away to choose
   some more. If fines are charged, the reader must pause at the counter
   until a staff member checks whether the books are overdue or not.
   The colour coding of transaction cards makes it easy to detect
   overdues. The transaction cards are removed from the books and put
   into pigeon-holes according to colour. If the books are not reserved,
   they may be shelved or put on a trolley.
   Overdues. All the transaction cards of a particular colour are
   gathered together when a certain number of weeks have elapsed since
   their use at the charging desk (i.e. when they would be overdue) and
   the batch of cards is sorted into numerical order by a computer.

Having sorted them, the computer then prints a list of missing numbers. The computer printout of missing numbers represents the overdues list. This is first checked against the renewals record, and then checked against the appropriate film which by now has been returned after processing. The film can be read only on a microfilm reader. The overdues assistant has to locate the appropriate transaction card number as it comes up on the screen, and then reads the book details and reader's name and address which appear alongside.

Renewals. If books are brought to the library for renewal the original transaction card is removed and the book reissued with a new transaction card. Telephone or postal renewals are tedious as they involve staff in writing down on mock transaction cards the transaction card number, date due, book details and reader details. Books are not renewed in this way more than once as it complicates matters too much.

Reservations. There is no physical record of the issues (except on film) and therefore no way of recording reserved books except by use of a visible index. Sometimes reserved books slip through because staff are not meticulous in checking the visible index.

3 *Advantages*

(a) Very quick discharging, therefore no queues
(b) Provides a record of which books are on loan and to whom
(c) Film record of loans less bulky than trays of Browne tickets
(d) Economical use of staff and counter space
(e) Reader keeps his or her ticket all the time, therefore no errors regarding wrong tickets.

4 *Disadvantages*

(a) Expensive equipment and stationery
(b) Possibility of mechanical breakdown or power failure
(c) Delay while film is being processed (and possibility of strikes), therefore a lengthy period during which one cannot check which books are on loan
(d) Telephone and postal renewals difficult
(e) Reservations difficult
(f) Loss of transaction cards while books on loan, or transfer of transaction cards from one book to another
(g) Possibility of blurred image on film
(h) Lengthy process to trace overdues
(i) Reader may forget his or her ticket
(j) Difficult to restrict number of books per reader.

Computerized issuing systems

Computerized issuing systems have been in use in larger libraries for many years. They have become increasingly sophisticated, however, and every day there seem to be new advances in this area. Therefore it may be helpful to the reader if two systems are described which illustrate how far things have moved since computerized issuing systems were introduced.

The data pen or light pen arrived with the early systems and is still going strong. In fact the early systems were referred to by the manufacturers' trade names, such as Plessey Pen and Telepen. Libraries using data capture systems have a bar code printer which resembles a typewriter. Striking the appropriate keys, either alphabetical or numerical characters, produces a bar code label of vertical black and white lines of varying thicknesses. This code can be 'read' by the data pen. In addition, the characters appear above the bar code in legible form so that they can be read by the human eye also.

At the time of registration, the reader is allocated a number which identifies him or her. A label is produced, using the bar code printer, which displays the reader's number in readable form but also shows that number translated into a bar code. The library member is issued with one ticket on which there are printed details of the library, written/typed details of the reader's name and address, and also the bar code label bearing the reader's number. Usually the ticket is made of card and it is inserted and sealed in a plastic wallet to make it more durable. Similarly each book or other item available for loan is given a number, like an accession number, and this too is shown on a bar code which is placed inside the book along with a date label. There are distinguishing features which identify certain codes as membership numbers and others as accession numbers so there is no confusion.

Examples of computerized issuing systems

The Plessey pen system

1 *Charging*

The issue terminal is equipped with a data pen to which may be attached a self-inking date stamp. There is also a card holder into which the reader's ticket is inserted.

Charging is accomplished by running the data pen horizontally across the bar code label on the reader's ticket and then across the bar code labels on the books to be borrowed. The date labels in the books are stamped with the date of return and the ticket is returned to the reader.

097 000000X

or to:

CAMBRIDGESHIRE LIBRARIES,
CENTRAL LIBRARY,
7 LION YARD, CAMBRIDGE CB2 3QD
Tel. Cambridge 65252-7

BOOKS MAY NOT BE BORROWED
WITHOUT PRODUCTION OF
THIS TICKET.

All changes of address must be
notified to the library and loss of the
ticket reported. A charge may be
made for replacement.

YOU ARE RESPONSIBLE FOR ALL
THE ITEMS BORROWED ON THIS TICKET

Fig. 6 (Note that this system is no longer in use in Cambridgeshire libraries)

The charge is in the form of electronic signals recorded initially on to a cassette or floppy disc. The information on the cassette is then transferred to magnetic tapes at a computer centre and subsequently fed into the computer. The transfer of information from the cassette can be done automatically using a Post Office modem or the cassette can be taken or posted to the computer centre.

2   *Discharging*
The discharge terminal is equipped with another data pen and this is used to read the books' bar code labels when they are returned. The reader's ticket is not required at this stage as the reader's name will be automatically deleted from the computer records when all books have been returned.

3 *Renewals*

Postal or telephone renewals necessitate the use of a keyboard terminal. if the book is not presented at the counter for renewal there is no means of reading its bar code label with the data pen. However, the book's number must be quoted by the borrower and the assistant can then manually key in this information on the keyboard terminal.

4 *Overdues*

The computer produces overdue cards which show the reader's number, name and address and the book number. These cards are ready for posting without involving the time and effort of library staff.

5 *Reservations*

The accession numbers of books which have been requested are fed in manually using the keyboard terminal. The computer includes a 'trapping store' which activates a flashing light at the discharge terminal whenever the bar code label of a reserved book is 'read' by the data pen. The issue terminal also incorporates a trapping store warning light in case a reserved book has slipped through the system and found its way on to the shelves. The reader wishing to borrow such a reserved book will be told to return it as quickly as possible as it is required by another library member.

6 *Additional facilities*

Provided the required information has been fed into the computer in the first place, the computer can produce all manner of statistical reports. In its initial stages, librarians tended to have too many reports at too frequent intervals. Economies are now being made in this respect and weekly reports appear to be the norm.

The onerous task of stocktaking can be accomplished quite simply and cheaply by taking a mobile data pen unit to the library shelves and reading all the stock's bar code labels. All other sources would be checked, such as books awaiting repair or binding, reserve stock etc. and then these records would be matched with the issue against the computer records of the library's total stock. A printout of missing items would then be produced by the computer.

Mechanical breakdown and power failure may affect the smooth running of the system but they do not constitute disaster. The data pen system is supported by battery-operated equipment, but the life of the batteries would not be sufficient to sustain the library's full service for a lengthy period. As a stand-by measure, input sheets are kept at the counter and the assistant would write down the reader's number and books' numbers. When the fault is rectified, these numbers are fed in manually using the keyboard terminal. Libraries which have adopted a data pen system use it in all of their branches and mobile libraries as well as at the central library so that all records are in the same computer memory bank.

7 *Advantages*

(a) Speed of charging and discharging
(b) Accurate reservations system due to the trapping store
(c) Computer-produced overdue notices
(d) All material issued on a single ticket and at a central point
(e) Statistical reports produced by computer
(f) Facilitates stocktaking
(g) Reduction in routine duties. Staff freed to concentrate on other aspects of library work
(h) Increased efficiency.

8 *Disadvantages*

(a) Expense, both on capital expenditure for equipment and running costs for computer time
(b) Staff at the computer centre are involved as well as library staff
(c) The speed of service at the issue desk makes the system more impersonal
(d) Human error may creep in; for example, the automatic acknowledgement of the trapping store light without taking the appropriate action.

An online computerized issuing system
A case study from the Anglia College of Higher Education.

Computer systems now available to libraries are very advanced indeed. They make the old methods described above seem very outmoded. However, it is probably only the larger libraries which can afford the computer hardware necessary for the latest systems.

Charging
In the Anglia College libraries (now totalling six on four sites), the issuing system is only one of many menu options available on the Adlib−2 Library Management System run on the 32 bit Zilog 130 computer.

  The basic equipment at the issue desk is a computer terminal with keyboard and an attached light pen. Some of the College's libraries are busier than others, and those have two or more issue terminals available for use at peak periods. The busy service point will also have the terminal(s) permanently in the issue mode. In the smallest of the site libraries there is only one terminal available for staff use so the librarian is constantly changing screens and choosing from a long list of options.

The main menu looks like this:

```
              ADLIB-2  LIBRARY MANAGEMENT SYSTEM

   Technical services              Acquisitions
   2  Cataloguer                   16 Head of acquisitions
   3  Authority file manager       17 Orders clerk
   4  Thesaurus manager
   Reference work                  Serials control
   7  Reference librarian          20 Subscriptions librarian
   8  Information officer          21 Serials receipts clerk
   Reader services                 22 Serials stock control clerk
   11 Reader services librarian    24 Management information
   12 Issue desk

   Use space bar, arrow keys, or type number to make selection.
   Enter 'h' for help or 'b' for bye.
```

Following the commands at the foot of the menu screen, the librarian would key in the number 12, or use the arrow keys or space bar to move around the menu options in order to highlight option 12, Issue desk. Pressing the 'Return' key then brings up on screen the Issue desk menu options shown below:

```
                           ISSUE DESK

   Issue desk operations           General enquiries
   2  Issue and catalogue          16 On accession number
   3  Discharge                    17 On title
   4  Renewal                      18 On borrower name or number
   5  Issue
   Reservations
   7  Place a global reservation
   8  Cancel global reservation
   9  Place a copy reservation
   10 Cancel copy reservation

   Amend availability flag         Choose another job
   13 Global reservation           27 Issue desk reports
   14 Copy reservation             28 Reader Services Librarian

   Use space bar, arrow keys or type number to make selection. Enter
   'h' for help, 'p' or 'm' for previous or main menu, 'b' for bye.
   Enter carriage return to execute selection.
```

Option 2, the Issue and catalogue facility, is very useful when a library is in the transition period from its previous manual systems to the new computerized one. It allows brief details of a book to be entered into the online catalogue at the point of issue. In an ideal world, of course, retrospective cataloguing of the entire stock of the library would have been completed so that all details would already be in the online system's memory store in advance of introducing computerized issuing. Option 5 can be used only when the book's details have previously been entered by the cataloguer into the online system's database.

As has already been stated, it is necessary for the borrower to produce a membership ticket bearing his or her own unique membership number in the form of a bar code label. The book must also have a unique bar code label representing the accession number of that particular copy. It also requires a date label.

If option 5 is selected, the following details appear on the screen of the computer terminal:

```
                          Issue an item
Borrower number:  [      ] [      ] [   ] [          ]

Expiry date:      [      ] Current loans:  [   ] maximum [    ]
                          Current res.  :  [   ] maximum [    ]

Accession no:     [      ] Catalogue no.:  [          ]
Title:            [                                    ]
                  [                                    ]

Issue date:       [      ] Return date  :  [          ]
Copy status:      [      ] Date last accessed:  [          ]
Copy location:    [      ] [              ]
Issues:           [      ]

F1        F2                          F7        F8
Query     Issue                       Help      Exit
```

On depressing the F1 key, the cursor moves into the borrower number box at the top of the screen. The number on the reader's ticket is entered either by scanning the bar code with the light pen or by typing in the number using the keyboard terminal. Pressing the F1 key again activates a search and information about the borrower is instantaneously called up by the computer and appears in the relevant boxes, for example:

Borrower no: [12345] [Mrs] [R E]   [BEENHAM]
Expiry date: 31/08/90 Current loans: [6] maximum [20]
                                    Current res. : [1] maximum [10]

The librarian at the issue terminal then presses the F2 key on the keyboard. This time the cursor moves into the box marked 'Accession no.', awaiting input of the information. As before, the accession number can be entered by scanning the book's bar code label with the light pen or by keying in the appropriate digits on the keyboard terminal. When the accession number is entered, and the process executed by pressing the 'Escape' key, the title of the book automatically appears on screen and can be checked to see that it tallies. The computer also shows the catalogue number of the book, a facility of benefit to the library staff who may need to call up catalogue or order records if a book should be lost or stolen. The issue date appears, this obviously being the date of the transaction. The computer has information in its memory store about the loan period of a specific book, so the correct date of return automatically appears on the screen. Library staff predetermine the loan period in accordance with expected demand and number of copies available and this information is entered into the computer at the time of cataloguing. In the Anglia College the maximum loan period is three weeks, with renewal facilities if the book is not reserved, and the minimum period is one hour, with several other variants between these two extremes.

Pressing the 'Escape' key completes the transaction and the information is then stored immediately in the computer's memory. At that point the date of return would be manually stamped on the date label of the book. If several books are to be issued to the same borrower, the F2 key has to be pressed for each one, the accession number entered and the 'Escape' key pressed to execute the issue. The reader's number is entered only once. The computer screen also shows how many books the borrower has on loan. When the predetermined number has been reached, the computer displays a message stating that no more loans are possible.

Discharging
To discharge a book one has to select option 3 from the Issue desk menu. This calls up the following screen:

```
                          Discharge an item
     Accession No.:    [        ]  Catalogue No. :  [       ]
     Copy location:    [    ]
     Return by date:   [        ]  Copy status   :  [      ]
     Date overdue sent:            Overdue status :  [    ]
     Date recall sent:             Date final recall sent:
     Borrower No.:     [       ]
     Current fines:
     Number of loans:
     ---------------------------------------------------------------------------
     Instructions: 1 Query on accession number to effect discharge
```

The assistant manning the computer terminal will depress the 'Q' key on the keyboard to move the cursor into the 'Accession No.' box. The accession number of the book is entered by scanning the book's bar code label with the data pen or by keying the information in via the keyboard. Pressing the 'Escape' key executes a search in the computer's memory and the relevant details appear on screen, thus effecting the discharge of the item. If the book is overdue, the computer bleeps a warning to the library assistant and the screen shows whether fines are chargeable. The computer also flashes up a message if the book is reserved by another library member and displays that person's membership number.

One does not require the borrower's ticket or membership number to discharge an item. The computer already has that information in its memory. It will be deleted only when all items have been returned. Displayed at the foot of the screen is up-to-the-minute information about the number of items a borrower still has on loan. If the borrower requests a verbal reminder about the authors and titles of books still outstanding, the information can be extracted by querying under the appropriate menu option, namely option 18, On borrower name and number,

Renewals

To renew a book, the assistant depresses digit 4 on the keyboard to highlight option 4, then the 'Return' key to execute the selection. The information which then appears on screen looks like this:

```
           Query Next Previous Update Current Output Bye
   ------------------------------------------------------------------
                      Renew the loan of an item
   Enter accession number:  [      ]   [      ]
   Return by date:          [      ]   Copy status:    [        ]
   Date overdue sent:                  Overdue status: [        ]
   Date recall sent:                   Date final recall sent:

   ------------------------------------------------------------------
   Catalogue number:        [      ]
   Borrower:                [      ]
   Expiry date:                        Current fines:

   ------------------------------------------------------------------
   Instructions: 1  Query on accession number
                 2  Update return by date.
```

Following the instructions which appear at the foot of the screen, the assistant will query on accession number by depressing key 'Q' on the keyboard and then entering the accession number. If it is a telephone renewal, the accession number must be entered manually via the keyboard. If the item is presented at the counter, the data pen may be used to scan the bar code label. Either way, the accession number appears on screen in the appropriate box. Pressing the 'Escape' key causes the computer to search its memory store and detailed information then automatically fills the screen. The predetermined loan period is shown, and the return by date. Further down, the book's title and catalogue number appear along with details of the borrower.

To renew the item, the assistant will depress key 'U' for 'Update'. The cursor automatically moves into the 'Return by date' box and the new date of return appears. Pressing the 'Escape' key executes the renewal and a message flashes on to the foot of the screen to give evidence that 'This record has been changed.'

If the book has been reserved by another reader, the information will flash up on screen and the assistant will be asked to depress a 'Y' (yes) or 'N' (no) key to indicate whether or not the renewal can go ahead. As with other systems, the date which appears on the book's date label must be altered to correspond with the information shown by the computer. If it is a telephone renewal, the reader will be told the new return by date and asked to write it on the date label. If the book is presented for renewal at the library counter, the assistant will restamp the date label.

Overdues

With an online computerized issue system, overdue notices are generated automatically by the computer. There is also the facility to produce early recall notices when a book has been reserved.

Reservations

The Issue desk menu shown earlier offers a number of options relating to reservations. Option 7, Place a global reservation, puts a reserve on every copy of an item in every site library when the assistant keys in the catalogue number along with the borrower number. The first copy returned will be sent to the requesting site library to satisfy the reservation. When the book is issued the computer will ask the assistant whether that reader's global reservation should be cancelled. Pressing the 'Y' key indicates a positive response and the global reservation is deleted.

Readers can also place their own global reservations via the online public access catalogue if all copies of the required book at all site libraries happen to be on loan at the same time. To do this the reader presses the F4 key on the keyboard and types in his or her own membership number. There are further details of this process in Chapter Six.

The library assistant can also go into option 8, Cancel global reservation, if the reader should obtain the item from another source in the meantime.

Option 9 allows the assistant to place a copy reservation. It may be considered expedient to reserve only the copy or copies of the book which are in one's own site library's stock. To do this one will enter the appropriate accession number or numbers along with the membership number of the borrower initiating the reservation. Issuing the particular copy to the reader will allow cancellation of the reservation. In addition there is the facility, via option 10, to cancel a copy reservation if the reader decides the book is no longer required.

Options 13 and 14 offer the assistant the facility of amending the availability flag for either a global or copy reservation. This is done when a reserved book is returned to the library. For a global reservation, the assistant will query by the catalogue number, and for a copy reservation the query will be by the accession number of the specific copy. A search is activated by depressing the 'Escape' key, whereupon the title of the reserved book appears on screen. Other details which are shown include the name and number of the first reservee and the site where the reader is based. Initially the signal in the field marked 'Availability' is 'E' for 'entered'. When the reserved book becomes available, the availability flag must be updated to 'A' for 'awaiting collection'. Every morning, at the Chelmsford site library, the computer produces postcards for all reservations showing 'A' in the appropriate field. These cards are printed with the full address of the reservee as well as details of the reserved book awaiting collection. The cards are therefore ready for posting. The computer automatically changes the availability flag from 'A' to 'P' to alert staff to the fact that a postcard has been sent. The book will be filed under borrower's surname on the reservations shelf behind the issue desk.

Using options 13 and 14, library staff can also check through all the reservations for a specific book simply by keying in 'D' for 'detail' and then keying 'N' for 'next' until the complete list is scanned.

When a borrower returns an item, a message to the effect that there is a reserved item awaiting collection will flash up on screen. Of course, the reader will already have been notified by post but may have come into the library before the postcard has been received.

Additional facilities

Issue desk menu options 16 and 17 allow one to enquire about the present whereabouts of an item by querying under either accession number or title. If it is on loan, the computer will show details of the transaction, including the name and number of the borrower, the date of issue and date of return. It also displays further details about the book such as ISBN, the library catalogue number and the site library where it is normally held.

Querying under option 18, On borrower name or number, will call up details of all items at present on loan to that borrower and also whether there are any current reservations. When students are permitted to borrow up to ten books at a time they do occasionally mislay one and come in to request a memory jogger. To be able to specify the authors and titles of all books on loan to the student assists greatly in the search for items temporarily mislaid.

Emergency back-up

There are times when the computer terminals are out of action. Sometimes this is done deliberately so that the system can be upgraded but occasionally there is power failure or a breakdown in the network. When this happens, the details of issues, renewals and discharges have to be recorded manually on back-up sheets and the information keyed into the computer via the keyboard once the system is up and running again. This is not as tedious as it might seem. There are pre-prepared back-up sheets for use in times of emergency. The issues/renewals are written on a sheet like this:

TODAY'S DATE	BORROWER NO.	ACCESSION NO.	R	BORROWER NO.	ACCESSION NO.	R
27/11/89	1807	632	R			
	1257	ZZ008258				

The discharge back-up form is even simpler because only the accession numbers need to be recorded.

Advantages of online computer issuing systems

1 Speed and accuracy of charging and discharging.
2 All renewals, including telephone renewals, easily dealt with.
3 Almost foolproof reservations system.
4 Computer-produced overdue notices and early recall notices.
5 All material issued on a single ticket.
6 Information instantly available at the touch of a key on a keyboard terminal.
7 Details of fines appear on screen so the assistant doesn't have to do any calculations.
8 No necessity for manual filing of membership cards.
9 Statistical reports can be printed as and when required.
10 Generally increased efficiency.

Disadvantages of online computer issuing systems

1 Expense.
2 Possibility of power failure or breakdown of the system with consequent need for an alternative means of recording transactions.
3 Necessity for library staff to keep changing screens when one terminal has to be used for many library operations.

Library bye-laws, rules and regulations

It has been stated that the applicant for library membership is usually required to sign a declaration of agreement to abide by the library's rules and regulations. The list of bye-laws, rules and regulations ought to be prominently displayed in the library so that the applicant knows what he or she is agreeing to.

Acts of Parliament empower public library authorities to make bye-

The basics of librarianship

laws. These bye-laws are drawn up by the chief librarian in consultation with the clerk to the council. They then need the approval of the library committee and the local council, and also the secretary of state. Bye-laws are prohibitive — that is, they tell people what they are not allowed to do — and they are enforceable by law. They are concerned with the prevention of damage to the library's property and the governing of behaviour on the premises.

Rules and regulations are informative — that is, they tell people what they may do. They are not enforceable at law, but wilful offenders may be blacklisted and banned from library use. There will be regulations governing eligibility for library membership, period of validity of tickets, loan procedures, hours of opening and so on. A model set of library rules and regulations was published in the *Library Association record* in August 1953.

Inter-library loans

An extensive and highly efficient network of library cooperation exists in the United Kingdom. Public and special libraries participate in the inter-library loan scheme and, to a lesser extent, in subject specialization schemes. There is also an international network of library cooperation. An individual library will try as far as possible to meet the needs of its own clientele. However, in these days of financial stringency, no library achieves complete self-sufficiency but has to rely on the back-up services of the inter-library loan network. This is of tremendous advantage to the individual reader as it means he or she has the stocks of most of the libraries of the United Kingdom and many overseas libraries at his or her disposal.

The inter-library loan network operates like a spiral with the individual library at the centre and the local, regional, national and international back-up services forming an ever-widening circle around it. Having ascertained that the required book is not in the stock of his or her own library, the reader will complete an inter-library loan request form. Figure 7 shows a typical example of such a form. The form is usually in triplicate so that one copy can be kept as the requesting library's own record.

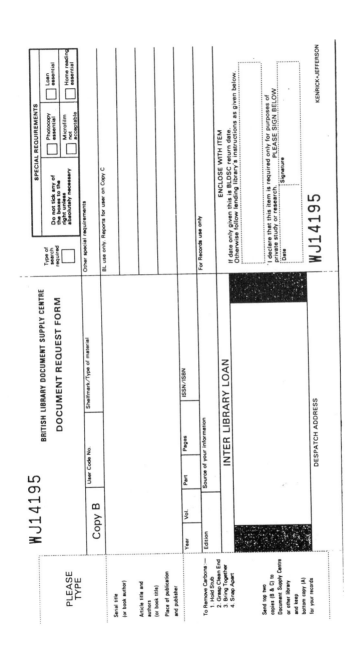

Fig. 7

The remaining two copies are forwarded initially to the appropriate county library headquarters where the union catalogue is consulted and, if possible, a library found within the county which can supply the requested book.

If the request cannot be supplied within the county, the appropriate regional library bureau will be approached. The bureau's union catalogue will be consulted to find a library within the region which can meet the request. LASER, the London and South Eastern Regional Library Bureau, has produced a microform catalogue for purchase so that the requesting library can do its own location seeking.

If this proves unfruitful, the British Library Lending Division will be approached. This is the library of last resort so far as inter-library loans are concerned. Larger libraries, such as county library headquarters, maintain a telex link with the British Library Lending Division, at Boston Spa, Yorkshire, so that the inter-library loan procedure can be speeded up. The British Library will supply the request either from its own vast stock or from the resources of another library within the United Kingdom which it will trace through its union catalogue. The requested item will be sent direct from the supplying library to the library which initiated the request. At local level, and to some extent at regional level, van services operate to deliver and return inter-library loan items. Requests supplied from further afield are usually sent and returned by post.

A library will maintain an accurate record of all items loaned to and borrowed from other libraries and will wisely provide some means of verifying the date on which material borrowed from another library was returned.

Some libraries, particularly special libraries, do not tap the local and regional networks but go direct to the British Library Lending Division with their requests.

Security in libraries

Despite the fact that books may be borrowed free of charge from most libraries, some antisocial individuals will steal rather than borrow them. A library may discover that an item is missing when it is reserved by a reader but cannot be traced by the staff. However, a more methodical way of determining the extent of book losses is to undertake stocktaking of either the entire stock or part of the stock. Some librarians are philosophical about book losses and consider them an inevitable adjunct of the open access system. Other librarians feel it is necessary to take measures which will prevent or discourage theft. Valuable items would normally be protected from possible theft by being kept in locked bookcases, or in a non-public area such as a stock room or librarian's office. Their availability would be made known by catalogue entries but borrowers would have to ask library staff if they wished to consult or borrow them.

In some libraries, shopping bags and briefcases must be deposited in lockers or a left-luggage area in the library foyer to prevent their use in smuggling out items which have not been issued. Other libraries allow bags to be brought in but an attendant is employed to check the contents as the reader leaves the library. Increasingly, however, librarians are turning to technological security devices. One such method requires that each book has a magnetic strip inserted into the spine and that a special exit door is fitted across which an electric signal is beamed. The book is desensitized at the time of issue but, if a book is removed from the library without being issued, its magnetic strip activates a warning signal at the library exit. However, problems can arise with some electronic detection devices because other metal objects such as belt clasps may activate the alarm signal. This is highly embarrassing for the innocent reader and for the apologetic library staff. There are systems available, which, according to the manufacturer, will be activated only by the sensitized device in the book and not by other metallic objects.

Care of library materials

Libraries of today look very attractive and welcoming, unlike the libraries which served previous generations. Library buildings are now planned to be aesthetic as well as functional; in addition, books are designed to look attractive. A great deal of thought and skill is expended on the design of dust-jackets and they are works of art in themselves. It is therefore one of the librarian's prime tasks to preserve the attractiveness of the stock for as long as possible.

The availability of plastic sleeves or jackets has simplified the task of protecting and preserving the paper dust-jackets. The principle on which they work is that the paper jacket is slipped between a layer of clear plastic and an attached paper backing sheet. This is then folded over to fit the paper jacket and fastened securely around the book's casing. The plastic sleeving material can be purchased either in continuous rolls of varying widths from which lengths can be cut or in flat sleeves of graded widths which are ready for use without cutting.

Another means of preserving books is to increase the strength of the casings by use of special reinforcing tape available from library suppliers. Libraries may also purchase books in specially reinforced bindings, and publishers sometimes produce library editions, particularly of reference works, which will cope with the frequent handling expected in library use.

Other library materials must be suitably treated at the outset to prolong life and fortunately many products are marketed which aid the librarian in this task. For example, one can purchase clear, adhesive plastic film for covering paperback books, laminating materials for covering illustrations and maps, and perspex covers for the protection of current issues of periodicals. The right kind of storage methods must also be used for the various types of library materials so that, as far as possible, the librarian prevents damage while still encouraging use. Very rare and fragile materials will, of course, be given extra care and protection and will often be housed in non-public areas to restrict handling.

It is important that library materials are handled with care throughout their life and several rules should be observed:

1   make use of book supports on shelves to prevent books toppling over or falling to the floor;
2   do not pull a book from the shelf by forcefully tugging the top of the spine;
3   do not suspend a book by holding its casing only;
4   do not force a book open, especially when it is new;
5   do not turn down the corners of pages to mark your place;
6   do not write or scribble in books or otherwise deface them.

Sheer common sense ought to be sufficient to guide people in the correct handling of library materials but damage is often caused by carelessness and negligence. Also, with the best will in the world, accidents sometimes happen and a book is dropped, or falls into the hands of a young child or puppy. The library staff must then take steps to remedy the damage.

Simple repairs can be undertaken by library staff and special materials are available for purchase from library suppliers. Torn pages may be repaired by using special transparent tapes obtainable from library suppliers. These tapes effect a permanent repair and do not discolour. Ordinary cellulose tapes such as Sellotape are not suitable for this purpose as they dry out, become discoloured and brittle, and cannot be removed without lifting a layer of paper and text. Cloth tapes may be used to repair damaged spines or to attach a casing which has become loose.

Years ago, many libraries had their own binderies equipped with simple stitching presses, guillotines and so on. For many years, however, librarians have made use of several firms of library binders who make an excellent job of rebinding damaged library books. They used to provide a choice of coverings such as cloth or rexine, and rebound books were clearly recognizable on library shelves. Now they can incorporate the book's paper dust-jacket into the binding so that the book's appearance is as good as new. Of course, the library has to submit the dust-jacket with the book. However, binding costs have risen in recent years and fewer books are being rebound. It was also common practice to have sets of periodicals bound but, in the interests of economy, many librarians now keep back issues in plastic or manila storage boxes.

The decision to have a book bound will be taken only if:

1 The physical condition of the book warrants binding. If pages are missing, or are badly torn or defaced, it is pointless having the life of the book prolonged. The margins must also be adequate as the binding process will reduce them.
2 The information in the book is still relevant. If the text is out of date it is foolish to bind the book. You may be able to purchase a new edition of the same book or another, more recent book on the same subject.
3 The book is still in demand. The amount of wear and tear in itself may be indicative of a book's popularity, but in addition some issue systems will enable staff to see how often and how recently a book has been borrowed.

Books to be bound are normally sorted by size because the machinery in library binding firms is so designed. The relevant issue stationery is sent to the bindery so that the bound books are ready for the shelves when they are returned.

Very specific binding instructions may be sent with the consignment, especially if the book or set of periodicals is one of a series which has been bound previously and there is need for uniformity of colour, style and lettering. A binding list would normally be completed to show authors, titles, classification symbols and so on. One copy would accompany the consignment of books and a second copy be retained as the library's own record of what had been sent. The list would be checked when the books were returned from the bindery. If the library maintained an accessions register, the fact that particular books had been bound would be recorded against their entries and the date and price of binding shown.

Binding procedure

To bind a book, or rebind it, the following steps would be followed:

1 Check that the book is complete, i.e. that no pages are missing. It is possible to photocopy a page of another copy to replace a missing one. Clean and repair pages if necessary.
2 Remove the book's casing.
3 Take the book apart so that the constituent sections are separated.

4　Assemble the sections in the correct order and sew them together over tapes or cords. Incorporate new endpapers.

5　Gently round the spine and then glue a piece of gauze over the spine to overlap slightly at each side.

6　Assemble the book cover with three pieces of cardboard (front board, spine and back board) glued to a covering material.

7　Attach the cover to the book, firmly fixing the tapes or cords and gluing endpapers to the front and back boards.

8　Do the gold tooling or lettering of the spine and front cover to show author and title. The binder will also put the classification symbol on the spine if instructed to do so.

Withdrawal and disposal of library materials

Library materials may be discarded when they are in poor physical condition, beyond repair and unfit for binding, or when the text is out of date or superseded by a new edition, or when they have outlived their popularity. One member of the library staff may act as stock editor and it will be his or her task to keep a constant vigil on the stock. He or she will decide which books to repair, bind, replace, relegate to reserve stock or withdraw. Which of these alternative courses of action is chosen will depend on:

1　Whether the book is still in print or now unobtainable. If the latter, it may sometimes be advisable to put the book into the reserve stock rather than withdraw it.

2　Whether the book is still in demand or merely gathering dust on the shelves. There is no point in trying to prolong the life of a book which has outlived its usefulness.

3　How much deterioration there is in the physical condition of the book.

4　Whether the book is out of date or of historical interest despite its age.

5　Whether it covers a subject area in which the library has an obligation to specialize. The life of such material would be prolonged by all possible means as there may be inter-library loan requests for it.

The procedure to be followed if the decision to withdraw has been taken would be:

1　Rubber stamp the book so that the word 'withdrawn' clearly appears on it.

2　Remove the issue stationery.

PERIODICAL AND REFERENCE BINDING

Date Sent | ••

No. of Vols. sent:	Code*	Item*	Rub No.*	
Lettering			Periodical	Books
	New Title			
	Bind to Patt. Vol.			
	Bind to Rub Supplied			
	MATERIAL SHADE			
	Bind Incomplete			
	Bind No. T.P./Index			
	Adverts Out			
	Adverts In			
	Bind Covers in position			
	„ „ tog. Front/Rear			
	Contents Front/Rear			
	Index Front/Rear			
	EDGES TRIMMED/UNTRIMMED			
	BOARD HEIGHT*			
	LETTERING—GOLD/FOIL			
	LEATHER T.P.—SHADE			
	Other Instructions:			

•• for library use
• for bindery use only   Price:

DUNN & WILSON LTD., FALKIRK

Fig. 8   Specimen of binding instruction form

3   Ensure that all catalogue entries pertaining to the book are removed if it is the last or only copy. The tracings on the main entry will direct the staff to the relevant added entries.

4   Notify libraries which have union catalogues in which your library's stock is represented (e.g. county library headquarters and/or regional library bureaux) so that their relevant catalogue entries can be removed.

5   Dispose of the book by offering it to other libraries or selling it if its physical condition warrants this, or offering it for recycling or pulping.

Simple accounts

Most libraries maintain a small cash float for the giving of change and, in addition, money is received in payment of fines and from coin-operated machines such as photocopiers and microform reader/printers. Petty cash may be used for the purchase of small items such as urgently required stationery items or postage stamps.

Accurate records must be kept of all money received and disbursed and normally the cash is balanced at weekly intervals. The records are often checked by auditors, so complete accuracy is essential.

Assignments

Written

1   Describe and evaluate *two* charging methods (issuing systems) suitable for use in:

(a) an industrial library, or
(b) a school library, or
(c) a large and busy public library.

2   What are the main requirements of a system for registering readers? What information is normally called for on a membership application form?

3   Describe briefly the processes involved in *four* of the following tasks:

(a) renewing expired tickets,
(b) replacing lost tickets,
(c) recording changes of address,
(d) locating reserved books,
(e) renewing loans of books,
(f) collecting fines on overdue books.

4 Describe a system for the identification and recovery of overdue books.

5 A reader has requested a book which is not in the stock of your library. Outline the procedure involved in tracing and supplying the requested book.

6 What principles should be borne in mind when deciding whether to bind or withdraw a book which is in poor physical condition?

7 List and describe the steps involved in withdrawing and disposing of books which are no longer required.

8 What measures can a library take to protect its stock from theft?

9 What is petty cash? From what sources is the library's petty cash received and how may it be disbursed?

Bibliography

Advances in library administration and organization, Vols. 1−4, 7−8, London, Jai Press, 1982−9.

Chirgwin, F. John and Oldfield, Phyllis, *The library assistant's manual*, 3rd ed., London, Bingley, 1988.

'Draft public library regulations', *Library Association record*, August 1953, 256−8.

Kumar, Krishnan, *Library administration and management*, Vikas, 1987. Distributed by Sangam, London.

— *Library organization*, Vikas, 1987. Distributed by Sangam, London.

Neal, K. W., *Introduction to library administration*, Wilmslow, Neal, 1975.

Ritchie, Sheila (ed.), *Modern library practice*, Buckden, Elm, 1982.

Chapter Eight

Shelving and storage of library materials

Many types and colours of shelving are now available, and forbidding dark wooden bookcases have been banished from most libraries. Wooden shelving is still popular but colours have become lighter and bookcases more varied in their design. Metal shelving is growing in popularity due to the wide range of colours and styles now on the market.

Materials which have to be housed in a library vary greatly in size and shape from very large atlases and maps to small books like the Observer series, flimsy pamphlets, filmstrips and so forth. Correct shelving of various types and sizes of stock is imperative if the items are to remain in good physical condition.

It is always preferable to have adjustable shelving so that the distance between shelves can be altered to suit the stock. The top shelves should be within easy reach of the library users and staff, and the bottom shelves should also be accessible without having to bend double. Bottom shelves which are tilted at an angle make it easier to see the books' spines.

Shelving of books

The average fiction book is crown octavo in size and requires shelving of the correct height and depth. Fiction books of larger format are published, so shelving has to be adjusted to suit.

Non-fiction books are normally larger in size than fiction, so bookcases designed for shelving non-fiction are deeper and the shelves further apart.

On the whole, librarians like to keep materials on one subject together so that library users can find everything in one place. However, this can lead to a very wasteful use of shelving. In the interests of economy it may be advisable to have separate sequences of shelving to house different sizes of material. The most common example of this is the separation of the oversize stock from the normal run of stock. This is usually termed 'parallel arrangement' as the sequences will be arranged in the same way (for example, the non-fiction in classified sequence).

Many kinds of book supports are marketed and these ensure that books remain upright on the shelves and do not topple on to the floor. Plastic-covered wire or metal supports are designed to clip firmly to the shelf itself or to the base of the shelf above. There are also L-shaped supports which sit on the shelf.

Shelving of multi-media items

Many of these items are, or can be, packaged in such a way that they will sit happily alongside the book stock. It makes sound sense to house all materials on the same subject together so that the information-seeker needs to go to one place only rather than trek to half a dozen different areas to discover the books, pamphlets, periodicals, portfolios, cassettes and slides on a chosen subject. However, there are factors which mitigate against a total integration of book and non-book stock. These are:

1 the susceptibility of certain materials, e.g. gramophone records, to damage if housed in open access areas;
2 the possibility of theft of easily pocketed items such as cassettes;
3 the rarity and value of some items compared with others and the consequent need for greater security;
4 the practical difficulties presented by a great variety of formats and sizes and the need for economy in shelving;
5 the need to preserve some materials from possible damage caused by dust, scratching, greasy fingerprints and so forth.

Shelving of special types of non-book media

Pamphlets

Perhaps the most common method of storing pamphlets is in pamphlet boxes. Usually these are made of plastic or stout cardboard which may be covered with colourful cloth or laminated paper. A label on the spine of the box identifies the contents and facilitates retrieval. Pamphlets may also be stored in wallets suspended inside filing cabinets and filed either vertically or laterally. Pamphlets which will be consulted or borrowed regularly are sometimes strengthened and protected so that they can be treated like the book stock. An individual pamphlet may be slipped into a hardback perspex or cardboard cover, or it may be stiffened by laminating. Such protection and stiffening allows the pamphlet to stand upright on the shelves beside books on the same subject.

Periodicals

In most libraries, the current issues of periodicals are displayed on specially designed racks. The periodicals themselves may be slipped inside protective plastic or perspex cases with transparent front covers. Back issues are stored in sets and may be bound when the correct number of issues and relevant indexes are to hand. Some display racks are designed so that the sloping display shelf lifts up to reveal storage space underneath for back issues. Otherwise, many types of storage containers are marketed and there is a wide range of attractive designs and colours to choose from. The binding of back issues is less popular now than it used to be, owing to the high costs involved, but in this technological age, it is becoming increasingly common to see microfiche or microfilm issues of periodicals. In many instances, microform editions are available for purchase and librarians may opt to buy these instead of the paper copies. In other cases, librarians pay to have their own paper copies microfilmed. Microform issues are more durable than paper copies and, of course, they have the tremendous advantage of taking up a minimum storage space.

Newspapers

Paper copies of newspapers present storage problems. The quality of the paper is often poor and it yellows and becomes brittle with age. In years gone by, it used to be quite common for back issues of newspapers to be bound into massive volumes which one could hardly lift. This practice has now been superseded by the microfilming of back issues of newspapers or the purchase of microform editions in lieu of paper copies. In some libraries, of course, the demand for back issues of newspapers is very limited so it is deemed sufficient to keep bundles of newspapers just sitting on shelves for a specified limited period before discarding them. They are often stored in a non-public area and staff retrieve copies requested by library members. This reduces the possibility of copies being misfiled or going astray.

Cuttings from newspapers and periodicals

Methods of storage employed for cuttings collections vary according to the purpose and life expectancy of the cuttings. Those of an ephemeral nature which will be discarded within a fairly short period may be roughly sorted, possibly by broad subject, into large envelopes or manila wallets and kept in filing cabinets. Alternatively, they may be put into cardboard boxes and stored on shelves. Cuttings which are to be stored for a long time may be kept in loose-leaf binders or albums or possibly individually mounted and laminated.

Duplicated paper materials such as handouts

Academic libraries may stock handouts produced by teaching staff. Sometimes these are not kept on open shelves as it may be considered undesirable for students to have access to them before the lecturer is ready to introduce the topic in class. They may therefore be kept in an area to which only staff (academic staff as well as library staff) have access.

It is common practice to file a single copy of each hand-out in classified sequence in a series of ring binders. Each hand-out may also have an accession number prominently displayed on it. Multiple copies, usually enough for one class of students or pupils, may also be available. The supply needs to be replenished when the multiple copies have been used, so a master is kept − usually for offset litho reproduction or for cutting a stencil on an electronic scanner.

Microforms

This is the generic term for all types of micro-reproduction. It includes microfilm, microfiche and microcard. All microforms require the use of an item of equipment which will enlarge the text and display it on a screen. It is worth noting that most machines are reader/printers, not just readers, and they can produce a paper copy of what appears on the screen.

Microfilm

Microfilm is a continuous length of film wound on to an open spool. A microfilm reader must be used to magnify the reduced image so that it appears in readable size on the machine's screen. The microfilm is wound from the full spool on to an empty take-up spool, via the lens system. After use it must be rewound on to the original spool. Modern machines have an automatic facility for fast-forward and rewind as well as a manual control for slower, more precise location of the required information on the microfilm.

Microfilms are supplied in their own compact cardboard boxes and can be housed on shelves or in drawers in a storage cabinet.

Cassetted microfilm

This consists of a miniature full spool and an empty take-up spool enclosed inside a cassette. Naturally, it requires a machine designed for use with cassetted microfilm. British Standards are available in this format. The rectangular shape of the cassettes is rather awkward but they can stand on shelves or be kept in drawers in a cabinet.

Microfiche

This is a flat piece of transparent film containing images greatly reduced in size. To bring them back to a readable size one needs a microfiche reader. Microfiches are best kept in individual envelopes — to prevent damage from dust and fingerprints — filed in drawers similar to catalogue cabinet drawers or in binders designed for the purpose.

Ultrafiche

Ultrafiche is a refinement of microfiche but with reduction/magnification 120 times the original. However, the ultrafiche format seems to have been abandoned in favour of traditional microfiche. Naturally, libraries prefer to standardize on equipment and would not want to purchase an ultrafiche reader as well as a microfiche reader.

Microcard

This is an opaque card with reduced images which again must be magnified on an appropriate machine before the text can be read. Microcard has also been superseded by microfiche.

Storage of specific types of non-print media

Slides (35mm transparencies)

A slide is a piece of 35mm film mounted in a cardboard or plastic frame. Occasionally the slide may be mounted between two pieces of glass to prevent damage being caused by dust or fingerprints, but this precaution would be taken only if the slide were irreplaceable or very valuable. Slides may be purchased individually, in a set, or in a tape/slide or cassette/slide package, and most sets or packages are supplied with an accompanying booklet or notes.

There are several methods of storing slides, the most popular being to keep them in individual pockets in transparent plastic wallets which are suspended in an ordinary vertical filing cabinet. The whole wallet may be lifted out and placed on or in front of an illuminated light box to facilitate previewing of the slides. Each slide must be identified with an accession/location number or symbol and its compartment in the wallet must be similarly identified. This makes it easier to see whether any slides are missing. Some plastic wallets contain a large pocket in which the accompanying notes can be stored.

Other commercially available wallets are made of a more pliable transparent plastic -- again with a separate pocket for each slide — and these can be folded to fit into a cardboard box. The spine of the box may be labelled so that it can sit on shelves alongside the book stock on the same subject. A well-known library supplier produces very attractive storage boxes, some of which are especially designed to hold slides.

In academic libraries, it may be deemed preferable to store some slides in projector magazines (carousels or slide trays) so that they are ready for immediate projection. This is done if a set of slides is in regular use by teaching staff because it ensures that the slides are always in the correct order and the right way round for viewing. The slides are never handled, they are kept dust free and they are ready for immediate use. Projector magazines are supplied in storage boxes which can be labelled clearly on the outside to facilitate retrieval. The boxes will sit happily on the bookshelves. The disadvantages of this method are that individual slides which might be useful in another context are not readily available and previewing is not as easy as with the transparent wallets.

Filmstrips

A filmstrip looks like a set of unmounted slides joined together to make a continuous length of film. Each picture is known as a frame. Most filmstrips are full frame but some are half frame, that is, they have two smaller pictures occupying the same area as would normally be filled by one. Filmstrip projectors are usually equipped with an attachment for showing half-frame strips. Filmstrips are normally supplied in their own plastic or metal cylindrical containers. These used to vary tremendously in size but now there is much more standardization. The title of the filmstrip will already appear on the lid of the container but it is advisable to mark the lid or base of the container with an accession number and classification symbol. A self-adhesive label should also appear on the filmstrip itself to ensure that each one is returned to its own container after use.

Again, there are several methods of storing filmstrips. The most common method is to house them in shallow drawers in a cabinet. Preferably, the drawers should be divided up into individual compartments to prevent containers moving about when the drawer is opened and also to make access to and return of filmstrips easier and quicker. Accompanying notes should bear the same accession number/ classification symbol as the filmstrip, and should be stored nearby.

A method of storage which allows one to browse and to see the entire stock of filmstrips on display together is to house them side by side on shallow shelves, or supported by strategically placed pegs, with the canister lids facing outwards. The filmstrips can be arranged in classified order with the classification symbols and titles prominently shown on the lids. The filmstrips may roll sideways a little as a canister is removed if they are housed on flat shelves. The pegs would normally be placed in a series of triangles so that no rolling could occur. The shelves also need a lip at the rear if they are not backed.

Alternatively, filmstrips and accompanying notes may be kept in a series of strong, transparent bags suspended from a rail, rather like clothes suspended on coat-hangers. This method makes issuing easy as the filmstrip and notes are borrowed in the packaging in which they are stored.

Equipment is available to facilitate previewing with minimum handling of the filmstrip. A typical example is a long length of transparent perspex with grooves at the side which is designed to hold the filmstrip rigid while it is held up to the light or placed in front of an illuminated light box.

Filmstrips may be converted into slides by cutting and mounting – either by machine or by hand. This allows one to show frames in one's own selected order and to discard frames which are not required.

Film-loops

A film-loop is a length of 8mm or 16mm film wound into a cassette in such a way that the end of the film is attached to the beginning. This allows the film-loop to be re-run after projection without having to rewind it. A film-loop projector is necessary for viewing.

Film-loops can be purchased from commercial suppliers. They are usually on specific topics, and are quite short in viewing time. They are supplied in their own boxes and can be labelled to sit on the bookshelves with the bookstock if required.

Films

16mm films are supplied in their own cylindrical containers, which are best housed vertically in racks which resemble bicycle storage racks. Vertical storage allows retrieval of a specific film without having to lift off several others, as would happen if they were stored horizontally on top of one another. You can also place the cylindrical container into an oblong storage box to allow vertical storage on ordinary shelves. Shelf supports prevent the films toppling over when one is removed from the shelves.

Films need to be rewound after use and should be checked regularly for damage.

Gramophone records and compact discs

Many libraries lend gramophone records to their clients, either as a free service or as a facility for which a reasonable fee is charged.

Gramophone records are very susceptible to damage through careless handling or by exposure to heat or dust. Normally, the gramophone records themselves will be stored upright in dustproof covers on shelves with upright supports at regular intervals. Usually they will be in a non-public area, for example behind the staff enclosure or counter. The record sleeves are displayed in browser boxes, usually in broadly categorized groupings such as spoken word, orchestral, solo instrumental, choral and so forth. Each sleeve bears an accession number which matches that on the corresponding record so that retrieval is easy.

Compact discs (CDs) are a relatively recent innovation offering better sound quality than the traditional gramophone record. As their name implies, they are more compact in size than their earlier counterparts but the storage arrangements may be similar. As the sales of CD players increase, so libraries will be considering their policy about offering their clients a loan service of compact discs. Eventually CDs may replace gramophone records in the same way that audio cassettes replaced audio-tapes.

Audio-tapes

Audio-tapes are reels or spools of magnetic tape on which sound has been recorded. They are much less common now as cassettes have tended to oust open-spool tapes. Hi-fi enthusiasts and connoisseurs of music used to prefer open-spool tape because it gave a better quality of reproduction than cassette, but now the compact disc offers even better sound quality. An open-spool tape recorder is required to play audio-tapes.

Audio-tapes are supplied in their own plastic or cardboard boxes with facility for labelling the spines. They will then sit quite happily on shelves alongside the bookstock if required. If audio-tapes are left on the shelves for long periods without being played, they suffer from print-through. To prevent this, the tape should be run through at intervals – not necessarily played but put through the tape recorder at the fast-forward position.

Audio cassettes

Cassettes are really audio-tapes but with both spools enclosed in a container to minimize possible damage to the tape caused by handling or dust. The tape is therefore very narrow and much thinner than that used on open-spool machines. Cassettes are supplied in their own little boxes and are referred to by their playing time: C30 (half an hour playing time), C60 (one hour) and C120 (two hours). C120 tape is extremely thin and it may stretch, crinkle or spill out of the cassette. Cassettes may pose storage problems for the librarian because of their size. A plastic rack which allows two rows of audio cassettes to be safely displayed on a normal library shelf may be purchased from library suppliers. However, the cassettes can be slipped so easily into a pocket or handbag that losses are high unless preventive measures are taken. Some librarians choose to house cassettes in display racks which are locked to prevent unauthorized removal. This allows borrowers to browse but it is tedious for staff to keep unlocking the case every time a cassette is borrowed or returned.

Alternatively, the cassettes themselves may be kept on closed access and only the empty cases left on open display. Otherwise, descriptive cards can be displayed which give details of the cassettes. These can also be colour coded to identify the type of cassette, for example, orchestral music, folk music or spoken word. Accession numbers usually provide the link between the display case or card and the actual cassette.

Cartridges
Cartridges are similar to cassettes but larger. They are less popular and rarely found in libraries.

Video-tapes
Video-tapes were similar to audio-tapes in appearance as they were magnetic tapes on open spool, the difference being that video-tapes record visual images as well as sound. A video-tape recorder (VTR) and a monitor (TV set) were necessary for playback. They are now rare, video cassettes and video-discs having superseded them.

Video-tapes were supplied in their own sturdy plastic boxes so they could stand firmly on ordinary shelves. As with audio-tapes, it was essential that video-tapes were run through the VTR from time to time to prevent print-through.

Video cassettes
Video cassettes superseded video-tapes in the same way that audio cassettes followed and replaced audio-tapes. Video cassettes must be played on a video cassette recorder (VCR), and a monitor (TV) is required for viewing. Video cassettes can record and playback colour pictures, provided the monitor also has the facility for colour. Video cassettes used to come in two main formats, Beta and VHS, but now the VHS system has virtually cornered the market. Video cassettes, in their dustproof storage boxes, will stand securely on the open shelves with spines labelled to show titles and classification symbols.

Video-disc
The video-disc is a more recent introduction. This resembles a

gramophone record but the sounds and images are 'read' by a computer and accessed via a VDU.

Computer programs

Many libraries offer computer facilities for the benefit of their clients, mainly for use with commercially produced discs which have been purchased and added to stock. However computer programs can be erased or damaged by inexperienced operators unless preventive measures are taken by the library staff. Usually a copy of the disc will be made available to the library member while the original is stored safely in a non-public area of the library. Discs may also be protected by the use of a tab which prevents the user accidentally corrupting the program.

Computer programs, or downloaded copies of them, may be shelved with other materials on the same subject, provided they are kept in suitable media storage boxes.

Maps and charts

Ordnance Survey maps can be purchased in a special format for library use. The maps are strengthened, laminated and folded to fit into a hardback cover so that, to all intents and purposes, they can be shelved like books.

Small maps should ideally be mounted and laminated and then stored in filing cabinets. Large maps and charts should also be laminated and then housed in map chests. Vertical storage is preferable as that enables a required map to be removed without much handling of the other maps. Some vertical storage chests have two pairs of 'elephants' tusks' on which the maps are suspended. Others utilize wooden rods to which the maps are attached, and some use clips or pegs. It is sometimes necessary to weight the bottom of each map with a piece of dowelling to prevent curling up.

Some libraries have horizontal map chests where maps are laid flat in drawers, but there is a tendency with these for smaller items to be pushed to the back and possibly crumpled as the drawer is opened and closed. Also, each map is likely to be handled while one is searching for the particular map whch is required.

Occasionally charts or maps are rolled up and stored in cardboard rolls housed in a structure like an umbrella-stand. This may make the loan of maps easier, but they do not stay flat for display purposes.

It is not wise to stick drawing pins into the corners of maps when displaying them. Ideally one should use a magnetic board and small magnets designed for display purposes.

Photographs

Photographs form an important part of local history collections. Ideally they should be mounted and possibly covered with non-adhesive protective plastic. Filing cabinets offer a satisfactory method of storage. Lateral filing is preferable to vertical filing as one does not have to lean over to reach items at the back of a drawer.

Illustrations

Illustrations should be mounted on card and laminated unless they are of ephemeral interest. They can be kept in classified order, possibly several on the same topic in a single manila wallet, and stored in filing cabinets. Again, lateral filing offers some advantages over vertical filing.

Portfolios

Portfolios are produced commercially − Jackdaws, for example − but they can be home produced. A portfolio is really a manila wallet containing several separate items related to a specific topic. The contents may include facsimiles of maps or bills, illustrations, pages of text and so on. Each item must be identified by an accession number and classification symbol to make it easy to refile any item which becomes separated from the rest of the contents. Portfolios are an awkward shape and do not sit happily on the bookshelves. They are best kept in filing cabinets in classified order.

Kits and packages

Academic libraries/resource centres may well have kits and packages in stock. They are usually teaching/learning aids comprised of a number of items containing information on a given topic. A kit may include a filmstrip, an audio cassette and some notes in print form, all stored together in a box or wallet. School libraries may stock kits which demonstrate the development of a manufactured product or the life-cycle of an agricultural or horticultural specimen.

For example, a kit devoted to cotton may contain samples of the cotton plant, cotton fibres at various stages and a piece of cotton cloth. The box might stand upright on the shelves with the books if its contents allowed this. Otherwise it would have to be stored horizontally, possibly in a cupboard. The contents of each kit should be listed inside the box and a regular check made to see that nothing has gone astray.

Models

Again, it is likely to be school or other academic libraries/resource centres which have models in stock. Their function would be as teaching/learning aids for use in the classroom. Their awkward shapes and sizes as well as their possible fragility make it essential for models to be housed in closed access areas, probably in cupboards or display cabinets.

Artefacts

Artefacts are man-made objects. Examples which might be found in a resource centre are tools excavated locally in archaeological digs. Again their shape and size makes them totally unsuitable for integrating with the bookstock and they are best kept in boxes, suitably labelled, in cupboards or display cases.

Realia

The term 'realia' refers to natural objects as opposed to man-made ones. Examples include geological specimens or fossils. Their storage problems and the solutions to them are similar to those of artefacts.

Storage of rare, fragile and secret materials

Some libraries are fortunate enough to have in stock rare items such as first editions of books or valuable manuscripts. Obviously these call for much greater security and also much more care in handling and storage. Such items may be kept in locked cupboards, bookcases or display cases to which some type of alarm device is fitted. Sometimes these materials need to be kept in conditions where the temperature and humidity are monitored and kept constant if possible. It is a problem for the librarian to find a happy medium between the need to protect rare items from damage and theft and the wish to allow as many people as possible to benefit from seeing them. To shut away such treasures in closed vaults seems a very negative solution.

Public libraries rarely stock secret materials but these may be found in government libraries or industrial libraries. Librarians of establishments which hold secret documents are usually bound by the Official Secrets Act, and they have to be extremely careful about the security of secret items. Obviously they will be kept under lock and key at all times and not be made accessible to unauthorized persons.

Assignments

Practical

1 Visit the Resource Centre of the Commonwealth Institute, Kensington, London, or a large resource centre in your own locality to see the tremendous variety of multi-media items in stock and the various methods of storing them.

2 Walk around the library in which you work or of which you are a member and note how many different types/sizes of shelving and storage areas there are. Consider the reasons for their provision.

3 Browse through the stationery and furniture catalogues of library suppliers such as Gresswell, Libraco and Librex. Note the variety of book repair materials and also the range of shelving and storage units available to libraries.

Written

1 Write a definition of each of the following:

    (a) parallel arrangement,
    (b) lateral filing,
    (c) microforms,
    (d) artefacts.

2 Describe and evaluate methods of shelving/storing the following:

    (a) oversize books,
    (b) large maps and charts,
    (c) gramophone records.

Bibliography

Cabeceiras, James, *The multimedia library: materials selection and use*, 2nd rev. ed., Academic Press, 1982.

Miller, Shirley, *The vertical file and its satellites*, 2nd ed., Libraries Unlimited, 1979.

Ritchie, Sheila (ed.), *Modern library practice*, Elm, 1982.

Weihs, Jean, *Accessible storage of non-book materials*, Oryx Press, 1984.

Chapter Nine

Information sources

In a previous chapter, it was stated that the chief service which libraries offer to their clients is the lending of books and other materials. Following close on its heels, the next most important service must be the provision of information and the stocking of requisite source materials which enable the librarian or the client to find facts as quickly as possible.

Faced with an enquiry, the librarian may have to turn initially to a dictionary for a definition of terminology or an encyclopaedia for a brief introduction to a subject. The word 'dictionary' is used loosely sometimes and one can find dictionaries which are really encyclopaedias and vice versa.

Dictionaries

Dictionaries can be divided into the following types:

1 Language dictionaries

    (a) National, i.e. the language of a particular country or countries. These can be English or foreign. National dictionaries can be subdivided into two types:

        (i) Etymological, i.e. showing the origin of words and tracing the development of meaning over the years, e.g. *Oxford English dictionary*, 20 volumes (1989).

        (ii) Current, i.e. giving only the present-day meaning of words, e.g. *The concise Oxford dictionary of current English*.

    (b) Bilingual, i.e. dictionaries which list the words of one language but give the meaning or synonyms in another language, e.g. *Cassell's Spanish-English English-Spanish dictionary*; *Langenscheidt's Standard German-English, English-German dictionary*.

2 Specialist dictionaries, which (like an extended glossary) list only those terms which pertain to a particular subject. Instead of just

giving synonyms, some give considerable information about each specific topic and so are more like encyclopaedias than dictionaries, e.g. *Illustrated Bible dictionary*, Parts 1 – 3; *New Grove's dictionary of music and musicians*, 20 volumes. Under the heading of specialist dictionaries one can include: dictionaries of synonyms; dictionaries of grammar and usage; dictionaries of abbreviations; dictionaries of prosody, i.e. rhyming dictionaries; dictionaries of Christian (personal) names.

3   Biographical dictionaries. These are of three kinds:

(a) International and general, e.g. *Chambers biographical dictionary* (includes living and deceased persons) and *The international who's who* (living persons only).

(b) National and general, which can be subdivided into two kinds:
  (i) Current – including only living persons, e.g. *Who's who*.
  (ii) Retrospective – including only deceased persons, e.g. *Dictionary of national biography*, and *Who was who*.

(c) Specialist, which cover persons concerned with particular professions, defined areas of knowledge or specified strata of society, e.g. *Burke's royal families of the world*, *Who's who in broadcasting*, *Who's who in art*.

Encyclopaedias

An encyclopaedia is a quick reference tool providing information on every branch of knowledge (general) or one field of knowledge (specialist).

The arrangement is usually alphabetical under subject headings which may be broad or specific. However, some encyclopaedias group topics together under very broad subject areas; for example, the *Oxford junior encyclopaedia* arranges subjects under broad headings such as 'The arts', 'Engineering' and so on, devoting one complete volume to each broad grouping.

The more scholarly encyclopaedias usually have lengthy articles written by subject specialists, and the articles are often signed (or initialled) by the writer. Popular encyclopaedias tend towards short articles on specific topics and these are not signed.

Most multi-volume encyclopaedias include an index (sometimes a separate index volume) which lists subjects alphabetically and gives the volume and page number where information can be found. The index usually has 'see also' references.

Illustrations, plates, maps and so on form a vital part of an encyclopaedia and should not be separated from the text to which they refer.

A select list of encyclopaedias:

General — one volume
1 *Hutchinson's twentieth century encyclopaedia*
2 *Pears cyclopaedia*
General — multi-volume
1 *Encyclopedia Americana*
2 *Encyclopaedia Britannica*
3 *New standard encyclopaedia* (Marshall Cavendish)
General — for young people
1 *Children's Britannica*
2 *New children's encyclopedia* (Grolier)
3 *Oxford junior encyclopaedia*
4 *World book encyclopedia*
Specialist
1 *Careers encyclopaedia*
2 *Hastings' encyclopaedia of religion and ethics*
3 *McGraw-Hill encyclopedia of science and technology*
4 *Van Nostrand's scientific encyclopedia*

Reference books

The choice of other reference sources to be consulted would be determined by the nature of the enquiry. These may include directories, yearbooks, almanacs, concordances, atlases and gazetteers. The number and range of reference books is vast and many years of study and practice are necessary before one can acquire the knowledge and expertise which reference librarians demonstrate. Nevertheless, the most junior library assistant and the most hesitant enquirer can begin to build up a basic knowledge of the main types and formats of reference sources.

Directories

A directory is a list of persons, organizations, professions, industries or trades. The list is systematically arranged, either in alphabetical or in classified order. Because the information in directories becomes out of date fairly rapidly, they are either published annually or new editions are brought out every two or three years.

Types of directory include:

1 Local directories — usually for the larger towns and cities only. These normally include:

   (a) a list of private residents, arranged alphabetically by surname;
   (b) an alphabetical list of streets, giving the name of the occupier of each property in each street;
   (c) a classified list of trades — similar to the *Yellow pages* telephone directory;

(d) lists of establishments such as places of worship, places of entertainment etc.

2 Professional directories — these are lists of qualified practitioners in particular professions, and include brief biographical details, and sometimes information about the profession itself. Examples are: *Directory of American scholars, Directory of directors, Library Association yearbook, Medical directory.*

3 Trade directories

    (a) General and national — i.e. all the trades and industries of a particular country. Arrangement is usually classified, or alphabetical, by the type of trade or industry, with an additional alphabetical list of individual firms; e.g. *Kelly's business directory,   Kompass UK.*

    (b) Specialist and national — i.e. concerned with one field of industry in a particular country; e.g. *Electrical and electronics trades directory.*

4 Telephone directories — each telephone directory covers the subscribers in a defined geographical area. The main list is alphabetical by name of subscriber but the *Yellow pages*, which is published separately, contains a classified list of subscribers arranged by type of industry or service. Telephone directories are now available in microfiche.

Yearbooks

A yearbook is a reference book which is published annually, and the word 'yearbook' is sometimes incorporated in the title. Yearbooks usually give up-to-date statistical information and may also include a review of the events of the previous year; e.g. *Statesman's yearbook.*

Almanacs

An almanac, sometimes spelt 'almanack', was originally an annual publication which gave astronomical information such as times of sunrise and sunset, the moon's phases and so on, but allied this to astrological predictions of the events of the coming year. The predictive element has now disappeared from the major almanacs but the astronomical information has been retained. *Whitaker's almanack* is the best-known example and it contains a wealth of information about the governments, education systems, products, imports and exports and so on of all the countries of the world. An example of an almanac which is concerned less with statistical information and world events and more about tide tables and so on is the *Nautical almanac.*

Concordances

A concordance is an alphabetical list of all the important subjects, persons, places which have been named in a particular work or in one author's complete works. It does not give any descriptive information about them but gives the context of each word and the source; e.g. *Cruden's complete concordance to the Old and New Testaments, Concordance to Tennyson* (Brightwell).

Maps and atlases

A map is a representation, usually flat, of the whole or a part of the earth's surface or of the celestial sphere. An atlas is a collection of maps bound together. The word 'atlas' was first used in this sense by Mercator from the figure of the mythological Atlas which was often used as the frontispiece of early collections of maps. It has come to mean any volume containing not only maps, but also plates, engravings, charts and tables, with or without descriptive text. It is sometimes used as the name of a volume in which subjects are presented in tabular form.

While it is generally recognized that atlases are essential in studying history, geography and other branches of social sciences, it is becoming increasingly apparent that many atlases are valuable also as general reference books because of the descriptive materials they contain in addition to maps. Today, maps are necessary companions to the daily newspaper, and radio and television news commentaries. They are used to verify names, places and events in the news, enabling them to be presented in their proper geographical context.

There are many sources of maps. Most of the general encyclopaedias include maps either in a separate volume or as illustrative material within the text; encyclopaedia yearbooks include up-to-date maps; many handbooks, almanacs, newspapers and periodicals also contain maps. However, the atlas is the reference book designed primarily to provide maps.

Atlases vary in quality and they vary in coverage according to the country of publication. In addition to topographical information, they may show administrative boundaries, the distribution of industries or population, the extent of settlement at a particular period and the use to which land is put.

Evaluating an atlas

1 The scope:

   (a) Is it worldwide in coverage, or is it limited to one or more regions?

   (b) Does it include all kinds of maps, or only maps of a specific nature?
   (c) Does it provide descriptive material about the various geographical locations?

2   The place of publication as an indication of emphasis.
3   The date of publication as an indication of its up-to-dateness.
4   The index:

   (a) Is there one comprehensive index for the entire atlas, or are there separate indexes for each volume or section?
   (b) Is the index a separate volume, or is it a part of the atlas?
   (c) Does it indicate pronunciation?
   (d) Is the reference to the location on a given map clear and definite?

5   The quality and content of the maps:

   (a) Is the scale indicated clearly?
   (b) Are the symbols distinct and easily read?
   (c) Are the projections in keeping with the purpose of the map?
   (d) Is the lettering clear and legible?
   (e) Is the colouring varied and well differentiated?
   (f) Are the names of countries given in the language of each country or in translation?

Explanation of terms

1   Scale — the distance as shown on the map in relation to actual distance. This is given as a ratio, e.g. 1:50,000.
2   Projection — the way in which the curved surface of the earth is portrayed on the flat surface of the map.
3   Elevation — the height of the earth's surface above sea-level. This can be shown by colour or by contour lines.
4   Reference system — the method by which one can locate a place on a map, e.g.:

   (a) degrees of latitude and longitude;
   (b) a grid reference.

Gazetteers

A gazetteer is a dictionary of geographical places. In addition to geographical location, it gives historical, statistical, cultural and other relevant information about those places. It may also indicate pronunciation. Because they provide a variety of factual material about places, gazetteers are important reference sources. Recent editions describe a place as it is now; old editions give historical information about it. The economic growth or decline of a town or city, as indicated by data on population, types of industries, schools and so on, will often be shown by the brief facts given in gazetteers over a period of years. Some gazetteers include entries for rivers, capes and other geographical features.

In using a gazetteer, it is important to note the publication date as an indication of the recency of the material, the system of pronunciation and the abbreviations used, the arrangement of the information, and any additional material — such as maps and tables — which may be included in appendices.

Government publications

The British government, through Her Majesty's Stationery Office (HMSO) and the Publications Division of the Central Office of Information, publishes about 9000 titles per year. There are more than 90,000 titles at present in print. Government publications include:

1 Parliamentary publications (all published by HMSO)
   (a) House of Lords publications

    (i)   Weekly information bulletin.
    (ii)   *Journal of the House of Lords* (1510 to date), published annually.
    (iii) *Official report of parliamentary debates* (Lords' *Hansard*).
    (iv) Papers and bills.

   (b) House of Commons publications

    (i)   Weekly information bulletin.
    (ii)   *Journal of the House of Commons*, published annually. Each volume has its own index. A general (cumulative) index is published every ten years.
    (iii) *Official report of parliamentary debates* (Commons' *Hansard*).
    (iv) Bills.
    (v)   Papers.

The *Journals* are large and expensive, so few public libraries stock them.

Hansard is published daily (printed overnight). It is often described as a verbatim report, but in fact it is discreetly edited. However, it is accurate and completely unbiased. The Commons'

Hansard and the Lords' *Hansard* are separate.

There is a weekly *Hansard* and separate weekly index, plus bound volumes (of uniform physical size so the number of the parts included varies) accompanied by an index. A consolidated sessional index is also published. The indexes include entries under subjects and under MPs' names.

(c) Commons' papers and Lords' papers. These are numbered serially each session; e.g. HC 298, 1969 – 70; HL 78, 1969 – 70.

(d) Command papers. These are papers presented to Parliament by a minister on his or her own initiative (in theory, they are presented by command of Her Majesty). Command papers also include:

> Foreign and Commonwealth Office papers.
> White papers, i.e. statements on government policy.
> Statistical reports, etc.

Command papers are numbered in series. We are now in the fifth series (1956 onwards).

(e) Bills, Acts and measures. Bills are printed on pale green paper and numbered serially within each session (in brackets for Commons' Bills, in parentheses for Lords' Bills).

Public general Acts are public Bills which have been passed by both houses and given royal assent. They are first published separately, then in bound annual volumes (appearing every March), including indexes.

> There are also tables and indexes to local and personal Acts (Acts arising from private members' Bills).

Measures of the General Synod are those passed by the General Synod of the Church of England and given royal assent.

2 Non-Parliamentary publications
These include:

(a) Statutory instruments – that is, regulations made by a minister under the authority of an Act of Parliament (delegated legislation). They are first published singly, numbered serially within each year, then in annual bound volumes.

(b) Reports – e.g., *Registrar General's statistical review of England and Wales*; *Kingman report* (1988) on the teaching of the English language; *Barclay report* (1982) on the role and tasks of social workers.

3 Periodicals

   (a) *London gazette* − published four times each week, with occasional special supplements, and with a quarterly index, it contains a comprehensive range of official information. (It was called the *Oxford gazette* from 1665 until 1910, when it changed its name to the *London gazette*.)

   (b) *Monthly digest of statistics* − detailed statistics on a wide range of subjects.

Obviously, librarians require the assistance of catalogues, guides and indexes to help them to find their way through such an array of government publications. Fortunately HMSO publishes a number of helpful guides. These include:

1 *Daily list* − published Monday to Friday, excluding Bank holidays. Contents:

   (a) Parliamentary publications.

   (b) Non-Parliamentary publications arranged alphabetically by department.

   (c) Publications sold but not published by HMSO.

   (d) Corrections to previous *Daily lists*.

   (e) List of statutory instruments issued.

Information given: author (corporate or personal), title, number of pages, size, ISBN, price. The *Daily list* is now accessible on Prestel.

2 *Monthly catalogue* − monthly cumulation of *Daily lists*. Contents:

   (a) Parliamentary publications, listed under (i) House of Lords, (ii) House of Commons.

   (b) Classified list − (i) non-Parliamentary, (ii) Parliamentary − arranged alphabetically by department.

   (c) Index.

   (d) Index of ISBN.

(Statutory instruments are included.)

The publication includes an alphabetical index of authors, editors, chairmen and subjects and there is also an index under ISBNs.

3 *Annual catalogue* − a cumulation of the *Monthly catalogue*, appearing four to five months following the end of the year covered. It excludes statutory instruments. The arrangement is the same as the *Monthly catalogue*.

4 Consolidated index to government publications − published every five years since 1936.

5 Sectional lists − these are lists of all the publications in print (and sometimes out of print) of individual departments − e.g. Department of Education and Science − or on special topics − e.g. construction; British Geological Survey. About 25 lists are currently available, free of charge.

6 Committee reports published by HMSO. These are listed under the names of the chairmen of the committees.

7 Weekly local government list − a weekly list of government publications from HMSO: a selection of interest to local authorities. Arrangement is under broad subject headings, e.g. education, housing, planning, public health, etc.

8 List of statutory instruments − monthly with annual cumulations. Arranged alphabetically by subject, with index of SI numbers, index of ISBNs and an alphabetical subject index. The subject index cumulates each month.

9 HMSO in print − a quarterly listing on microfiche. There is also an HMSO database accessible via BLAISE-LINE which covers publications from 1976 to date and is updated monthly.

Bibliographies, indexes and abstracts

Some reference enquiries involve a systematic search of published bibliographies, indexes and abstracts. These provide a short cut to finding out which articles have been written or books published on a specific topic or by a given author. They are invaluable tools in any reference department or academic library, or anywhere where serious research is undertaken.

Bibliographies

Some of the prime information retrieval tools which librarians use are bibliographies. A bibliography is a list of books. However, not all bibliographies cover the same field or are arranged in the same manner. There are bibliographies which cover one particular subject, while others cover many or all subjects. Some bibliographies are arranged alphabetically and others are classified. The number and range of bibliographies is vast, so in the compass of this chapter one can describe only a few examples.

British national bibliography (BNB)

In this country the major bibliography is the *British national bibliography* (*BNB*) which commenced publication in 1950. It is compiled from the legal deposit copies of all new publications/editions, which United Kingdom publishers must supply free of charge to the British Library.

The bibliography, therefore, claims to be a complete list of all new UK publications. *British national bibliography* is published weekly and the last copy of each month contains author/title and subject indexes covering the entire month. Interim cumulations are published which supersede the weekly and monthly parts and there is an annual cumulation available in hardback or microfiche format. Since the autumn of 1989, *BNB* has also been available on CD-ROM, including a back-file covering the years 1950 to 1985 and a current file from 1986 onwards which is updated quarterly.

The arrangement of the bibliography is like a classified catalogue:

1   It has a classified sequence in which each book is represented by a full catalogue entry with the Dewey classification number as the heading. The entries are arranged numerically from the 000s to the 999s in keeping with the Dewey scheme. A typical entry might look like this:

> 025.4'028 − Documents, Abstracting
> *Rowley, J.E. (Jennifer E.), 1950−
>   Abstracting and indexing/Jennifer E. Rowley − 2nd ed. −
>   London: Bingley, 1988 − (176)p : ill ; 22cm
>   Previous ed. 1982 − Includes bibliography and index
>   ISBN 0-85157-411-4 : £16.00 : CIP entry (June)
>   Also classified at 025.4'8
>   I.Ti   B88-20654

The items of information given in the above entry are:

(1) Dewey class number, (2) subject, (3) author, (4) title, (5) edition, (6) place of publication, publisher and date, (7) number of pages, illustrations and spine height, (8) notes, (9) international standard book number, (10) price, (11) cataloguing in publication information, (12) alternative class number, (13) information about additional catalogue entries (tracings), (14) *BNB* running number.

2   The second sequence in the bibliography is an alphabetical index of authors and titles. The book given as an example above would have the following index entries:

> (a) Rowley, J.E. (Jennifer E.), 1950−
>   Abstracting and indexing/Jennifer E. Rowley. − 2nd ed
>   − Bingley. £16.00: CIP entry (June)
>   025.4'028   Issue 1980 ISBN 0-85157-411-4

(b) Abstracting and indexing/Jennifer E. Rowley — 2nd ed
     — Bingley. £16.00: CIP entry (June)
     025.4028   Issue 1980   ISBN 0-85157-411-4

3   The third sequence in the bibliography is an alphabetical index of
    subjects which shows the appropriate Dewey classification number
    for each subject:

    (a) Abstracting. Documents   025.4'028
    (b) Documents
        Abstracting   025.4'028

    To discover which books have been published on a particular topic,
    one would consult the subject index to discover the Dewey number
    and then turn to that number in the classified sequence to find full
    details of the books. Of course, if either author or title is already
    known, one can turn directly to the author/title index to discover
    brief details of the book, but for full bibliographical details one
    would have to turn also to the classified sequence.

    British national bibliography is more or less comprehensive in
    its coverage of new UK publications/editions but it does not include
    music or the majority of government publications as these categories
    are covered by other bibliographies. Reprints are also omitted.
    Included in the bibliography's coverage is advance information about
    forthcoming books, details of which are supplied by more than 1000
    British publishers.

British books in print (BBIP)
The name of this bibliography adequately describes its coverage —
namely, a list of all books in print and on sale in the UK. It therefore
includes not only new publications but books published a number of years
previously which are still in print. The printed edition of *British books
in print* is in four hardback volumes published annually but most libraries
prefer to stock BBIP in microfiche format as it is updated monthly. The
arrangement is in one straightforward alphabetical sequence of authors,
titles and keywords. There is no subject guide to *BBIP* so one must know
either the author or the title or a keyword which appears in the title before
one can trace further bibliographical details. Examples of entries (1,
author and 2, title) from *BBIP* are:

1 Rowley, Jennifer, Abstracting and Indexing. D8. 176.
    2 r.e. £16.00 Bingley (6.88)   0 85157 411 4
    The items of information included in the author entry are (1) author,
    (2) title, (3) size (i.e. demi-octavo, 176 pages), (4) edition, (5) price,

(6) publisher, (7) month and year of publication, (8) ISBN.
2 Abstracting and Indexing (Rowley) D8. 176. 2 r.e.
£16.00 Bingley (6.88) 0 85157 411 4

British books in print is now available on CD-ROM as *Whitaker's bookbank*. To use this, the enquirer keys in the search terms, author and/or keywords, on a keyboard which resembles a typewriter. Depressing the F2 key activates a search, and subsequently pressing the F10 key causes the information required to be displayed on the screen of a computer terminal. If linked also to a laser printer, the information on the screen can be printed out simply by depressing the F5 key. *Whitaker's bookbank* is updated monthly in the same way as *BBIP*.

Books in print
This bibliography is the American equivalent of *British books in print*. It is also published in hardback and microfiche formats, the latter being updated monthly. There are two alphabetical sequences, one under authors, the second under titles.

Books in English
This is a bibliography compiled from British Library Bibliographic Services records of all new British publications plus records of books in the English language added to the stock of the Library of Congress in Washington.

The arrangement is alphabetical and the information given includes author, title, edition, publication data, physical description (e.g. number of pages), series, Library of Congress classification, Dewey classification and ISBN.

Books in English is published on microfiche at bi-monthly intervals, each issue being cumulative, and there is a full annual cumulation.

The British Library commenced publication of *Books in English* in 1971 in ultrafiche format, but subsequently changed to standard microfiche which increased its usefulness.

A cumulation covering the period 1971−80, consisting of over 1.1 million records, is still obtainable, along with a cumulation covering 1981−5.

Specialist bibliographies
Almost every subject field has its own specialist bibliography or bibliographies. Some are large and scholarly works while some are designed as simple guides to source material for the student or the person in the street wishing to read up on a particular topic.

British catalogue of music
The catalogue covers new music published in Great Britain along with foreign music available in this country or acquired by the British Library. Like *British national bibliography*, the *British catalogue of music* is mainly compiled from legal deposit copies received by the Copyright Receipt Office of the British Library. It is published in annual bound volumes, with two supplements per year. The catalogue is arranged in two separate sequences:

1 a classified sequence arranged by the Dewey classification scheme (proposed revision of the 780 music class);
2 an alphabetical index of titles, composers, arrangers, librettists etc.

The coverage is comprehensive apart from some types of pop music and modern dance music. There is a ten-volume cumulation covering the years 1957 to 1985.

British catalogue of audiovisual materials
This catalogue, published by British Library Bibliographic Services Division, is based on the stock of the former Inner London Education Authority's Centre for Learning Resources. In addition, information is gleaned from publishers and from the British Universities Film Council.
   The catalogue is arranged in three sequences:

1 classified sequence arranged by Dewey numbers;
2 an alphabetical index of titles, series, and originators;
3 an alphabetical subject index which gives the relevant Dewey number for each subject.

The arrangement and method of consultation is therefore identical to *British national bibliography* but the information in the main entries differs from *BNB* because of the nature of the non-book media. Here is a sample of an entry from the classified sequence:

   027.625 − Children's libraries. Guidance for users.
      The junior library. − London, Slide Centre, 1967.
      3p; 33cm
      24 slides: col.
      (293-4)
      Leaflet contains teacher's notes.

The information in the above entry includes (1) Dewey classification number, (2) subject, (3) title, (4) place of publication, publisher and date, (5) number of pages (in the accompanying leaflet) and its shelf height, (6) number of slides in the set and the fact that they are coloured, (7) annotation or further notes about the item.

The catalogue covers filmstrips, slides, films, film-loops, portfolios, posters, charts, overhead projection transparencies, kits, cassettes, gramophone records, work cards, educational games, spirit masters and so on, but excludes video recordings and most 16mm films, which are listed in the *British national film catalogue*, and also musical sound recordings.

Supplements to the main catalogue were published in 1981 and 1983.

British national film catalogue

Listed in this three-volume catalogue are films and videograms, two volumes being devoted to those suitable for schools and the other volume listing material suitable for management. It commenced publication in 1963 and appears quarterly with an annual cumulation. The arrangement is in two main sequences:

1 non-fiction films arranged in classified order by the Universal Decimal Classification scheme;
2 fiction films arranged alphabetically by title.

There are also indexes of subjects, titles, distributors and so on. The information about each film includes the producer and distributor, running time, and whether sound or silent, black and white or colour. Feature films and newsreels are excluded from the catalogue's coverage as they are dealt with in the *Monthly film bulletin*.

Other specialist bibliographies

As has been stated previously, practically every field of knowledge has its own specialist bibliographies and they are far too numerous to list. It must suffice to name just a few examples:

1 *Bibliography of nursing literature*, Vols. 1−4, London, Library Association, 1968−86.
2 *Bibliography of Scotland*, Vols. 1−6, National Library of Scotland, 1976−82.
3 Borchardt, D. H. and Francis, R. D., *How to find out in psychology*, Pergamon, 1986.
4 Oleksiw, S., *Reader's guide to the classic British mystery*, Blandford Press, 1989.
5 Padwick, E. W., *Bibliography of cricket*, 2nd rev. ed., London, Library Association, 1984.
6 Selden, R., *Reader's guide to contemporary literary theory*, 2nd rev. ed., Harvester Wheatsheaf, 1989.

Indexes to periodicals

Periodicals are important as information sources because they are published more frequently than books and are therefore more up to date. However, it would be a time-consuming task for the student or researcher to sit down with piles of periodicals, frantically scanning contents lists to try to trace articles on a chosen topic. Fortunately, the researcher does not have to do the spadework as, in most cases, it has already been done and published indexes provide a short cut to discovering what has appeared in periodicals. Again, there are too many indexes to list them all so it must suffice to consider a few of the better-known ones.

Contents pages in education

One of the simplest indexes to periodicals in terms of its compilation is *Contents pages in education*, a monthly publication in paperback format. Its title discloses the fact that its coverage is restricted to the field of education and that its arrangement consists of a series of contents pages of a specified list of journals. These contents pages are arranged alphabetically by the title of the journal, but they are also numbered consecutively. At the back of each issue there is a subject index and an author index which make use of that running number to link the index item with the appropriate contents page. The publication also includes a complete list of all the journals scanned, plus a list of those included in that particular issue.

British education index

The major index covering the field of education is *British education index*, now produced by the Brotherton Library at the University of Leeds in three quarterly paperback issues with a bound annual cumulation. The index can also be accessed online through DIALOG File 121. More than 250 educational journals are regularly scanned.

British education index contains an author index arranged alphabetically by surnames, followed by an alphabetical subject index. Preliminary matter includes a list of the journals scanned along with clear instructions for the user.

An example of the information to be found when searching under subject is as follows:

School Libraries
  The final frontier: independent learning and the role of the library/ Sally E. Gibbs *School Librarian*, Vol. 37, no.1: Feb. 89 p10−11.

The example gives (1) subject heading in bold type, (2) title of the article, (3) author, (4) name of the periodical, (5) volume and part number, (6) date, (7) page numbers.

In the author index there is an entry under 'GIBBS' which repeats items (2) – (7) above and then lists all the subject headings under which the article has been indexed; for example:

Gibbs, Sally E.
> The final frontier: independent learning and the role of the library/Sally E. Gibbs *School Librarian*, Vol. 37, no.1: Feb 89 p10 – 11.
> Secondary Education/School Libraries/Library Role/Independent Study/General Certificate of Secondary Education.

Education index

This is the American counterpart of *British education index* though its scope covers other English-speaking countries as well as North America. The arrangement is akin to that of a dictionary with authors and subjects in one alphabetically arranged sequence.

British humanities index

The index is a guide to articles appearing in a list of more than 300 periodicals and newspapers. According to the index's own blurb, the term 'humanities' is interpreted broadly to include the arts, economics, history, philosophy, politics and society. Articles on science and technology which are written for the layman rather than the specialist are also included.

British humanities index is published at quarterly intervals in paperback format but these issues are superseded by a hardback annual cumulation. The index is an alphabetical list of subjects with related headings and 'see' and 'see also' references. The annual volume also includes an alphabetical index of authors. The information given about an article is as follows:

Libraries, Public: Great Britain
> Charging for public library services. Stephen J. Bailey. Policy and Politics, 17 (Jan 89) p.59 – 74. refs.
> Mild after bitter. (Public library expenditure 1987 – 8). Peter Mann. Bookseller, (24 Feb 89) p.619. ref.

The above entry shows:

Subject heading
Title. Author. Name of periodical.
Issue number. Date. Page numbers.

If the article is illustrated, the abbreviation 'il.' is given and if it includes a bibliography, the abbreviation 'refs' appears.

Current technology index

Because of the need to be really up to date in the field of technology, *Current technology index* (previously known as *British technology index*) is published monthly but also has an annual bound cumulation. Its subject coverage spans all branches of engineering, along with chemical technology and manufacturing. The index is arranged in two sequences:

1 alphabetical subject index which gives details of titles of articles, authors and sources;
2 author index which quotes the source of the article and also gives the first word or phrase of the subject heading under which it is listed in the main sequence.

Times index

The times newspaper group publishes its own index to *The times*, *Sunday times*, *The times educational supplement* and *The times higher educational supplement*. The index is published monthly in paperback format with a hardback annual cumulation. It is arranged in one alphabetical sequence of subjects, persons and places. The source of the item is shown by the date of the issue, the page number and column number; for example, Jan. 28 6 g.

Citation indexes

A citation index is 'an ordered list of references (cited works) in which each reference is followed by a list of the sources (citing works) which cite it'. In other words, if a person doing research in a particular field knows of one book which is useful, he or she can trace other authors who have referred to that book in their published work. Their books will consequently be of use to the researcher as they are bound to cover the same subject area. The two prime examples of this kind of reference tool are *Science citation index* and *Social sciences citation index*.

Abstracts

Indexes to periodicals are extremely useful tools for discovering which articles have been published on a given topic but they give only subject headings and titles of articles as clues to their content. An abstracting service, on the other hand, gives a précis of each article, so it provides a much more informative guide. Most subject areas are covered by abstracting services and the following are examples.

Anbar abstracts

Anbar abstracts is the major abstracting service for the fields of business and management. It has been published since 1961 and at present there are five different journals, each covering a specific area of management. These are (1) accounting and data processing, (2) management services and production, (3) marketing and distribution, (4) personnel and training, (5) top management.

Each one is published in 12 separate issues which together comprise one annual volume to be stored in its own ring binder. Each issue has its own index but there is also an annual cumulative joint index which covers all five of the abstracting services. In addition, there is a bound annual cumulation of the abstracts themselves in what is called *The compleat Anbar*. Over 300 management journals are regularly scanned. The abstracts themselves are arranged in a classified sequence and are identified by a unique Anbar reference code. To discover which journal articles have been written on a specified topic one must first consult the 'keyword register', an alphabetical list of subjects which shows the relevant classification code against each; for example:

Management styles 2.02

One then has to look up 2.02 in the index (monthly or cumulative) to discover the Anbar codes for the abstracts; for example:

2.02 Management Styles & Techniques	
Autonomy, maintaining control and allowing	OX 3
Change, changing computer systems means business	OX26
Change, four types of large-scale	OX 2
Change, phases employees experience through	OX67
Culture, customer v. product-driven	OY57
Culture, evaluating an organization's	OX 4
Culture track to organizational success, the	OY98
Deregulation, mgt style for surviving	OX66
Entrepreneurship in large firms	OY99
Ethical standards, raising organizational	OX88
Innovate (newstream) mgt	OX49
John Harvey-Jones on qualities managers need	OZ70
Managing without managers	OX85
Manufacturing competitiveness, renewal/resurgence of	OX50
Organizational development intervention brings prosperity	OZ 0
Reluctant managers	OX92
Turnaround managers must be autocrats	OY50

To discover the source of the article 'John Harvey-Jones on qualities managers need', one must locate abstract OZ70 in the list of abstracts, that is:

OZ70   Manage with passion: love your factory
Sir John Harvey-Jones in Works Management (UK), Oct 89 (42/9): p.18 (4 pages)
The flamboyant ex-chairman of ICI reveals his beliefs about the main qualities managers need (e.g. the ability to listen) and what their attitude to their job should be; laments the prevalence of systems that punish failure 'grotesquely' and give relatively poor reward for success and sees management's task as that of maintaining the highest rate of change that is feasible to provide more and better from less. Advocates personal development profiles and annual progress/planning reviews for all managers. Refers to works managers in the article but his views have wider application.

Discovering the existence of a pertinent article is only part of the process because the customer will not be fully satisfied until the article is actually obtained on his or her behalf. The library's own journal holdings will be checked first but, if a blank is drawn, the interlibrary loan service may be used. The normal routine for non-Anbar items is to apply to British Library Lending Division for a photocopy of the required article. However, Anbar offers a very rapid service for any articles listed in their abstracts. Libraries subscribing to *Anbar abstracts* may fax or telephone Anbar and, by merely quoting the abstract number, in the example above OZ70, can have a copy forwarded in that day's post. The article may be purchased at a privileged rate by any subscriber or alternatively borrowed for a short period by libraries subscribing to the comprehensive service.

Children's literature abstracts

The Children's Libraries Section of the International Federation of Library Associations publishes *Children's literature abstracts* at quarterly intervals. The coverage includes journal articles on children's reading, children's books, their authors and illustrators, book selection and children's literature awards. The journals scanned, both English and foreign, are listed in each issue. Abstracts of relevant books and pamphlets are covered in separate issues. The abstracts themselves are arranged under broad subject categories and each is identified by a running number. The annual index of authors and subjects provides the key to these running numbers.

Library and information science abstracts (LISA)

LISA is published monthly by the Library Association. The relevant journals which are regularly scanned total approximately 550, covering 60 countries and 34 foreign languages. The abstracts are arranged in classified order using a classification scheme devised by the Classification Research Group which utilizes upper and lower case letters and numerals in its notation. Each abstract is also identified by a running number. For example:

HykGuAz — Secondary school libraries. Influence of local government reorganisation. UK   89/5622
    School libraries on the move: managing library changes in English local authorities. Peggy Heeks. [London], British Library Research and Development Department, 1988, 71p. refs. bibliog. (Library and Information Research Report No. 69) (ISBN 0-7123-3166-2).
    Reviews secondary school library development in England, drawing on 2 pieces of research: the Berkshire Libraries for Learning (BELL) project which ran from Sept. 85 — Aug. 87 and an overview of development in 83 English local authorities, as revealed by returns to the Office of Arts and Libraries (OAL) during 1985/86, and case studies of change in 8 of these: i.e. Avon, Bexley, Bradford, Cornwall, Cumbria, Devon, Gloucestershire, and Hertfordshire. (J.S.)

Each issue of *LISA* contains a subject index and a name index which link with the classified list by means of the abstract number. The indexes are easily identifiable because the pages have a distinctive border. The entries in these indexes for the example shown are:

1 Subject index
    (a) Local government
            Influence on secondary school libraries   5622
    (b) Secondary school libraries   5620 — 5622
    (c) School libraries
            Secondary schools *see* Secondary school libraries
2 Author index
    Heeks, P   5622

In addition to each issue's indexes there are also annual and five-yearly cumulated indexes.
    LISA is also accessible online through DIALOG and ORBIT, permitting retrieval of approximately 90,000 records spanning 1969 to date. A complete back-file is also available on CD-ROM.

Reference works of unusual format

Some reference works are not published as bound volumes but in separately produced parts. One such work is *Keesing's contemporary archives* which is an authoritative source of information on current events throughout the world. To ensure that the information is up to date, printed pages are posted to subscribers at weekly intervals and these must be inserted into the loose-leaf binders provided. Indexes of subjects and of names are similarly supplied at regular intervals with accompanying instructions about the discarding of superseded indexes.

Croner publications produce a number of reference works in loose-leaf binders with a frequent updating service. These include *Croner's executive companion* and *Croner's reference book for employers.*

Another format of reference work is that of printed cards or slips which have to be filed in drawers or binders; again new items have to be inserted and old ones discarded to ensure currency of information. One such service is Extel Financial Card Services, which covers current information about industrial firms, including company profits and share prices.

Extel offers a variety of services covering company news from the UK, Europe, North America, Australia, Hong Kong, Japan, Thailand and the Middle East. The UK listed service covers about 2750 companies listed on the Stock Exchange, and the Extel cards, or loose-leaf information sheets, are updated and circulated to subscribers on a daily basis. For other services, the frequency of updating varies from twice weekly to weekly or fortnightly.

Microfilm and microfiche formats are now commonplace in most libraries. Several bibliographies, indexes and abstracts are available in microform editions and one can usually purchase complete back runs as well as the current issues. One example of a reference source in microform is Barbour microfile. Its coverage is of technical products, building plans and designs and other topics related to the construction industry. The microfiches contain the actual journal articles or pages from manufacturers' catalogues. To access the required fiche one must first consult printed indexes in bound volumes. The alphabetical subject index gives a reference number and the number, in turn, leads to the appropriate section in the subject list. Each entry listed under the appropriate subject heading has a number which refers to the fiche itself. The Barbour microfile is updated three times a year.

British Standards are available in cassetted microfilm format.

Basic reference books

Time and space do not allow the inclusion of a comprehensive list and survey of all reference works available. However, the following is a list of basic reference books broadly grouped by Dewey's ten main classes.

1   *General knowledge and librarianship*
      Aslib directory
      Everyman's dictionary of abbreviations
      Guinness book of records
      One-volume encyclopaedia:
      Pears cyclopaedia
      Multi-volume encyclopaedias:
      Encyclopedia Americana
      Encyclopaedia Britannica
      Everyman's encyclopaedia
      Encyclopaedias for children:
      Children's Britannica
      Macmillan children's encyclopaedia
      Oxford junior encyclopaedia
      World book encyclopaedia
1(a) *Newspapers and periodicals*
      Abstracts, indexes, directories, etc.:
      Abstracts:
      Anbar abstracts
      Children's literature abstracts
      Library and information science abstracts
      Indexes:
      British education index
      British humanities index
      Current technology index
      Times index
      Directories and guides:
      Ulrich's international periodicals directory
      Willings press guide
      Catalogues of library holdings:
      British union catalogue of periodicals
      Essex union list of serials (on microfiche)
2   *Religion*
      Atlas of the Bible (Phaidon Press)
      Cruden's complete concordance to the Old and New Testaments
      Hastings' encyclopaedia of religion and ethics
      Illustrated Bible dictionary
      Oxford Bible atlas
      Oxford dictionary of the Christian church

3   *Social sciences*
      Directory of directors
      Dod's parliamentary companion
      Hansard
      Municipal yearbook and public services directory, vols. 1 and 2
      Statesman's yearbook
      Whitaker's almanack
      Education:
      Careers encyclopaedia
      Education authorities directory
      Education yearbook
      University calendars and handbooks
      World of learning
      Post Office:
      Telephone directories

4   *Languages*
      See the section on dictionaries, pp.159

5   *Science and technology*
&   British Standards (manuals or microfiches)
6   Croner's reference book for employers
      Illustrated medical dictionary (Dorland)
      Jane's all the world's aircraft
      Jane's fighting ships
      Kempe's engineers yearbook
      Kompass United Kingdom
      McGraw-Hill encyclopedia of science and technology
      Machinery's handbook
      Medical register
      Van Nostrand's scientific encyclopedia

7   *The arts*
      Encyclopaedia of sports and games
      Encyclopaedia of world architecture
      Grove's dictionary of music and musicians
      Kobbe's complete opera book
      Oxford companion to music
      Oxford companion to the theatre
      Who's who in art
      Wisden cricketers' almanack

8   *Literature*
      Brewer's dictionary of phrase and fable
      Fiction index
      Junior fiction index

Oxford companion to classical literature
Oxford companion to English literature
Oxford dictionary of quotations
Sequels, vol.1: Adult books, vol.2: Junior books
Writers' and artists' yearbook

9 *History*
Annual register of world events
Britain: an official handbook
Chambers' dictionary of dates
Historical atlas of Britain
Keesing's contemporary archives
Times atlas of world history
Victoria history of the counties of England

9(a) *Geography*
Gazetteer of places in Britain (Bartholomew)
Ordnance Survey maps
Times atlas of the world

9(b) *Biography*
Burke's royal families of the world
Chambers' biographical dictionary
Dictionary of national biography
International who's who
Who's who
Who was who

10 *Local information*
Ordnance Survey map(s) of the locality
Telephone directory of the locality
Thomson local directory

Compilation of booklists and bulletins

Most libraries produce their own booklists and bulletins from time to time. These are usually offered free of charge to library members as part of the library's promotional services. The bibliographies may be lists of recent additions to stock, works by a particular author, fiction of a particular type or non-fiction covering a specific subject. Bibliographies are sometimes produced to accompany exhibitions and displays, or to relate to extra-library activities such as children's story hours, film shows or outings, or for special events such as National Library Week.

The home-produced bibliographies will normally relate to a library's own stock and will be compiled from information gleaned from the library's catalogue. Sometimes, the bibliographies are straightforward lists of authors and titles but they may also be annotated to include a short summary or appraisal of each book. Printing costs are high so libraries often produce their own booklists and bulletins using photocopiers, offset-litho or other duplicating machines. A few libraries employ staff trained at art college so that the artwork, lettering and general standard of production of all publicity and display materials is high.

Special libraries, particularly academic and industrial libraries, will circulate home-produced bulletins to their own clientele in an effort to keep them up to date in their own field of expertise. Abstracts bulletins supplement published abstracts and have the advantages of being more up to date and based on the individual library's own holdings. They can also cover internal reports and foreign language materials which would not be encompassed by published abstracts. It must be appreciated, however, that a great deal of staff time is taken up in reading, summarizing and evaluating books and periodical articles if an abstracts bulletin is to be produced.

A simpler method, though less informative, is to produce a titles bulletin whereby only the titles, authors and sources of periodical articles and books are given. The titles are usually grouped under subject headings so that the reader does not have to peruse the entire list to find the items relevant to his or her subject field.

One popular form of current awareness service involves the photo-copying of the contents lists of specified periodicals. The photocopies are then sent to particular individuals who require to be kept informed about current literature in their specialist field.

Libraries with ready access to a computer can produce printouts of titles or abstracts and operate a service known as SDI, selective dissemination of information.

Recent technological advances have greatly increased the speed and scope of information searching. Their importance is so great that they warrant a separate chapter (see Chapter 12).

Audiovisual materials and equipment

Libraries have always been repositories of knowledge in whatever formats were available. Thus, libraries of ancient times stored clay tablets, papyrus rolls, parchment scrolls and so on. As they have become readily available, libraries have also kept newspaper cuttings, charts, maps, mounted illustrations and photographs. In recent years, the range and diversity of formats has increased dramatically and public libraries stock and offer for loan slides, filmstrips, gramophone records, audio cassettes, video cassettes, compact discs and, in some instances, framed works of art.

Academic libraries house an even wider range of audiovisual media to meet the needs of pupils, students and staff. Their stocks may include

Fig. 1 A home produced bibliography

films, film loops, overhead projection transparencies, wallcharts, video cassettes, computer programs, models, kits, workcards, handouts, educational games, nature specimens, artefacts and realia (for example, fossils).

It is unfortunate that some institutions separate the printed materials from the non-print media and maintain a library and a resource centre as two separate entities under completely different management. This is not a sensible arrangement as the person seeking information normally wants it and happily accepts it in whatever format is available. In fact a variety of formats is often more helpful than a single format. For example, the child doing a project about birds will require books to give background information, a record or cassette to hear bird-song, and a film to appreciate bird flight. How much easier it would be for a pupil if all the various media were listed together in the catalogue and housed together in one area.

Non-print media are extremely useful sources of information but, despite Marshall McLuhan's predictions of several years ago, the book has not yet been ousted. It must be remembered that books are still the most important resources for learning.

Multi-media items are often more susceptible to damage than books and their varied shapes and sizes can cause shelving problems. They also require equipment for their use. Many libraries provide carrels equipped with power points so that audiovisual equipment can be used. The use of headphones with audio equipment ensures that other library users are not disturbed.

Some of the multi-media items named above will be quite familiar but others may need further description and explanation.

Films
Commercially produced films are 16mm and require a 16mm cine projector. The newer projectors are self-threading which makes things easier for the projectionist. Home-produced films are usually 8mm and require an 8mm projector.

Film-loops
A film-loop is a short length of film enclosed in a cassette with the end of the film spliced on to the beginning so that it requires no rewinding. Film-loops are commercially produced and usually deal with one precise topic.

Filmstrips
A filmstrip is a continuous length of 35mm film containing a consecutive series of frames. They may be full-frame (equivalent in size to a 35mm slide) or half-frame. Most filmstrip projectors incorporate a masking device for showing half-frame strips. After use the filmstrip has to be rewound ready for the next showing.

Video cassettes
A video cassette recorder can be found in many homes in the affluent countries of the world, so the reader will be familiar with the appearance of a video cassette and will know that it reproduces visual images as well as sound.

Fig. 2 Video cassette recorder

Overhead projection (OHP) transparencies

The overhead projector allows the projection of information or illustrations on to a screen behind while the teacher remains facing the class. In direct use, the overhead projector can replace the chalkboard. The teacher writes or draws directly on to the acetate roll covering the glass platen of the projector, using a water-based pen. The roll can be wiped clean after use and reused. On the other hand, the teacher may use pre-prepared acetate sheets, either home-produced using a spirit-based pen to ensure permanence, or produced on various kinds of document copying machines or purchased from a commercial firm. The latter are often beautifully coloured and of very high quality. Librarians may keep stocks of pre-prepared OHP transparencies which they have classified, catalogued and made available for loan.

Kits

School libraries usually stock a variety of kits. They are normally boxes containing samples covering, for example, the production of cotton from its plant stages through to finished cloth.

Handouts

These are duplicated notes distributed by a teacher to the class which cover the main points of a lecture or lesson and replace or supplement the student's/pupil's own notes.

Further information on resource centre equipment, including reprographic machines and methods, may be found in Chapter 12, and the storage of software is covered in Chapter 8.

Assignments

Practical

1   Go to your local reference library and locate a copy of each of the following reference works. Thoroughly peruse each one and then write short notes describing and evaluating two of the works listed:

(a) Brewer's dictionary of phrase and fable,
(b) Fiction index,
(c) Oxford book of quotations,
(d) Roget's thesaurus,
(e) Sequels,
(f) Statesman's yearbook,
(g) Whitaker's almanack,
(h) Willing's press guide.

2 Information retrieval exercise. Write the answer to each question
in the 'answer' column and give the name of the reference book you
used in each case in the 'source' column. Use a different reference work
for each question:

No.	Question	Answer	Source
1	Name the oldest extant castle in Britain.		
2	Name one British library which subscribes to the periodical *Graphics world*.		
3	Who is the MP for the Chelmsford constituency?		
4	What is meant by the phrase 'a dog in the manger'?		
5	What does the acronym Aslib stand for?		
6	Which school did the Rt Hon. Margaret Thatcher attend?		
7	Who wrote the book *Pathways for communication: books and libraries in the information age*?		
8	Peter Mann wrote an article about public library expenditure 1987−8 entitled 'Mild after bitter'. In which periodical did this appear?		
9	Give the author, title, publisher and publication date of any book about the history of cricket from 1890 to 1914.		
10	What is the English equivalent of the German word *Frühling*?		
11	To which tribe did the Biblical character Gideon belong?		
12	Give three words which have the same meaning as 'restitution'.		
13	What are the Christian names (forenames) of the composer Tchaikovsky, and how old was he when he died?		

14 What is the regulation size of
a tennis court for a doubles game?

15 The disease of rickets is caused
by a deficiency in the diet. What
is lacking?

16 Who wrote: 'A traveller by the
faithful hound, Half-buried in
the snow was found'?

17 What is the meaning of the proof
correction symbol 'w.f.'?

18 Where is the headquarters of the
World Health Organization?

19 Of what larger company is the
Tetley Tea Co. a subsidiary?

20 What is the correct way to
address an envelope to the
Archbishop of Canterbury?
(Only the heading need be given,
not the full postal address.)

Written

1 Name two bibliographies which cover British publications and write short notes about each.

2 List and describe the various guides to British government publications.

3 What information can be found in the following types of publication? In each case, name a reference work as an example:

    (a) almanac,
    (b) biographical dictionary,
    (c) concordance,
    (d) etymological dictionary,
    (e) gazetteer.

4 List ten works of reference which one would expect to find in a library's quick reference collection.

5 What is the difference between an index to periodicals and an abstracting journal? Name and describe one example of each.

6 There are several types of dictionary. Describe four different types and cite an example of each.

7 List the types of audiovisual materials which might be stocked by a large library/resource centre. Assess the reasons why libraries stock audiovisual materials.

Bibliography

Bromley, D. W. and Allott, A. M. (eds.), *British librarianship and information work 1981−85*, London, Library Association, 1987−8.

Cabeceiras, J., *The multimedia library*, 2nd ed., New York, London, Academic Press, 1982.

Department of Education and Science, *Future development of libraries and information services*, London, HMSO, 1982.

Dority, G. K., *Guide to reference books for small and medium-sized libraries, 1970−82*, Englewood, Libraries Unlimited, 1983.

Dove, J., *The audio-visual*, London, Deutsch, 1975.

Guide to reference sources for the small library, compiled by Karen Beales . . . [et al], Winchester, Hatrics, 1981.

Katz, William A., *Introduction to reference work*, Vols. 1 and 2, 5th ed., New York, London, McGraw-Hill, 1987.

Library Association, *Guidelines for reference and information services to public libraries in England and Wales*, London, Library Association, 1981.

Miller, Peter, *Production and bibliographic control of non-book materials in the United Kingdom*, London, Polytechnic of North London, 1985.

Ollé, J. G., *Guide to sources of information in libraries*, Aldershot, Gower, 1984.

Pemberton, J. E., *Bibliographic control of official publications*, Oxford, Pergamon, 1982.

Rowley, Jennifer, *Organizing knowledge: introduction to information retrieval*, Aldershot, Gower, 1987.

Teague, S. J., *Microform, video and electronic media librarianship*, London, Butterworth, 1985.

Walford, A. J., *Guide to reference material*, Vols. 1−3, London, Library Association, 1987−90.

Chapter Ten

Library cooperation

From 1850, when the British public library service was born, until the early decades of the twentieth century, each library was an entity, serving or trying to serve the needs of its own membership and purchasing books to meet their primary demands. However, a combination of circumstances made it increasingly difficult for an individual library to be self-sufficient. These circumstances included:

1 a tremendous increase in knowledge and a corresponding growth in publishing;
2 the spread of education from primary through to university level which led to greater and more diverse demands on the public library service by a much more literate public;
3 the advance of technology with its effect on industry and commerce and the necessity for employers and employees to develop new skills and techniques;
4 increased opportunities for travel and international economic co-operation, which demanded up-to-date information about foreign countries.

These factors altered and increased the demands on the library service. It became impossible for an individual library to meet all the requirements of its own clientele and so calls for organized schemes of library cooperation began to be heard. The loudest call came from the Kenyon report in 1927 which recommended:

1 a system of voluntary cooperation between all types of public library authority, whether county, county borough, municipal borough or district;
2 the creation of regional networks based on large urban libraries;
3 cooperation between special libraries, e.g. industrial, commercial, academic;

4 the creation of a national central library to coordinate the entire cooperative system.

The National Central Library came into being in 1931, and by 1937 a system of regional library bureaux had been set up to cover the whole of England and Wales. The problem of discovering what resources were available in the participating libraries was overcome by the production of union catalogues at the bureaux and at the National Central Library. A number of non-public libraries participated in the cooperative scheme and they were known as outlier libraries.

The middle of the twentieth century saw further developments in library cooperation which included schemes for cooperative purchase and subject specialization and for the exchange and redistribution of withdrawn books. The National Lending Library for Science and Technology and the National Reference Library of Science and Invention were set up, both of which are now incorporated into the British Library.

In more recent years the advance of technology has brought major improvements to the networks of library cooperation. These include the use of telex and fax to speed up interlibrary loan requests, computerized cataloguing and bibliographic services, the availability of microform editions of union catalogues such as the LASER catalogue of the London and South Eastern Regional Library Bureau, and the easy production of photocopies.

The picture may appear rosy but there were some thorns in certain areas. Some of the union catalogues at regional library bureaux were comprehensive and reliable but others were incomplete. Some libraries leaned too heavily on the interloan network and shirked their own responsibility in book purchasing. Also, the heavy demands on the interloan scheme sometimes meant long delays in getting the required material.

The basis of a national interlibrary loan network must surely be a cooperative scheme of acquisition and storage. It would be a hit-and-miss system if one were merely to hope that a requested book might have been bought by some library somewhere in the country. A methodical scheme of cooperative purchase ensures there are no gaps in acquisition and no unnecessary duplication. A degree of duplication is inevitable as each library's first concern must be for its own readers and their demands with regard to stock.

The first of the subject specialization schemes was set up in London in 1948. Twenty-eight libraries agreed to specialize in certain subject areas (represented by Dewey classification numbers) so that jointly they would achieve good coverage of all publications on all subjects. The scheme included not only book purchase but the acquisition of withdrawn items from other libraries and permanent storage of all materials in their allotted subject fields.

A larger scheme based on the South Eastern Regional Library system was inaugurated in 1949 whereby 85 libraries agreed to purchase jointly all books listed in *British national bibliography*. Other regions followed with similar schemes of cooperative acquisition, the aim being to make each region self-sufficient. However, some of these regional schemes were reduced in completeness when the British Library came into being in 1973.

By law, UK publishers must submit a free copy of every book published to six designated libraries, including the British Library. These legal deposit copies are available as a back-up to the interloan scheme.

Concurrently with the reduced activity of regional schemes for acquisition and storage of materials came local government reorganization and the incorporation of previously autonomous borough libraries into the appropriate county library systems. County library authorities are therefore much larger and more powerful than they were, and some have initiated their own schemes of acquisition and storage which will make them as self-sufficient as possible.

Cooperative purchase of new publications has to be supplemented by schemes for the acquisition of out-of-print and rare materials. Material discarded by one library may be urgently required by another and some method is required whereby libraries are informed of available items. To coordinate this work, the British National Book Centre (BNBC) was set up in 1948. Libraries notified BNBC of their discarded items and lists were then circulated to libraries in Britain and later to exchange centres abroad. Foreign materials are also obtained through exchange agreements, principally between the national libraries of the countries concerned.

Local cooperative schemes

Sheffield pioneered the idea of a local cooperative network in the 1930s. The 12 original libraries participating in the scheme have now been joined by more than 50 others. The range includes public, academic, industrial, commercial, research association and chamber of commerce libraries. Cooperation is on a 'give and take' basis with each participating library fulfilling an obligation to subscribe to a minimum number of periodicals and to carry a bookstock of a stipulated minimum size. The organization is called the Sheffield Interchange Organisation, hence its acronym, SINTO. The union catalogue of the holdings of participating libraries is maintained by the Department of Commerce, Science and Technology of Sheffield public library. The backbone of the cooperative venture is the interlending of materials, but activities have included the monitoring of withdrawn stock, the compilation of a union list of periodicals, the production of several indexes and the sponsoring of information research projects.

Since the formation of SINTO, many other local networks have been set up in various parts of the country. Many of them are known by their acronyms, such as CICRIS (Co-operative Industrial and Commercial Reference and Information Service), LADSIRLAC (Liverpool and District Scientific, Industrial and Research Library Advisory Council), ESSNET (the network based at Essex County Library) and HERTIS. HERTIS is the Hertfordshire Technical Library and Information Service based upon the Hatfield Polytechnic library and using resources from the county as a whole. It has its own staff and they offer information tracing, consultancy and advice. As in most schemes, there is a charge for membership and a small service charge to cover copying and postage of any materials.

Regional cooperative schemes

Most cooperation at regional level has been channelled through the regional library bureaux. Nine regions were formed; these were Northern, West Midlands, Wales and Monmouth, London and South East, East Midlands, North West, Yorkshire, South West and Scotland.

Other informal schemes of regional cooperation have been set up in various parts of the country. One such network is the Yorkshire Cobook Scheme in which 11 autonomous library authorities have agreed to a cooperative book purchasing scheme.

The largest of the regional schemes is LASER (London and South East Region), which has recently computerized its listings and made them available online to participating libraries. The scheme's computer is called the Viscount and stores perhaps the largest database of books in a cooperative scheme in the world. Member libraries pay a subscription and have a representative on the policy board. LASER has a van delivery system that speeds up the delivery of requested items to the requesting libraries' central collection points.

Regional schemes provide over 60% of library requests and make UK libraries the most efficient in the world in meeting reader needs in a cost-efficient manner.

The national network

At the hub of the national network of library cooperation stands the British Library Document Supply Centre (BLDSC) in Boston Spa, Yorkshire.

It was set up in 1973 by amalgamating the stocks and services of the National Central Library with the National Lending Library for Science and Technology. The BLDSC is the library of last resort for interlibrary loans in that local and regional sources should be tried first before it is approached. It has its own vast stock:

Journals (Serials)	211,000 titles
Books (Monographs)	2,821,000 volumes
Reports in microform	3,270,000
Other reports	375,000
Doctoral Theses (US)	425,000
Doctoral Theses (UK)	85,000

Virtually all UK universities and the Council for National Academic Awards supply their doctoral theses for microfilming.

Conference Proceedings		265,000
Translations	over	500,000
Local Authority Material		23,300
Music		117,000
Russian Science & Technology Monographs	over	200,000
Microform		Roll microfilm: over 1,700 miles (2,700km) Microfiche (other than reports) 300,000

Statistics supplied by BLDSC's *Facts and figures*, April 1990

From this stock, most of the 3.3 million requests made to the Supply Centre every year can be met. In addition BLDSC maintains a union catalogue and can trace other sources if its own stock cannot meet the need. It publishes a list of its own periodicals holdings, entitled *Current serials received*. The library subscribes to more than 55,000 periodicals, and also has in stock about 70,000 sets of periodicals which are no longer in publication, so most requests for photocopies of periodical articles can be met from BLDSC's own resources. In addition, however, the British union catalogue of periodicals gives major locations for a vast number of periodicals.

The British National Book Centre, which coordinates a national and international scheme for the exchange or redistribution of unwanted stock, is also housed in the BLDSC buildings at Boston Spa. The centre has been renamed the Gift and Exchange Division.

Making an application to borrow from the BLDSC is straightforward. It sells vouchers for use as application forms and the requesting library types in the fullest bibliographical detail possible. To this is added the library user number and the address to which the item is to be sent. The form allows for special requests to be made, for example to state if a photocopy is acceptable or the original is essential, or searches are to be made overseas. The forms are in triplicate; the top two copies go to BLDSC and the requesting library retains the bottom copy. It is best to type these forms so that all copies are clear and easily readable.

Whether borrowing or lending material, careful records must be made so that items can be traced quickly and returned to the owner. Failure or loss will lead to charges being made.

Aslib and special library cooperation

Aslib, the Association of Special Libraries and Information Bureaux, was founded in 1924 by a group of librarians working in research stations. It is now made up of industrial libraries (about 59%), university and college libraries (about 14%), public libraries (about 11%). These are all corporate members. There are also a sizeable number of personal members (about 16%).

Aslib was influential in the development of several areas of inter-library cooperation, notably the establishment of the National Central Library, the provision of a union catalogue for London libraries, the compilation of location indexes of European and Russian scientific journals, the publication of the *British union catalogue of periodicals* and the *British National Bibliography*.

Aslib maintains its own information service for use by its members and also administers an interlending service between participating libraries. Other services include panels of translators and indexers on whom members may call, research and consultancy services related to special libraries and the organization of courses on various aspects of information work. Aslib's publications include the *Aslib directory* and the *Index to theses*.

Assignments

Practical
Discover the extent of participation of your library (the one in which you work or of which you are a member) in local, regional and national networks of library cooperation.

Written

1 Write brief notes on the following:

(a) British Library Document Supply Centre,
(b) Aslib,
(c) regional library bureaux.

2 What are the full names of the organizations represented by the following acronyms?

(a) CICRIS,
(b) LADSIRLAC,
(c) NANTIS,
(d) SCONUL.

3 What are the advantages of:'

(a) Cooperative acquisition and storage of materials?
(b) Union catalogues and union lists of periodicals?
(c) The interlibrary loan scheme?

Bibliography

Harrod, L. M., *Librarians' glossary of terms used in librarianship, documentation and the book crafts and reference books*, 5th ed., Aldershot, Gower, 1987.

Jefferson, G., *Library co-operation*, 2nd ed., London, Deutsch, 1977.

Montgomery, A. C., *Acronyms and abbreviations in library and information work*, 4th ed., London, Library Association, 1990.

Office of Arts and Libraries, *Current library cooperation and coordination*, London, HMSO, 1986.

Plaister, J. M., *Computing in LASER: regional library co-operation*, London, Library Association, 1982.

Chapter Eleven

Understanding the purposes, uses and production of library publications and the legal aspects of copyright and public lending

There is no doubt that libraries are part of the communications industry; simply by providing an information service they qualify for that definition. The role of libraries in communication goes much further than simply answering questions, however.

Many libraries attempt to predict their users' questions and have material ready for sale, or hand-outs to answer them:

1 Libraries know that new members will want information about their services and therefore produce a reader's guide that can be taken away and studied at leisure.
2 To help with their general education programme, libraries often produce displays on topics of current concern and support these with reading lists.
3 Library members' attention is drawn to new material by issuing lists of recent additions to stock.
4 Posters are produced advertising special activities.
5 Libraries keep specialists up to date by publishing reviews of the literature in specified subject areas and circulating copies.
6 Guides are published to periodicals either held by a library or by a group of cooperating libraries.
7 Some libraries extend their range of publishing to cover local history pamphlets, consumer news sheets, etc., thus being publishers in the truest sense of the word.

These are just a few of the reasons librarians have for producing publications; you should be able to add several others on looking round your own library. It is a good bet that if asked why libraries produce so much material of this type, the librarian would answer by saying that it all helps members to make fuller use of the stock, is part of the information dissemination process or forms part of the library's cultural and educational role.

The best format

In Chapter Twelve we shall look at the technical side of the many methods of printing and copying available to the librarian. The factors that will affect the decision can be summarized as follows.

Volume of copies to be produced

1　Very small: use photocopier, particularly if the copy consists chiefly of copies of pre-printed matter, e.g. contents lists of journals.
2　Small − say up to 500: use a stencil and absorption duplicator. If available, small offset litho machines are equally cost-effective.

　　In many towns there are small print shops offering offset litho or other quality reprography at low costs. Sometimes for smaller libraries they provide an opportunity to obtain short runs quickly at reasonable costs.
3　Very small, but colour wanted: spirit duplication is the only cheap system, but copies are limited in number. Recent advances in colour copying make it possible to get covers printed at commercial print shops at reasonable prices. Some large councils have purchased colour copiers for central use and libraries can make use of these effectively. Prices are, however, still high for quality − in the region of £1 per A4 sheet is common.
4　Medium to large runs − 1000 plus: use in-house offset-litho or outside traditional printing. Use the latter particularly if stitching or binding is required since the printer will usually have facilities for folding, cutting, and binding.

Appearance

The advent of desk top publishing (DTP) has dramatically changed library publishing. Using standard personal computers (PCs) and a DTP program such as Pagemaker, it is possible to achieve very professional layout and design standards. With more advanced equipment linked to the PC, for example a scanner and laser printer, masters of top quality can be made by most people.

With a scanner it is possible to put pictures into the PC and 'paste' them into the text at an appropriate point. Scanners are like small desk top copiers; you lay the item to be scanned face down and the machine copies it not to paper but to the disc on the PC. By using an optical character recognition (OCR) software package linked to the scanner it is possible to copy text into the word processing package and save typing. However, always think about copyright when considering this procedure.

For all the text and pictures held within the PC, changes can be quickly and easily made and updating material is no longer the long task that it used to be. The combination of a DTP package and a laser printer allows various typefaces, sizes and lines to be put into the finished work. This saves hours of time in preparing artwork.

Even using a very basic word processing package, high quality results can be achieved if a good printer is available. If the printer is described as being of 'letter quality', ink jet, or is a laser printer you can expect the best results.

Clearly if the final master copy is good, all the copies will be of a high standard.

1 Average quality, or cheap and cheerful, standard duplicating can be obtained by using an electric stencil cutter. Some quite good covers can be produced from Letraset or DTP originals. Line drawings are possible, but photographs are rarely successful on an electric cutter.
2 Good quality copies can be achieved by using offset litho with originals made either by typing/printing directly on to a master, or by producing the master on a photocopying machine. Using a DTP system and scanner real print effects can easily be achieved. Type sizes and styles can be mixed, multi-column layouts are easy and illustrations can be incorporated. With the aid of golf-ball or daisy-wheel typewriters, a good range of typefaces and different type sizes can be used on the same page. A 'print' effect can be obtained by reducing the typewritten page by, say 50% on a photocopying reducing machine before making the master. Covers and title pages can be very elaborate, including logos, if a 'paste-up' original is made before the master is produced. Photographs and so on are possible but their quality is sometimes disappointing.
3 High quality – professional printing is essential. Often this is not as costly as you may think, and small local printers can be a very good 'buy' for leaflet production. Photographs and other illustrations can be introduced more easily by using this method.

Speed of production

1 'Yesterday' – most library work falls under this heading. The fastest method is photocopying, followed by duplicating, then offset, then printing.
2 'Tomorrow' – a reasonable job can be done using any method except printing.
3 'Next month' – usually all methods will compete in this time scale.

Cost

This is so often volume dependent that no easy answer is possible. When many thousands of copies are required, in-house offset-litho or outside printing may well be the best bet. For small volume, absorption duplicating is usually much cheaper than photocopying.

Preparing material

Regardless of the reprographic system used to produce the end product, the ways in which the material is prepared are similar.

Collection of material

The material may be in the form of a bibliography or in normal prose. Whatever it is, it will require a list of headings under which the information is to be provided. The chapter headings of a book are a good example. Once the material is collected, these headings may well need to be modified either by adding or removing whole headings or by providing sub-headings. Often the material will be collected on cards or loose-leaf paper so that internal reorganization is quite an easy matter and rewriting is cut to a minimum.

First draft

The form of this depends on circumstances. Some people will produce a manuscript draft and work on and polish that; others will dictate their material and get a first typewritten draft to work on. In either case plenty of space should be left between lines (two to three in typed material) so that changes and corrections can be made clearly and easily. If possible colleagues should be asked to comment on this draft.

Second draft

This is normally typewritten on one side of A4 paper, in double-line spacing with wide margins to accommodate corrections. At this stage the insertion of illustrations is considered and suitable places in the text marked. Spelling should be standardized throughout the text, and the size of headings shown. The pages should not be bound or stapled together, as this makes insertions and corrections difficult. Pages (or folios as they are often called) should be numbered and if any extra pages are added later, these should be numbered 2a and so on.

The final length of the publication can be judged and printing methods can be discussed. The format of the final product also has to be considered. A5 and A4 are popular sizes in libraries because of their ease of production. However, one does see A4 folded twice to give a 'pocket leaflet'.

The cost of these operations has to be considered as well.

Final copy
For printing it is usual to produce final copy on single-sided A4, in double spacing. However, some less traditional methods call for different techniques. By setting tabulators on the typewriter or columns on a DTP system, three columns (or more) can be produced for two-fold A4 either to go on a stencil or to be reproduced by offset-litho. Similarly, A5 leaflets can be produced. Great care is needed to produce clean copy; this is essential if it is going directly on to an offset master for every fingerprint will be printed. The stencil is perhaps the most flexible form (after plain paper), since correction fluid can be used to remove errors. However, corrections may be apparent as unclear letters on the final print.

Printing and proofs
When using in-house offset-litho, the final copy is the end of the road; the copies are made from that master. In outside printing (most of which is still offset-litho) other stages usually take place. These are:

1 Galley or slip proofs. The printer will represent your original in a typeface you have selected with appropriate headings, italics, etc. Sometimes actual 'type' will be set but increasingly printers are using photosetting. Galleys are often just columns of print up to two feet long. These are checked for accuracy, and this is the last chance to make changes without great cost. (See British Standards Institution publication BS 5261, Part 2.)

2 Page proofs. The galleys are made up into actual pages with page numbers, headlines, etc. The positions of illustrations are shown. These pages are nowadays laid out on a board, ready for negatives to be made for printing.

3 Increasingly outside printers are able and willing to take copy from a customer on a computer disc straight from DTP software. This means that costs can be reduced; labour charges are kept down by the printer not have to set text for you. Changes are also easy since increasing or decreasing the amount of content is an electronic matter and you can see the effects on page layout on your own computer VDU immediately. There is the possibility of using the printer's own graphic staff to help improve covers etc. while still using the basic text from your computer.

Correcting proofs
The British Standards Institution has produced BS 5261 Parts 1 and 2

(1975 and 1976) and these are generally regarded as the 'bible' for proof correction.

Many local printers have a much smaller list of basic symbols that their staff are used to seeing and should be asked for copies of these if they undertake work for the library.

Binding
Most library materials are 'saddle stitched', that is, stapled through the folded edge. Some libraries use 'perfect' binding for booklets, but this tends to be expensive in comparison. In perfect binding all pages are cut as separate sheets and then glued together within the casing.

Copyright and libraries
In producing new library publications or allowing users to copy parts of items held within the library stock, attention must be paid to the legal requirements of the Copyright Act 1989. Libraries lend many types of copyright works including books, music, artistic works, gramophone records and cassettes. Some libraries also lend films and video tapes. The loan of these materials by libraries is in no way restricted by copyright law and there is usually no need to seek the permission of the copyright owner. Unfortunately the Copyright Act has made some confusion about the lending of some materials, for example CD and video recordings, and at the present time negotiations are under way with the licensing authorities acting for the rights' owners to resolve this situation. The Copyright Act includes a definition of the term 'library'. It is a very wide definition which really includes all types of library except commercial lending libraries which presumably have indirect profit-making motives.

Besides the lending of materials, most libraries offer a photocopying service and in this connection definite rules must be complied with if a library is to provide a copy of a periodical article without infringing copyright laws,

1 The library must be non-profit-making;
2 The person requesting the copy must satisfy the librarian that it is required for research or private study;
3 Only one copy of the article may be produced for any one person;
4 Only one article in a publication may be copied;
5 The person supplied with the article must pay the library a sum which covers the cost of its production;
6 A form of declaration should be completed and signed by the person requesting the copy. The form is normally set out as follows:

COPYRIGHT ACT
FORM OF DECLARATION AND UNDERTAKING
(Statutory Instrument 1957 no.868)

To. The librarian

PLEASE USE BLOCK CAPITALS

1)   I, (name). . . . .
of (firm) . . . .
(address) . . . .
. . . .
(postal code). . . . . .   Telephone . . . . . .
hereby request you to make and supply to me a copy of
the following periodical article which I require for the
purpose of research or private study.

NAME OF PERIODICAL . . . .
VOLUME/ISSUE NUMBER . . . DATE . . . PAGES . . .
AUTHOR OF ARTICLE . . . .
TITLE OF ARTICLE . . . .

2)   I have not previously been supplied with a copy of the
above-named article by any librarian.

3)   I undertake that if a copy is supplied to me, I will not
use it except for the purposes of research or private
study.

Signature. . . . .
Date   . . . .

Similar restrictions apply to copying parts of books, plays and musical scores, but in addition:

1 The part copied must not be a substantial part of the original.
2 If the name and address of the copyright owner are known to the librarian, he or she must seek that person's permission to make the copy.

Microform copies of entire works may not be made without the permission of the copyright owner, and the copying of gramophone records is not permitted at all.

Under the Copyright Act 1989 a number of bodies have been set up to collect fees for the copying of materials. In academic libraries, for example, it is possible to buy an annual licence from the Copyright Licensing Authority that will allow multiple copies to be made for classroom use provided they are given to students. Similar arrangements are in hand for electronic recordings from television. In time these will probably spread to other types of library.

Public Lending Right (PLR)

The Public Lending Right Act was passed in Great Britain in 1979 and two statutory instruments relating to the PLR scheme appeared in May 1982 (no. 719) and March 1983 (no. 480).

The Act of Parliament was passed in response to a demand by authors that they should receive payment from libraries for the loan to the public of books which those authors have written. This is on the grounds that sales of their books would increase and therefore the authors would receive a larger sum in royalties if members of the public were not able to borrow books free of charge from the public library. The 1979 Act recognized the authors' right to payment but the details of how the money was to be levied and paid to authors were not fixed until Statutory Instrument 480 received parliamentary approval in 1982.

The scheme operates in the following way. The author must complete a separate application for each book he or she has written in order to register in the PLR scheme. If a second or subsequent edition is published, a new registration form must be submitted. Payment will not be made to authors who are not registered. Joint authors up to a maximum of two must register on the same application form as the main or first-named author. Payment will not be made to any of the co-authors unless all are registered. If one of the co-authors dies before registering in the PLR scheme, the other(s) cannot register either and therefore have to forego payment. An illustrator of a book is deemed to be a co-author and is therefore eligible for registration, but editors, compilers and translators are not eligible. Co-authors have to agree the proportion of payment which each is to receive and this is stated on the registration form. Authors must register in their own name and not use a pseudonym or maiden name under which the book may be written.

Payment of the author is based on the number of times the book is borrowed and purchased by libraries. This raises the anomaly of reference books or books put into the lending stocks of some libraries and the reference collections of others. A further anomaly is that payment is based on loans from public libraries. Loans from university, college, school, industrial and other special libraries are not considered. Furthermore, to be eligible for the PLR scheme a book must have a minimum of 32 pages, or 24 pages if it is mainly poetry or drama.

The method for determining the number of loans is as follows. Sixteen public libraries are selected as a sample and these libraries send a monthly issue record to the PLR office. Ten of the selected libraries have book issues of more than 500,000 per year, the remaining ones have fewer than 500,000. The record is in the form of a magnetic tape or cassette, therefore the libraries chosen are ones operating a computer-based issuing system such as data pen. The PLR office extracts the information about loans of registered books from these tapes so the participating libraries are involved in very little extra work. The PLR computer compares the file of registered authors/registered editions of their works with the file of loans computed from the 16 libraries. The use of ISBNs makes this task easier, but where a book has no ISBN some other identification such as a BNB or LASER 'ff' number is used.

The resultant figure is grossed up so that payment can be calculated. There is a fixed minimum payment and a fixed maximum payment. The sums paid are taken from a central PLR fund. Payments to authors commenced in the spring of 1984.

Assignments

1   Collect three different samples of library publications and comment on their method of production.

2   List the ten symbols in BS 5261 that you think are likely to be the most used ones.

3   Use a word processing system and try to see how this eases production when compared to traditional typing. If available try a DTP system on a similar basis.

4   Outline the headings of a library booklet you would like to produce. Give reasons for the quantity of copies you suggest should be made and select the appropriate printing method.

Bibliography

British Standards Institution, *BS 5261*, Parts 1 and 2, London, British Standards Institution, 1975 and 1976.

Hansen, Richard E., *Manager's guide to copying and duplicating*, London, McGraw, 1980.

Jennett, Sean, *The making of books*, 5th ed., London, Faber, 1973.

Writers and artists yearbook 1990, London, A. and C. Black, 1990.

Guidelines in pamphlet form have been produced by The Library Association for:

Copyright in industrial and commercial libraries (2nd ed., 1990)
Copyright in National Health Service libraries (1st ed., 1990)
Copyright in polytechnic and university libraries (2nd ed., 1990)
Copyright in public libraries (2nd ed., 1990)
Copyright in school and college libraries (2nd ed., 1990)

These are available (free to Library Association members) from the LA's Professional Practice Division.

Chapter Twelve

Information technology in libraries

Information Technology (IT) is a term that covers a multitude of things. Originally it was applied to the use and application of computers, but recently the definition of what is a computer has become more complicated. The problem is illustrated by considering most modern photocopiers – they have processors more powerful than the computers of the era when the term 'IT' was first used. In this chapter we have used the term 'IT' widely, to embrace the newer definitions and to include more traditional office machines since their use is related to the new equipment.

Online computer services

Most library services have means of accessing the ever-increasing number of specialist databases that are 'hosted' on large computers, often in other countries. To use these services a number of items of equipment are required. These include a personal computer (PC) (or terminal capable of accessing the public telephone system), a modem that allows you to transmit from your PC to the host computer and therby access the particular database that is of interest, a printer and the permissions necessary to get into the database.

The use of a PC is best since it allows (with prior permission to use the database) the downloading of information from the database into the PC for later scanning by staff in order to check its suitability to meet a user's request. This is an important feature since once the information is loaded into the PC it enables the costly telephone links to be broken and all further manipulation of the data to be done locally. It is easy to use a standard word processing package to present the results of the search in an attractive way for the end user.

Access to databases requires that the library registers with the database host. Normally the initial registration is free and a password allowing access is issued. Some hosts require a guaranteed amount of use and so an advance payment in anticipation of use has to be made. The library also, in most cases, has to purchase manuals to train staff in the use of the database, including how to identify the detailed contents of each database on the host computer. If you want the host to print off material found during a search, you will be charged an additional fee. Sometimes it is more economic to print at the host than to pay telephone bills while the data is transferred down the telephone line to your computer. The deciding factor will be the speed at which that transfer of data can take place.

Speed of transferring data between the host and your PC is determined by the quality of the modem you are using and the host computer. The modems most commonly used are able to operate at 1200 baud − this is the speed of Prestel − but some are much slower at 300 baud while very expensive ones can go over 2400 baud. A baud is a measure of the number of 'bits' per second that can be sent down the telephone line. Some hosts have a number of entry points, called ports, to their computer and can set each of them to a different baud rate. Often a different telephone number is allocated to each port so that you dial into the port set for the speed of your modem. Some hosts only have a set speed and you can go no faster than that regardless of the modem.

As we said above, many hosts are based outside the UK. Users of those will join the British Telecom (BT) Package Switching System (PSS) that allows you to dial all over the world using software and networks provided by BT. Again there is a fee for this service and a password is needed before any connections can be made.

Examples of the hosts available are as follows.

1   DataStar. They provide 200 databases at charges ranging from £20 to £80 per hour of connect time. They allow the downloading of information into a PC but charge a fee for this facility. The databases are varied but are strong in business, company, and biomedical information.

2   DIALOG. The world's largest host, based in the USA. Over 400 databases are hosted on their computers. They do not charge a joining fee or minimum use fee, but an annual fee for updates etc. is payable (£35). Database charges vary from £10 to £150 per connect hour. They also host a low-cost version of their system, called the Knowledge Index, which gives access to 80 databases at a flat fee of around £18 per connect hour.

3   ESA/IRS. Hosted on the European Space Agency's computer and marketed in the UK by the Department of Trade and Industry (DTI). Some 100 databases are hosted, chiefly dealing with technical subjects. Charges are lower than many other systems.

4 LEXIS/NEXIS. LEXIS is a full-text database giving law information for the USA, England, Scotland, Ireland, France, the Commonwealth and the EC. NEXIS is a full-text information system based upon newspaper and magazine articles. Charges are fairly high but the information is very good. A prepayment is usually necessary.

5 ORBIT. Contains around 100 databases, mainly scientific and technical patents. Charges are around £100 per connect hour.

6 BLAISE. The British Library host that allows access to a number of useful sources of information for librarians. The chief one is the MARC data that gives all the bibliographic information contained in the *BNB*. This allows online searching to create subject lists and find publication details. It is also possible to order items that users request directly from the BLLD via BLAISE.

Using the systems

When using these systems, it is necessary to define exactly what it is that the user requires since both the telephone charges and the database royalties can be high. In fact the procedure is very much the same as when answering a reference enquiry − you must ask questions to get a very specific idea of what is required. There is no point in connecting (or logging-on) to a host and hoping that you can work it out as you go along.

Most hosts allow you to search by a number of clearly defined fields (an area of the record that is specially indexed). Some of these are freetext, every word is indexed; some are controlled as in a thesaurus and specific definitions are expected. The terms can usually be combined by what is known as Boolean logic, that is to say that the words, 'and', 'not' and 'or' as well as brackets can be used to define the search closely.

An example might be that a user asks for information on engineering. This is too wide and would find many thousands of records on a specialist database. After questioning it might be reduced to motor engineering − still too large − and later to car engines − still too large, possibly. You could end up with a request for engines for Ford motor cars and pistons in particular. The searcher would look at any thesaurus and might find that 'pistons' is indexed and that 'automobile engines' is used also. So the search could look like this:

'pistons and automobile engines and Ford'

This instruction tells the computer that each term must be in every record before it is acceptable. If the instruction had been:

'automobile engines or (pistons and Ford)'

the computer would have given any record for automobile engines and also any records where Ford and pistons were given – a much wider result than the first.

Teletext services

Teletext was invented by the BBC, which saw the possibility of being able to provide subtitles to their programmes for the benefit of deaf people. The concept has been developed into the most widely used electronic information system in the country. Millions of television viewers use the CEEFAX and ORACLE services of the BBC and IBA to get sporting, political, holiday, programme, weather and business information every day.

The system uses a small computer to hold the pages of information that are then transmitted as part of the picture signal. To enable this to happen, several of the 625 lines that make up the UK television picture have been 'removed' and converted to carry that data for the teletext pages. The frequency with which each page is transmitted varies so that index pages are sent more frequently than other pages.

A television equipped to receive teletext (or in more modern sets Fasttext) is required and this set will have a handset that allows both channel changing and access to the pages of information. The user keys in the page (e.g. p.100 for the main menu) and waits for that page to be next transmitted. Once the microprocessor in the television receives the page it puts it on the screen, either blanking out the picture or superimposing it over the picture, depending upon the user's decision. He or she can then move through the pages by keying in the next page number.

Fasttext is a more advanced system in which the microprocessor can store several pages at once. You can also program it to link special pages that you use regularly and it will hold them in the latest updated version all the time. This means that for many pages you get almost instant page changes, unlike the older version where 20 seconds or more can be spent waiting for a page to arrive.

Libraries find the system useful since it gives current news, stock market prices and so on to users at a very low cost. It is also easy to use and so training is virtually nil.

Prestel

A similar service to teletext is the Prestel system originated by British Telecom in 1979. This uses a main frame computer linking the television or special Prestel set by telephone line. Its operation is similar to Teletext but is much faster since there is no wait for a cycle of pages to be sent. Many thousands of pages are available and there are also special user groups on the system. To gain access to these you need to join and pay a fee, as for online systems.

There are hosts on Prestel for educational users that allow computer software to be downloaded. A base for legal information is also available.

Since Prestel is an interactive system − you can send messages from your keypad − it is possible to place orders for goods and services direct to anyone putting up a page. Businesses often use it for booking hotel rooms or tickets for journeys. Many Prestel information packages can be recorded on to a blank floppy disc inserted into the microcomputer; the charge for this facility appears on the screen. Alternatively, numerous commercially produced programmes on floppy disc are available for purchase and the microcomputer and monitor can be used for playback of these programmes.

Costs are charged on the normal telephone bill and include the calls and the hosts' charges for using their services. You have to join the Prestel service and obtain a password.

Fax services

Another information transmission system that is rapidly becoming important in libraries is the facsimile transmission or fax service. This uses standard telephone lines and a special machine that looks and works a little like a small photocopier. The machine scans a page of text and converts it so that it can be sent over the telephone to a similar machine anywhere in the world. At the other end it is printed out and is ready for immediate use. The charges are standard telephone calls plus the price of the paper that you print out on to − once the machine has been paid for, of course.

The advent of fax allows libraries to deliver periodical articles from one branch to another quickly and could, therefore, save on subscriptions. Interlibrary loans of a few pages in length can easily be made by this method. Some libraries are offering fax as a service to the community and making a profit on the activity.

The cost of fax machines varies according to features such as speed of transmission and error-correcting facilities, but at a basic level can be less than £800. Indeed a small machine just launched (1990) offers the businessman or home user a combined fax, answering machine and telephone for that price. The error-correcting facility is useful since it enables the two machines to talk to each other to ensure that noisy telephone lines have not distorted the signal. Distortion will lead to incorrect data being printed out.

Telex

Telex is another development in the field of telecommunications for transmitting text, and it is proving its worth in quite a number of libraries. The equipment consists of a teleprinter, which resembles a typewriter, and a dialling unit. Each telex machine is connected by direct line to an automatic telex exchange.

Each subscriber's installation is given a telex number and an individual identification signal known as the answer-back code, both of which appear in the UK *Telex directory*. The *Telex directory* is arranged in two sections: the first has entries in subscriber order (like a telephone directory); the second is arranged in answerback order. A telex subscriber can contact any other telex subscriber in this country merely by dialling. When the call is connected, the distant machine automatically sends its own answerback code for identification by the caller as a check that he or she is through to the number required. The sender then types the message on the telex keyboard and the typed message appears in black and white on a roll of paper on both the sender's machine and the receiver's machine. Subscribers in the UK can communicate at any time of day or night, even when the receiving library is closed and the machine unattended. The receiving machine automatically identifies itself, and then records the message on the telex roll to be read and dealt with later.

Advantages of telex

1 Speed of communication. It is much quicker than the postal service and is excellent for interlibrary loan requests.
2 Flexible timing. There is no need for a human recipient to be present at the time of communication as the message is recorded and stored. It is useful where one library's hours differ from another's.

Disadvantages of telex

1 Possibility of breakdown of machine or failure due to power cut.
2 Slips of telex paper can be easily lost or defaced. Requests, if not dealt with speedily, may be forgotten if no other record is kept. Telex operators usually have to spend a lot of time chasing requests.
3 Open to error. The operator may make more mistakes when using a keyboard than when writing by hand.
4 Cost. There is a connection charge and an annual rental plus a charge for each call at rates which vary according to the distance between centres. In order to cut costs, some libraries have machines with the facility of pre-producing messages on perforated tape. This tape can then be fed into the machine when the telex connection is made to ensure that the message is transmitted at the maximum speed.

Computers

In many libraries computers are used extensively by staff and members through the computer cataloguing systems or OPAC systems. Computers are not new in libraries; some of the largest computer systems in the world are holding library information. (See Chapter Six).

The advent of the PC in its cheap form has offered additional opportunities for libraries to extend services. Many now hire out software for use in PCs and have machines on open access for users. Many academic libraries encourage students to prepare course work by using word processing packages and by so doing they get used to the operation of computers. Indeed, in some colleges teaching packages have been prepared and placed in the library to enable students to study part of their course by computer-assisted learning methods (CAL).

Some public libraries are buying commercially available CAL packages and offering them either for use within the library or at home. Copyright is a significant problem in this respect; some libraries consider the difficulties too great and have stopped buying software.

It is helpful in doing library work to understand some of the terminology of computing. Some of the more commonly used terms are explained below:

VDU   Visual Display Unit, or the screen upon which the images appear. This may be green, brown, white or full colour.

Hardware   those parts of the computer that you can touch: the keyboard, screen, printer etc.

Software   those parts that make the computer work, often called programs or operating system. Confusingly some modern software is in the form of hardware. (It comes in the form of a 'chip').

Hard disc   the storage system that is inside (but can be a separate hardware box outside) the computer that stores your information. Hard discs come in various sizes and are measured by megabytes (mb); e.g. 80mb is a large hard disc for a PC but very small for a minicomputer.

Floppy disc   a small storage disc that usually contains a program or stored information. It is easy to transport or post. Easily damaged.

Program   software that makes things happen within the computer; e.g. a word processing package is a program. You load it from a floppy disc, usually on to your hard disc, and then use it.

Network   a way of linking computers so that they can work together. There are many different names, both brand names of systems and types of networks. One of the more common is local area network (LAN), often used to link a single library's computers together. When a network links computers over large distances it is called a wide area network (WAN).

Memory that part of the computer that allows it to manipulate data, often called the 'brain' of the computer.

Port a socket on the back of the computer that allows connections to be made to other hardware or computers.

Operating system usually a form of software on a chip that allows the computer to run all the activities that make it work. The two most used are MS DOS and UNIX.

Chip small devices that carry instructions or circuits and make up the working parts of modern computers. Memory is held on a chip and fixed to a board.

Board a board carries the chips and other parts of the computer and provides links between the various elements fixed to the board.

Electronic mail services

Electronic Mail (Email) is a system that has been around for many years, and the largest in the UK is the Telecom Gold service of British Telecom. That can be used as a traditional Email service but it also has facilities for sending fax and telex messages. Therefore in one service the library can have access to many. It can also enable you to use some databases similar to those mentioned above. A PC is used for access.

One of the services most used is the mailbox facility where you can join a group (such as LANET – the Library Associations Network) and have an 'address' or box number that any other member can use to send messages to you. Likewise you can send electronic mail to all other members.

Charges depend on the range of services you choose to use, but basic charges are telephone line charges, a registration fee and a charge per unit of data transmitted.

Many versions of Email exist and it is common for groups of librarians in a library service to have their PCs linked in an area network so that they can exchange information electronically. Once this is done, a local Email service can be put into action for those groups of people. This allows instant communication and response without any paper intervention or postal delay. The use of passwords can also mean that information can be fully confidential. These PCs can, of course, also be linked into the library computer system and out into the wider world of online searching. The networking possibilities of the computer increase each day and it is slowly getting easier to make different types of computer talk to each other.

In universities and polytechnics a computer network called JANET (Joint Academic Network) is in place to allow research papers and ideas to be 'published' in the form of an Email or bulletin board (see below).

The library services of those institutions also use the system to make their OPACs available to each other.

Bulletin boards

There are several commercial bulletin board services (BBS) available. Mostly they are for commercial use and allow companies to keep customers up to date with product information. Some are put up by computer clubs and specialize in software and ideas for the particular make of computer concerned. They are a little like Email in that once you are a member you can leave messages and read messages – but they are open to all, hence the title of bulletin board.

Details of these services are published regularly in the computer journals.

CD-ROM

CD-ROM stands for compact disc-read only memory. It has had an increasing impact upon the library world since it moved from being a superior type of record to a data storage system. Companies are now publishing encyclopaedias and databases in the CD format. A special CD player (similar to but slightly different from the CD player used for records) is linked to a PC and the contents of the CD-ROM are then accessible on the computer screen. This information may include text, pictures or moving images as well as sound. To give an idea of the storage capacity, one recently published encyclopaedia, containing many volumes, filled only about 20% of one CD-ROM disc.

Perhaps the most common CD-ROMs available in libraries are *Whitaker's bookbank* and the MARC databank from the BL.

Once linked to a printer, the computer and CD player offer fast searches and printouts, without any telephone connections. Full colour is available on many discs. The discs are small (about the size of a 45rpm record), silver coloured and coated to protect the information encoded on them. They are tough and handle well, making them suitable for use in public places.

At present it is difficult to network most of the systems available and so a separate player is needed for each location. Some libraries have invested in a carousel player that takes several discs and allows the user to select one at a time – this saving loading the discs one after another. It also helps prevent accidental damage while a disc is not in the player.

Office machines and equipment

Office practice forms part of the day-to-day routine in all types of library; therefore office machinery will be included in a library's inventory. Of prime importance, of course, is the typewriter, which will be used for correspondence, compilation of booklists and bulletins, typing of readers' tickets and 101 other routine tasks. The electric typewriter ensures even pressure and produces a more attractive appearance. Offset-litho masters must be produced on an electric typewriter using a special litho ribbon with a high grease content. A golf-ball typewriter is very useful as a variety of typefaces can be used, thus giving a very professional look to home-produced reports and booklists. Modern typewriters of this type are often fitted with an erasing tape which enables typing errors to be corrected by using a special back-spacing key, retyping the incorrect letter to obliterate it and then typing the correct letter on top. This gives a much more satisfactory result than that achieved by the use of erasers or erasing fluid. Sophisticated typewriters are available, such as the varityper, which produces a layout like a page of a book with straight margins at both sides of the text, and the tape-typewriter, which produces punched tape. Larger libraries will have word processors which may be linked to a DTP. This allows professional quality to be achieved by ordinary library staff. It certainly allows typists who are not the most skilful to produce better quality work since error correction is very easy with word processors; also most come with a spelling checker, which can also be an aid in correcting errors. However, total reliance on this latter feature is a mistake since it checks wrongly spelled words but not correctly spelled words used wrongly.

Other office equipment to be found in libraries may include the following.

Adding machines or calculators are used to cope with statistics related to petty cash, issues, membership and so on. Some machines have a visual display and others produce a paper printout.

Addressing machines/addressographs are used in libraries which offer a regular postal service to their clientele. Each client's address is typed on a mini-stencil protected by a cardboard mount, and these are filed in sequence ready for use on the machine, which acts like a mini-printer. A similar feature is available in the better word processing packages. This allows for names and addresses to be stored once and then used on many occasions, both by filling in spaces in letters to personalize them and also to produce the address block for posting.

Franking machines are obtainable from the Post Office and other suppliers. They enable letters and parcels to be weighed by library staff and franked to show the correct amount instead of sticking on postage stamps. Franking machines offer the advantages of dispensing with the purchase and stocking of sheets of stamps of varying values and also of speeding up delivery — franked items go straight to the sorting office.

Telephones are essential and are used to receive reference enquiries and telephone renewals as well as for outgoing calls by library staff.

Reprographic equipment

Reprographic equipment of one kind or another is to be found in practically every library. The most common item of equipment is the coin-in-the-slot photocopier provided for public use. The term 'photocopier' is loosely used as most of these copiers do not work on photographic principles.

Electrostatic copying machines

The electrostatic process, sometimes known as xerography, was invented in the USA in 1938. Machines are available for purchase or rental from manufacturers and a fee is paid for each copy produced. The rental charge includes a maintenance agreement and engineers come at very short notice to repair faults. On balance, most libraries prefer to own their equipment than rent it.

The type of copier required by most libraries is a simple, basic machine which will produce a single-sided copy from an original book, periodical or document. Large and complex machines are available which will automatically produce double-sided copies and will collate multiple copies of successive pages. Some machines also have a reduction and/or enlargement facility, for instance A3 to A4 and from A4 to A5 and vice versa. However, the majority of libraries would not make use of such complex features and prefer the small, table-top models which will do a basic job satisfactorily.

Method

The original, which may be an opened book, periodical, document or illustration, is placed face downwards on the glass platen of the machine. A rubber blanket or lid is then brought over the top of the original to cut out extraneous light. Machines have indicators so that the original and resultant copy are correctly aligned.

When the power is switched on, the money or photocopy card inserted and the print button pressed, a light source within the machine shines on to the original. The image is then reflected via a series of mirrors on to an electrically charged, rotating selenium drum. The charge on the drum is discharged over those areas which correspond with the white or background areas of the original but the charge remains on those areas corresponding with the black text or illustrations. What remains on the selenium drum is therefore an inverted, invisible latent image.

Next a carbon powder or toner is shaken over the selenium drum. The powder adheres to the parts of the drum where the electrical charge remains but does not stick to the drum where the charge has been dispersed. The inverted image now appears in visible form on the drum. A sheet of copy paper is drawn into the machine from the feed tray and the paper is electrically charged before it comes into contact with the selenium drum. The carbon powder transfers from the drum to the paper because it is drawn by an opposite electrical charge. At this stage the powder is just 'sitting' on the paper and would be easily smudged, so before the copy appears in the take-up tray the image is fixed by exposure to heat. The selenium drum is automatically cleaned by rotating in contact with a brush so loose particles of powder are removed in readiness for the next copy to be made.

As described, the process appears to be lengthy but it is really very rapid and the copy is produced in a few seconds. As stated earlier, the main purpose of electrostatic copiers is to produce single copies, but they will produce multiple copies very rapidly. Most machines are fitted with a preselect button so that one can set the required number. The machine will stop automatically when the correct number of copies have been ejected. However, if multiple copies are required, other types of reprographic equipment may be preferable because of their economy.

Advantages of electrostatic copying

1 Simplicity of operation. The process is a direct one from original to copy without the production of any intermediate master.
2 Speed of production of copies.
3 Copies are of a high quality with dense black on white or, on appropriate machines, in full colour. In fact, the intensity of the image can be adjusted so that the copy is sometimes better than the original.
4 Run-off paper is not expensive unless special coated paper is used for colour work or covers.
5 Copies do not fade, even when kept for a considerable period.

Disadvantages

1 Difficulty may be experienced when coloured originals are copied on black and white machines as certain colours, notably blue, do not copy well.
2 If the machine is in constant use the selenium drum may not be cleaned sufficiently and stray particles of carbon will appear as minute black spots on the copies. If this problem worsens, the copies will tend to have a dirty appearance.

3 Paper sometimes becomes jammed in the machine, and great care must be taken in removing it, otherwise the selenium drum may be damaged.
4 Rented machines are expensive in the long term.

Spirit duplicating machines

Spirit duplication is probably the cheapest and easiest of the reprographic methods available. The quality of the copies produced, however, does not compare favourably with some other methods, notably offset-lithography. Nevertheless, a spirit duplicator could be very useful in a children's library for the production of project work-sheets or quiz forms. Sometimes the process is referred to by the name of Banda, but this is really a trade name for one make of spirit duplicator, Fordigraph being another. The method is outlined below.

Materials and equipment

One can purchase blank paper masters from commercial suppliers. The master has a glossy side coated with kaolin and an uncoated reverse side. It is also necessary to have a supply of 'carbons'. These have no carbon content but resemble typewriter carbon paper, hence the loose usage of the term. Actually, they are sheets of paper coated with aniline dye which is commonly dark blue or purple, although rainbow packs are obtainable which include red, blue, green, yellow, brown and black. There is also a choice of long-run or short-run carbons to match the number of copies to be produced. A short-run carbon is suitable for up to 100 copies and a long-run carbon will produce about 300. In addition, a supply of coated, non-absorbent run-off paper is required on which the copies will be produced. Lastly, one needs a spirit duplicating machine and a supply of spirit solvent with which to top up the solvent container incorporated in the machine.

Preparation of a master

To prepare a master manually, a master sheet must be placed on top of a carbon so that the glossy side of the master and the dye-coated side of the carbon are in contact. Using a pencil or ballpoint pen, the text or diagram is written, printed or drawn on the uncoated upper surface of the master, using firm pressure on a hard smooth surface. This transfers the dye from the carbon to the coated side of the master, leaving a reverse image of what appears on the upper surface. Coloured work is achieved by using different colours of carbon for various parts of the image.

The master may also be produced by using a typewriter, but a backing sheet should be used. The typescript will be fuzzy and indistinct without the smooth, firm surface which the backing sheet offers.

A further method of producing a master is to use a thermal (heat) copier. To do this the original image or typescript must be on a single sheet of paper and it must have a carbon content. A special hectofilm unit is required. This is just a dye sheet attached to a master sheet to make a combined unit especially designed for use with a thermal copier. The original must be placed image-upwards in a carrier and the hectofilm unit placed on top of the original. The hectofilm unit will probably have a tissue interleaf and this should be removed. The carrier containing both items is then fed into the rotating rollers of the thermal copier and as it proceeds through the machine it activates an infra-red light. The heat produced causes the transfer of dye to the master at those areas which correspond with the carbon image on the original. Masters produced on a thermal copier are of one colour throughout. Nowadays one can purchase pre-prepared masters and sometimes these are incorporated into educational books.

Production of copies
The spirit duplicating machine is prepared for use by placing a stack of run-off paper in the feed tray. It is wise to fan the paper to separate the sheets and let air in between them, otherwise several sheets might stick together and clog up the machine. The fluid control button should then be moved to the 'on' position and the priming button pressed several times. This causes spirit fluid to moisten the felt pad in the duplicator. The prepared master is clamped around the metal drum so that the dye image is outermost. Then the drum is rotated manually, or automatically if an electrically operated duplicator is used. At each rotation, one sheet of paper is fed into the machine where it is dampened with the spirit solvent. The moistened paper then comes into contact with the master and the spirit solvent causes the transfer of one layer of dye from the master to the copy paper. The copy is then ejected into a take-up tray where it quickly dries. As more and more copies are produced, so the amount of dye on the master is reduced layer by layer until the image on the copy paper becomes quite faint. To compensate for the decreasing amount of dye, one can adjust the pressure control knob and press the copy paper more firmly to the master.

Advantages of spirit duplication
1   The equipment is cheap compared with that for other methods and the materials are comparable in cost.
2   The preparation of masters is simple and speedy.

3 Multi-coloured copies are easy to produce and there is no problem with register.
4 Errors on the master can be erased by gently removing the layer of dye with a razor blade.
5 No skill is required in operating the machine.
6 Machines are robust and need very little maintenance.

Disadvantages

1 Copies are not of high quality. The text may appear slightly fuzzy, especially if the characters are as small as those produced by typewriter.
2 The number of copies that can be produced is limited.
3 Copies tend to fade, especially if left exposed to daylight or if some of the colours are not strong to begin with.
4 The operator needs to exercise care in handling materials to prevent dye from colouring the fingers.

Absorption duplicating machines

Absorption duplication is probably better known by trade names such as Roneo and Gestetner or by the term 'stencil duplicating'. One may occasionally hear it referred to as 'cyclostyling' or 'mimeographing'. It is a widely used method which produces good quality copies at very reasonable cost. The method involves the following procedure.

Materials and equipment

A stencil is the basic requirement for this process and it can be of several types:

1 A stencil designed for use with a typewriter. This consists of a thin sheet of paper, similar to tissue paper but coated with wax, which is attached to a thicker paper backing sheet, and with a sheet of carbon as an interleaf between the two.
2 A thermic stencil which is similar in appearance to the ordinary stencil but has a thinner wax sheet. There is no carbon interleaf but instead a sheet of tissue is attached to the unit so that it completely covers the upper surface of the waxed sheet. Thermic stencils are specially designed for use with a thermal copier.
3 A paper-based or plastic stencil designed for 'cutting' on an electronic stencil cutter. On the latter a wax coating covers a thin sheet of plastic which is attached to a paper backing sheet. Plastic stencils are especially good for reproducing half-tone illustrations.

The run-off paper must be thick and absorbent to cope with the thick layer of ink deposited on it by the duplicator. The duplicating machine and a supply of ink are the final requirements.

Preparation of a master

To enable ink to penetrate the wax sheet and thus come into contact with the copy paper, the wax coating must be removed in areas corresponding to the required text or diagram. One can do this manually by using a stylus or a cutting tool designed for that purpose, but the most common method is to use a typewriter. The ribbon must be disengaged so that the metal type strikes the wax sheet directly. This ensures that the wax is cleanly cut and the characters are sharp. Problems can arise if an inexperienced typist strikes the keys too strongly as enclosed letters such as 'o' tend to drop out. Also, continued contact with the waxy surface may clog up the type. To prevent these problems arising, some stencils are covered by a thin transparent plastic top sheet which meets the type yet does not prevent the cutting of the wax surface beneath. A carbon interleaf allows one to see what has been typed.

If a thermal copier is to be used in the preparation of the master, a special thermic stencil must be employed and the original text or diagram must be pre-prepared on a single sheet. The image must also have carbon content in order to activate the thermal copier. The original is placed face upwards on the stencil's backing sheet, the wax sheet is then placed over it and the tissue sheet on top of that. The thermic stencil is then fed through the rollers of the thermal copier where it activates an infra-red lamp. The heat melts the wax on those areas which correspond with the image areas of the original, and the melted wax is absorbed into the tissue sheet.

An electric stencil cutting machine has twin cylinders which rotate together on the same plane. The original, which must be a single sheet of text and/or illustrations, is clamped around the left hand cylinder and a special stencil fastened around the other cylinder. As both drums rotate, a photo-electric scanning device travels line by line over the surface of the original, detecting light and dark areas. Whenever the scanner 'reads' an image area it activates a stylus which correspondingly travels line by line across the stencil. The stylus emits tiny sparks which cut minute holes in the surface of the stencil.

Production of copies

If the stencil has a carbon interleaf, that must be removed. The top edge of the stencil is then attached to the cylinder of the duplicating machine using the slots or perforations provided. The waxed sheet must be in contact with the cylinder. While the stencil is held taut, the cylinder is slowly rotated until the bottom edge of the wax sheet can be clamped in position. Wrinkling or creasing of the wax sheet must be avoided. The ink supply will have been checked and the cylinder rotated manually a few times while the inking lever is depressed. This ensures an even ink flow. The paper backing sheet can then be removed (leaving only the wax sheet around the cylinder). A supply of copy paper should be fanned out and stacked in the feed tray and this must be raised to the correct level for feeding into the machine. One or two copies may be produced manually to see whether the image is properly aligned and the margins are correct. The machine can then be switched to automatic and it will produce the number of copies stipulated by the preset counter. With each rotation of the cylinder, ink is forced through the holes in the waxed stencil and this ink is deposited on the copy paper as it is fed into the machine.

One stencil will normally produce up to 5000 copies though it is claimed that 7500 copies may be obtained from a good quality stencil. If a stencil is carefully removed from the cylinder after use and blotted to remove excess ink, it can be stored and reused.

Advantages of absorption duplication

1 Equipment and materials are cheap.
2 Stencils are easily prepared by a variety of methods.
3 Errors on the stencil are easily rectified by coating with correction fluid and then writing or typing on top.
4 Duplicating machines are easy to operate.
5 A considerable number of copies can be produced from one stencil.
6 A good black-and-white image is achieved and there is no fading even when copies are stored for a lengthy period.
7 Stencils are reusable.

Disadvantages

1 The layer of ink deposited is thick and this necessitates the use of absorbent copy paper with a rough texture.
2 Multi-colour work is difficult. The cylinder must be thoroughly cleaned before another colour of ink is used or the whole cylinder must be lifted out and replaced by another.
3 The operator may get ink on hands and clothing.

Offset-litho machines
The basic principle of offset-lithography is that grease and water are

mutually repellent. Legend has it that the principle underlying lithography was discovered quite by chance by a Bavarian printer named Senefelder (c.1796). One day he was sitting on a large stone on a Bavarian hillside eating his picnic lunch when it began to rain heavily. He stood up and began to collect his belongings when he noticed something odd about the stone he had been sitting on. Although the rain was falling on the stone, it was not completely wet but showed a pattern of parallel lines where the rain water was not being absorbed by the porous stone. He realized that the lines corresponded to the ridges of his greasy corduroy trousers. Some grease had been transferred to the surface of the stone and the grease was repelling the rain water. Senefelder pondered over this fact as he walked back to the printing shop and decided that the principle could be put to use in printing.

Lithography as a printing process dates from the nineteenth century. Porous Bavarian limestone was used as this absorbs grease and water equally. The stone was first levelled to give a perfectly flat surface, then grained to give either a fine or coarse finish. The artist then drew, sketched or painted on the grained surface using greasy crayon, pen, brush or even a finger. Normally black crayon or ink was used so that the artist could see the image, but otherwise the colour was of no importance. As the surface would pick up any grease, the artist had to be careful not to leave unwanted fingerprints or greasy marks on the stone – they would show up in printing. However, chemicals could be used to remove unwanted grease or to 'fix' the required greasy drawing.

On completion of the drawing, the stone was placed in a flat-bed printing machine, where it was wetted by damping rollers. The water was absorbed by the non-image background areas but rejected by the greasy areas. The stone was then 'inked-up' by the inking rollers and this time the greasy ink adhered to the greasy image but was repelled by the dampened background areas. The impression cylinder then pressed paper against the stone and the image was transferred to the paper.

In later years zinc or aluminium plates were used instead of stone as these were cheaper, less heavy and easier to store. The metal plates were grained to give a roughened surface which would hold ink or water.

Offset-lithography

With offset-lithography, there is no direct contact between the plate and the copy paper. Instead the image is first transferred to an intermediate surface, that is, a blanket roller, and it is this which comes into contact with the copy paper. The image is the right way round on the master, reversed on the blanket cylinder and the right way round once more on the copy paper. The first offset-litho machine (1875) was a flat-bed machine in which the image was transferred from card to metal and then to paper. Rotary machines are now used in which the image is transferred from a master or plate to a rubber blanket stretched tightly around the blanket cylinder and then to the copy paper.

Making a master or plate

1   Direct image masters. Paper masters are available on which the image can be produced manually using a special pen containing greasy ink or by a typewriter using a special offset ribbon which has a high grease content. The image should be on the surface of the plate, so it is important to use an electric typewriter which gives even pressure. Typing errors cannot be obliterated with a normal erasing fluid as this would print and appear as a blotch on the copies. Special erasers are available which gently remove the greasy letters ready for retyping. Care must be taken not to get greasy fingerprints on the master.

2   Paper plates produced by an electrostatic plate-maker. The original, which may be a single typed or manually produced sheet, a montage or a book or periodical, is placed face downwards on the glass platen of the electrostatic copier. A rubber blanket or hinged lid covers the original to cut out extraneous light and then, at the push of a button, paper is fed into the machine and charged with electricity. A light then scans the original and the light is bounced back on to the charged paper. Light is reflected from the white or background areas of the original and action of the light on the paper dissipates the electrical charge. No light is reflected from the black or image areas, so the charge remains in the paper in areas corresponding to the image. When a coloured original is used, the machine can 'read' the colours only as different intensities of black or white, therefore some colours, particularly blue, do not reproduce well. As the powder is shaken on to it, the toner particles adhere to the electrically charged areas of the paper, thus forming a visible image. This image is then fixed by the action of a chemical solution and dried by heat before it emerges as a plate ready for printing.

There are various qualities of paper plate for short (150 copies), medium (1000 copies) or long (3000 copies) runs.

3   Metal plates produced by a photographic process. Sensitized aluminium plates produced photographically or on a plate-making machine utilizing ultra-violet light give the longest runs (25,000 to 40,000 copies) and the best quality copies. Professional printers use only metal plates. These plates can be stored and used again time after time provided they are wiped over with a gum solution after each use to prevent oxidization.

4   Polyester plates. These are a fairly recent innovation and give good

results. Up to 5000 copies can be produced from a polyester plate. Plates can be stored and reused.

5   Litho scan plates produced on an electronic scanner. With this method, the original text, illustration or montage must be on a flat sheet of paper. This is clamped around the left-hand cylinder of the electronic scanner. A blank plate is then clamped around the right-hand cylinder. When the machine is set in motion a scanning device travels backwards and forwards over the original as it rotates, and transmits an electronic signal whenever it 'reads' a black or image area. This signal activates a sparking device which cuts holes in the rotating plate to correspond with the image areas of the original.

Printing or duplicating on an offset-litho machine

The paper, polyester or metal plate is clamped around the plate cylinder on the machine. Fountain solution (water with additives which make it less miscible with ink and slow down evaporation) is transferred from the fount tray via a series of fountain rollers until it comes into contact with the plate. The background areas of the plate are dampened by the fountain solution but the greasy image areas on the plate repel the fountain solution. The plate then comes into contact with the ink, which has been carried by a series of inking rollers from the ink-tray. This time, ink adheres to the greasy image areas on the plate, but is repelled by the wet non-image areas.

The plate cylinder is then brought into contact with the blanket cylinder where the ink image is transferred to the rubber blanket. The image is in reverse as it appears on the blanket roller.

Paper is then fed into the machine from the feed trays and the paper is pressed against the blanket roller by the impression cylinder. The image is thus transferred to the paper and appears the right way round. There is a preset counter to ensure that the correct number of copies is produced.

Only a very thin layer of ink is transferred from the blanket to the paper. Consequently, the machine will print on to very thin tracing paper (like fine greaseproof paper). However, it will also print on to three-sheet card or on to self-adhesive labels on backing sheets.

Cleaning the rubber blanket

Most offset-litho machines now have the facility for cleaning the rubber blanket and rollers automatically. A bottle containing blanket wash solvent is incorporated in the machine and the process is activated by depressing and holding a lever.

Colour printing

A wide range of coloured inks is available for offset-litho printing. The ink tray would be removed, the rollers and blanket cleaned automatically with blanket wash and a new ink tray containing the required colour of ink inserted. A separate plate is required for each colour. The first colour would be printed and then the paper would be fed back into the machine for printing with the second colour.

Register is quite accurate on most offset-litho machines, so good quality four-colour work can be produced.

Advantages of offset-litho

1 Copies are of excellent quality. The first copy is as good as the last, and all are as good as the original.
2 Illustrations and colour work can be of comparable quality to letter-press printing.
3 Direct masters are cheaper than most stencils and are as easy to prepare.
4 Indirect masters are very quickly and easily made and are quite cheap.
5 Many qualities of paper can be used, including thin, cheap paper.
6 The method uses very little ink, and copies are virtually dry on delivery.
7 Copies are long lasting and do not fade.
8 Automatic machines ensure that the operator does not get ink on hands or clothing.

Disadvantages

1 The capital cost of equipment is high (from about £3000 for a complete system of basic offset-litho duplicating machine and plate-maker/fixer – and much higher for a more sophisticated set of equipment).
2 Skill is required in operating the machine.

Thermal copying machines

Thermal copiers have already been mentioned in connection with the production of masters for use with other reprographic methods. The machines, though small, have many uses. These include:

1 Making one-off opaque copies from a single sheet original. The quality of reproduction is not high and appears greyish rather than true black on white. Copies are liable to fade if left exposed to sunlight.
2 Making overhead projection transparencies. These are quickly and

easily made and provided one has a good original the OHPs are of high quality.
3 Making masters for spirit duplication.
4 Making thermic stencils for absorption duplicators.

Method
The original must be a single sheet — you cannot copy direct from a periodical or book — and the image must have carbon content. The original is placed in contact with the copy paper, acetate sheet, hectofilm unit or thermic stencil, and in most cases the two are put into a carrier. The carrier is merely a cardboard backing sheet with a gauze or plastic top sheet and its purpose is to assist the copy to travel through the rollers of the machines. The electric power is switched on, the dial set to control the speed of travel and then the carrier is fed into a slot in the machine and taken up by rollers. This activates an infra-red lamp inside the machine and the heat from the lamp is intensified by the carbon areas of the original. This intensified heat is radiated back to the copy paper where the sensitized coating is 'scorched' in those areas corresponding to the image areas of the original.

Thermography is a simple method which is of most value when only one copy or master is required. It would not be used for the production of multiple copies as the machine must be fed manually before each copy is produced.

Dual spectrum machines
These machines, though quite small in size, incorporate two processes in one. At the top of the machine is a glass platen on which the original is placed in contact with a light-sensitive intermediate sheet. The original may be a single sheet, a periodical or a book. The lid of the machine is adjustable so that it can cope with varying thicknesses of original. The purpose of the lid is to prevent extraneous light affecting the light-sensitive paper. A timing control is set prior to pressing a push button which activates a light source within the machine so that the correct exposure can be given. When the lamp switches itself off, the intermediate sheet can be separated from the original. At this stage there is only a latent image on the intermediate, that is, the light sensitive coating has been affected by exposure to light, and an image corresponding to the image on the original is present but is invisible to the naked eye. The next stage of the process involves the feeding of the intermediate sheet, which is in contact with a sheet of copy paper, through the lower part of the machine, which is really a thermal copier. The action of the infra-red lamp causes the transfer of the latent image to the copy paper.

In some ways, the dual spectrum machine overcomes some of the drawbacks of the ordinary thermal copier in that it can cope with a greater variety of originals and these can be in coloured non-carbon inks. On the other hand, it is a two-stage process and therefore is more time consuming and more expensive.

Dyeline copying machines

Dyeline or diazo machines are seldom used in libraries. Their main purpose is to produce copies of large plans or maps such as would be needed in an architect's office or town planning department.

Method

The original, known as a translucency, is normally a line drawing on a sheet of translucent paper which resembles tracing paper or greaseproof paper. A thin sheet of polyester film may be used instead. A sheet of sensitized paper of identical size is then required. This paper is coated with diazonium salts.

The original is placed on top of the sensitized paper so that both are facing upwards and the two are fed together into the machine. Inside the machine is a rotating pyrex lamp which emits ultra-violet light. The light is reflected from the non-image areas of the original, causing the chemicals in the sensitized copy paper to become inert. Where no light is reflected, that is, in areas corresponding to the image on the translucency, the chemical coating remains, leaving a latent image on the copy paper. In order to render the image visible, the copy paper must be developed.

Machines differ in the developing process. The most common method is to expose the copy paper by passing it through a trough of developing fluid. The other methods utilize ammonia gas, heat or pressure. If ammonia gas is used, care must be taken to duct the gas through an external ventilator to prevent the operator being overcome by fumes. Ammonia-developed copy paper is capable of producing images in black, blue, sepia or reddish-brown.

Advantages of dyeline copying

1 Fast, and low cost reproduction of large print areas.
2 Ideal for maps, building layouts, and similar drawings.
3 Originals can be changed easily for updating.

Disadvantages of dyeline copying

1 The original must be translucent.

2 Materials have a short shelf life, as the sensitized coating deteriorates with time.
3 Copies are the same size as the original. There is no facility for reduction or enlargement.
4 Copies fade, especially if left exposed to sunlight.
5 The ammonia method of developing poses problems of smell and fumes.

Assignments

1 Compare any two methods of printing used in your library or in one close by.

2 Try to use an electronic source of information and practice searching − note the problems and good points.

3 Compare the use of fax and Telex machines as a means of sending information between libraries.

4 Compare, if possible, the use of a bibliography in print form to the use of one on CD-ROM.

Bibliography

Adams, Roy T., *Information technology and libraries*, London, Croom Helm, 1987.

Batt, Chris, *Information in public libraries*, London, Public Libraries Research Group, 1990.

COPOL, *Information technology and polytechnic libraries*, London, Council of Polytechnic Librarians, 1986.

Fothergill, Richard and Butchart, Ian, *Non-book materials in libraries*, 3rd ed., London, Bingley, 1990.

Hartley, Jill, *New electronic information services*, London, Gower, 1987.

Rowley, J. E., *Computers for libraries*, 2nd ed., London, Bingley, 1985.

Teague, S. J., *Microform, video and electronic media librarianship*, London, Butterworths, 1985.

Tedd, Lucy A., *An introduction to computer-based library systems*, 2nd ed., Chichester, Wiley, 1984.

Index